Biblical
CHRONOLOGY DECIPHERED

Biblical
CHRONOLOGY DECIPHERED

BC DATES SOLVED

GERALD JOHNSTON

Library of Congress Control Number: 2021922151

PAPERBACK: 978-1-956803-37-2
EBOOK: 978-1-956803-38-9

Ordering Information:

For orders and inquiries, please contact:
1-888-404-1388
www.goldtouchpress.com
book.orders@goldtouchpress.com

Printed in the United States of America

CONTENTS

Dedication vii
Acknowledgments vii
Foreword ix
Preface..xi

Chapter 1   Introduction 1
Chapter 2   Solving the Chronology 5
Chapter 3   Theoretical Eleven 27
Chapter 4   Accuracy of the Result 33
Chapter 5   Designs in Time 39
Chapter 6   The Mystery of Elijah 47
Chapter 7   Bones of Elisha 51
Chapter 8   Valley of Decision 59
Chapter 9   The Exodus 63
Chapter 10   Paran 71
Chapter 11   Galeed 73
Chapter 12   The Year 1111 BC 81
Chapter 13   King David 87
Chapter 14   The Millennial Reign 97
Chapter 15   Natural Aging of a Supernatural Creation 103
Chapter 16   "Don't Chop the Throttle" 107

Appendices...115
            Anno Domini History 117
            Number Correlations 127
            Moses' Tabernacle 133

Glossary 141

DEDICATION

One of the most difficult parts of this book for me is the dedication. There have been many people influencing and shaping my life through the years, and it is not possible to include them all, so here I will only list three: my mother Sammy Lou, my dad Gerald Sr., and my lifelong friend Gregory. These three are no longer walking on this earth, but their memories will always walk on with me.

ACKNOWLEDGMENTS

Not every book that needs to be written has a good writer as was the case with this work. Without the help and encouragement of others this book would not have been. I would like to thank the following persons for their contributions:

Ms. Patti Hughes, Ms. Callie Kinsman, Mr. Clay Pinner, and Mr. Jimmy Carter for their diligent reviews, writing insights, and recommendations that greatly improved the grammar and manuscript.

Dr. Mark Thrasher for his honest assessment of the first edition that led to this second one. Dr. Thrasher also graciously supported me by programming two phone apps to help share my studies.

Mr. Blaine Wills who is one of the most giving friends I have ever known and who has encouraged and supported me through the most troubling days of my life and in writing this book.

And finally, Dr. Frank Anders for reading and affirming my work, for writing the Foreword, and for being my doctor, my flight instructor, and my friend.

You have all been instrumental in this project and in my life. I am forever grateful.

FOREWORD

In the sixteenth chapter of this, Gerald Johnston's monumental effort to reveal God's perfect Word by showing His perfect timing through the ages, he recounts what appears to be our "chance" meeting for the benefit of advancing his new career in aviation. His recollection of the persons, times and places of that meeting are exactly as mine. A friend and fellow pilot had called me about Gerald. We were both Designated Pilot Examiners and liked to promote General Aviation, especially in helicopters.

My friend told me that Gerald needed some advanced instrument training in his Robinson helicopter like those I had been teaching in for over twenty years. He also told me that Gerald was in considerable financial straits, a condition I had suffered many times earlier in my life. I was an Airline pilot and Army Special Forces veteran living in Denver, Ray was a Corporate Pilot and also a US Army Special Forces veteran living in Los Angeles. Gerald was living in Houma about 80 miles from Lafayette.

I'm not a statistician or a mathematician but….the probability of the three of us without prior planning, being in the same room at the same airport in the same city at the same hour and day with the will to accomplish a major change in Gerald's life is infinitesimal. Gerald was a Christian, as were Ray and I.

The Lord can and routinely does orchestrate such astonishing "coincidences" for His servants. Gerald has devoted many thousands of hours to understand the ancient Hebrew and Aramaic writings necessary to produce the Chronology. My hope and prayer is that it will strengthen the faith of those who know that God's Word is true and perfect, and with prompting of the Holy Spirit, help those who are near to discovering that fact.

Frank Anders M.D.
COL (Ret) U. S. Army Special Forces
Airline Transport Pilot (Ret)

PREFACE

Someone once said, *"If your theology and your science don't agree, you either have bad science, bad theology, or both."* This was a broad statement since the terms *"science"* and *"theology"* were being applied to an understanding of Earth's age. Science was referring to a study of Earth's origin based on the fossil record, rock formations, radiometric dating, and other methods, while theology is a belief system based upon spiritual values. Reconciling these two is nearly an impossible task being both approaches require theory, and theory involves the possibility of error. Furthermore, science assumes Earth formed by natural processes through time, but the Bible says all things, including time itself, were created supernaturally.

Science can be applied to many subjects, from something as complex as studying rocket engines to something as simple as the chemistry of making soap, and its methods can even be applied to a study of the Bible, as done in this book. This approach will show the Bible is cohesive and structured, while revealing its claimed age for Earth, however, it cannot prove the claim.

Again, this book is not a study of science as used in the opening statement, but rather a study of the Bible using the scientific method with the goal of establishing *"good theology"*, such that the scope of this book is greatly reduced: logical processes are followed to discover the exact biblical timeline of human history. Earth's age cannot be proven by any scientific approach, but the Bible can be proven to be well-ordered, and its record both detailed and precise. This work is not an opinion but rather a theoretical result, an accurate chronology from which understanding can be gained.

While going through the solving and validating chapters, the math may seem laborious to some since not everyone is inclined to mathematics, however, the ideas used are simply basic arithmetic: adding, subtracting, multiplying, and dividing. Even so, many people just do not like numbers, and unfortunately that is the language of much of this content, yet the message is still for everyone. With this in consideration, every attempt has been made to keep the message flowing easily by using graphic displays.

After a brief introduction, the steps to solving the chronology are presented, followed by the chronology and its theoretical solution, validation and accuracy, and lastly new discoveries from its use. Theological reasonings are given as needed to support all assumptions, and some chapters build on previous ones, so please be sure to read in order. The final chronology is a most useful tool for study by both the lay student and the scholar. Its benefit in solving biblical mysteries as well as in uncovering some textual mistranslations will become apparent and enlightening; this book reveals many insights from the ancient texts.

CHAPTER ONE

INTRODUCTION

When first considering publishing this work, and knowing it would involve much, I decided to first test the waters to see what interests there were. I received various feedback from acquaintances: "Why are you doing this? What is your purpose? Are you trying to make money, or is it for something else? What do you hope to achieve? Is this topic unique?" These were good questions and make a great starting point. In this introduction I want to spell out the purpose and explain what the chronology is, what it is not, and talk briefly about preconceptions. Obviously from the book's cover, it is apparent I believe the Bible contains enough information to produce an exact and detailed biblical chronology, and although I am sure I have done that, I am equally sure some will disagree. Therefore, it is important to begin by addressing some potential arguments, but first, it is necessary to define my use of the term "Bible" for readers of different religious backgrounds.

Throughout this book, the word, "Bible", will be referring to the Christian Bible in general and the Old Testament, or Hebrew Tanakh, in particular, being the chronology is based there. The Bible is many different things to people: to some it is the word of God, while to others it is a fairy tale, to some it is an inspirational fiction, and yet to others it is just an old book someone gave them, a dust collector. No matter what your view, it remains one of the oldest books available to most any reader, at least for any reader in a country where it is not banned. Many see the Bible as a tool for controlling masses of people, however, it seems people are much freer in places where the Bible is also free. Religion is a tool for controlling masses, but not the scriptures. The Bible is a well-preserved collection of ancient stories and records with a message for mankind.

There are numerous opinions, disputes, and divisions over its content, yet it is still the best-seller ever. The Bible contains many truths, but not leading all to the same conclusions. This is apparent being two distinct religions, Judaism and Christianity, are based on it, and within these are even more divisions. Christianity, for example, has a wide field of beliefs among its members. While supposedly based on the same text, Christianity has produced countless denominations due to disagreements on various subjects, such as the length of a Jubilee cycle, length of Jesus' earthly ministry, timing of the rapture, water baptism, and even on the Lord's Supper, to name a few. These differing views prompted me to start studying for myself; I was on a quest for the truth and recommend the same for you. Have you ever heard people say, "the Bible can be interpreted so many ways"? I certainly have and have pondered the reasons. Were many interpretations intended by its authors, or were these due to incongruencies, or alternatively, to misconceptions?

Sometimes, the bridge between fact and theory can simply be knowledge – an understanding of the evidence. I suppose it is possible for something to be a fact to some and a theory to others, and similarly, in some cases the difference between faith and knowledge is small and vague: we know facts, we believe facts. If we consider how a child learns language, we find they learn not only by observation, but also by belief or trust: while watching their parents, a baby might hear, "Hand me that glass, you dropped your glass, fill my glass with ice." The young child associates the object with the sound, and after several experiences over time, adds glass to her or his vocabulary. Having no previous words to refer, the child must accept the association of sound and sight by belief, and therefore belief is fundamental to learning. Babies probably make the connections even quicker if they have a trustworthy theater, thereby reducing the effects of doubt. Later, as they try and learn to speak, a warm and patient audience enhances the process.

As adults, we continue learning language, but the process becomes somewhat different. We live in a broader arena and encounter more diverse contacts, and some of them use words incorrectly. No problem though, we have a vocabulary for comparison, and an additional reference, the dictionary, however, this tool itself changes through misuse of words over time. The points are, humanity is influenced by consensus, and babies do not read dictionaries, they learn by faith and reason, these are facts. A baby can only theorize a word's meaning until she or he learns it. We learn from each other based on communication, perception, trust, and judgment. Faith is integral to who we are and what we know, or think we know. Along this subject, I will share a couple of short personal stories.

I have a friend who can be somewhat difficult at times, so anytime we visit I usually let him choose the topic of our conversations. During several past visits, he consistently chose the Bible, knowing I enjoyed the subject, but he always took the role of teacher, and I just listened. Finally, after too frequent of lessons and having lost patience, I spoke up,

"I have a question?"

"Sure, what?"

"How many times have you read the Bible?"

He paused, "I've never read it."

The room became deafly silent as I explained I had read it nine times, then the deer-in-the-headlight-look overtook him, and the subject was changed. That was a while back. Since then I have read the entire Bible additional times, have learned Hebrew and Aramaic, and have read the Tanakh six times in Hebrew and the Aramaic parts three times, or more. Having read it so much, and in other languages, surely, I should know something, and this leads to my next story.

I once met a well-educated preacher, an elderly scholar who had been trained at Oxford University and was well versed in the Bible, both its languages and history. He told me a story about moving to Mississippi, and of one of his early first trips to an old country church where he met the pastor, an uneducated man. The pastor told him, "I'll tell you what the Bible says, it says behave yourself." The scholar continued, "You know, he didn't know the Bible, but he did know God!"

The Bible contains much information, and my understanding is limited; however, I continue to learn. I have preconceptions and opinions like everyone, but I tried diligently to keep them out of the chronology. I wanted to produce an accurate biblical record of human history on a concise timeline with all critical references listed, but not necessarily what your preacher thinks, nor your neighbor, nor anyone else, including me. You do not need anyone's opinion to prove the chronology. The references are given on the timeline, allowing you to easily look them up and form your own opinion. These come from the Bible, allowing it to be its own authority.

Christianity and Judaism are based on the Tanakh, and Islam also finds its roots in those early records. I hope to write to a general audience with the goal of sharing a reliable and accurate biblical chronology, demonstrate its amazing self-confirmations, and to explain its usefulness. It will be helpful if you could put any preconceptions aside as you read, as this would ease my job of communicating. Preconceptions cause people to jump to conclusions and this brings up another worthwhile story.

I worked one summer as an intern engineer at a meat packaging plant. On a tour of the facility, I was taken just inside the door of a blast chiller for a moment, where the temperature was minus forty Fahrenheit. This was a chilly experience to say the least. Anyway, some years later I was in a conversation with some people I had just met from Alaska. One man mentioned he had once been in a temperature of minus ten degrees and explained how brutally cold that was. I spoke up, "I know. I was once in minus forty degrees." Being shocked, he asked, "When and where?" With straight face I said, "One summer in northern Mississippi." You could almost see preconceptions rising and opinions forming in his mind.

One dispute against a biblical chronology argues there are discrepancies between the books of Genesis and Chronicles. The argument is the record in Chronicles omits persons mentioned in Genesis, and then concludes the intent of the biblical record is not to provide a chronology. This is simply a misunderstanding. A detailed study shows the lineages in Chronicles were intentionally abbreviated to list only the qualifying ancestries for priests or kings, contrasted by Genesis chapters five and eleven, where the word *fathered* (Hebrew יולד) is used. Genesis continues with the father's remaining years after he *fathered* (Hebrew הוליד), and gives the total years the father lived, making it absolutely clear these are presented as true genealogical and chronological records as opposed to the descendent qualifiers in Chronicles.

Another rhetorically contends, "How long was a day back in Genesis? Doesn't the Bible say a day with the Lord is as a thousand years and a thousand years as a day? How can we know the days were 24 hours?" A good response to this demonstrates the need for a chronology. The argument being made is based on Peter's words in the New Testament written years after the Hebrew Tanakh was completed and simply do not apply. If you are a Christian, you should understand that the Old Testament was a completed document. It had to be complete so that Jesus could fulfill it entirely, and therefore, in the stand-alone Tanakh, a day is simply a day.

The chronology developed in this book comes from timelines taken from the King James Bible, and their source is the Masoretic Hebrew texts; these disagree with the Samaritan Pentateuch and the Septuagint accounts of Genesis. In reviewing all three sources, a spreadsheet was used to compare the differences and appears to show the Samaritan Pentateuch and the Septuagint versions were also based on the Masoretic account, but with adjustments for certain key events, primarily Noah's flood. Without getting elaborate, the Hebrew timeline from the King James version is assumed to be correct and is used as the basis for the chronology.

Summarizing, the chronology is a result of applying the scientific method to solve the timelines in the Bible. In the scientific method, data are gathered and arranged, hypotheses are drawn, predictions are made, and the predictions are then tested to evaluate the hypotheses. This chronology is a theoretical result, but it is not a scientific result, or certainly not by the modern definition of science. Math has been removed from the definition of science by some for over a century, and the supporting evidence for this chronology is purely mathematical. However, as you will see from the numerical correlations presented, the overwhelming confirmations are astounding. There has certainly been a design to the time-claims in the biblical record, and this fact leads to "what the book is not". This book is not a debate about Earth's age based on presently accepted dating methods or their validity, but rather it is a presentation of the Bible's distinct assertion of a recent creation. Science is a study of natural phenomena and processes, and the scientific dating of Earth assumes the forming processes were natural, while the Bible presents a supernatural origin. All answers to the age of Earth are opinions, or beliefs, and none can be proven.

The point I hope to have communicated is you are about to discover for the first-time the true biblical chronology. Of course, this is an opinion and may sound conceited, but that is not the intent. I decided to publish this work because it is unlike any other. This book presents an intriguing chronology, exact to-the-year. You may be thinking, "If this is so, why hasn't anyone discovered it before now?" Maybe the answer is no one spent the time or did not believe an exact chronology was possible. Perhaps no one believed it was important, or maybe earlier attempts lacked the advantage of tools now available in the computer age. Early tries might have been made prior to discovery of the Babylonian artifacts that establish the exact date of Babylon's fall. Whatever the reasons, the numbers strongly support this being the correct biblical chronology. It is an unmatched tool for its purpose in Bible study.

The best answer might instead be that God did not want an exact chronology revealed until now. With this I ask you to set aside any doubts and read with an open mind. Do not jump to conclusions without having all the facts; do not be like the man from Alaska. The precision of the chronology reveals much, not only of biblical history, but also of major events in our world today. Some chapters contain many numbers, but the math is not exceedingly difficult, and the study is most worthwhile.

I recommend that chapters two through five be given sufficient attention to prove and understand the chronology's development before proceeding to the remaining chapters. The detailed timeline is presented after chapter two and is intended to be a reference for chapters six through fifteen and for future studies. Please become only become briefly familiar with it while reading chapters two through five or otherwise you might be overwhelmed. There are many biblical references and tracing them all while reading will certainly slow the learning process. If an area is questioned, look those sources up, otherwise read at least chapters two through five before scrutinizing the work. Once you finish the book, the chronology's role as a reference will be apparent and welcomed. Please also read the Appendices as they contain helpful and interesting insights. Thank you for your interest in the Bible and this chronology, and please enjoy while keeping the theme of the Preface in mind.

CHAPTER TWO

SOLVING THE CHRONOLOGY

Solving the chronology begins with a thorough perusal of the scriptures to gather all pertinent data and to arrange it in proper order. The number of years from the creation of Adam to the birth of Abram, or Abraham, is determined by simply adding the years found in Genesis chapters five and eleven. The Bible states the years each patriarch lived until he fathered his son, the number of years he lived afterwards, and further gives the total number of years of the father's lifetime, such that no misunderstanding should arise. Abram was born 1948 years after Adam was created. We are also told Abraham was one-hundred-years old when his son was born (Genesis 21:5), therefore, Isaac was born 2048 years after creation.

Genesis chapter twenty-two provides one of the most amazing and pivotal events in the Bible: God asked Abraham to offer his son Isaac as a human sacrifice. God's ultimate purpose was not to sacrifice Isaac, but rather to test Abraham's faith and to establish his covenant (Genesis 22:16-18). The story explains God stopped Abraham just before he killed Isaac and provided a substitute sacrifice, a ram caught in a thicket. The chronology will show the name Israel traces its beginning to this very act. This incident is not only critical to God's covenant with man, but also to the chronology. We are not told Abraham's age when he offered Isaac, nor are we told Isaac's age, except that he was one hundred years younger than Abraham, and these omissions will be shown to be the only unknown in biblical history.

The Exodus from Egypt was a major event in the Bible. The captive Israelites left Egypt on Passover (Exodus 12:40-41), but this might not have been the first one. Isaac being passed over exactly 430 years earlier could be considered the first Passover. This theological position connects the offering of Isaac with the very day of the Exodus and is crucial to deciphering the chronology. We are told the following:

> *Now the sojourning of the children of Israel, who dwelt in Egypt, was four hundred and thirty years. And it came to pass at the end of the four hundred and thirty years, even the selfsame day it came to pass, that all the hosts of the LORD went out from the land of Egypt.* Exodus 12:40-41 KJV

The words, *"who dwelt in Egypt,"* are merely identifying the children of Israel, but the word *"sojourning"* possibly introduces confusion as translated, implying they had sojourned 430 years in Egypt. We must understand they did not dwell in Egypt 430 years, but rather had been established as a people those years, some of which were in Egypt. Exodus chapter six proves they could not have been in Egypt much longer than 250 years and shows that Jacob was born after the 430 years began, thereby providing further insight into the name Israel.

The Israelites left Egypt on Passover at the end of 430 years, on *"the selfsame day"*, meaning at the time of Passover. The name Israel must be a covenant name that began when God passed over Isaac to the substitute sacrifice on what was truly, the very first Passover.

Some scholars contend the 430 years began when Abram received the initial promise (Genesis 15), however, afterwards when he was ninety-nine years old, the Bible still spoke of the covenant being established in the future (Genesis chapter 17). Others argue the covenant was established the year before Isaac was born when Abram's name was changed to Abraham, but Genesis 17:19-21 disproves that. The covenant was established when Abraham offered Isaac (Genesis 22:16-18). For Christians, New Testament verses further confirm Isaac's being offered was the event establishing the covenant and beginning the 430-year interval (Acts 3:25 and Galatians 3:17).

We now have the number of years from Adam to Isaac, 2048 years, and the number of years from Isaac being offered to the Exodus, 430 years, but we do not yet have an age for Isaac when offered, nor for Abraham. If we had either age, the other would be known, but as of now we have neither, therefore, this becomes the first unknown on the timeline.

Proceeding, another lengthy span to the puzzle is found: there are 480 years from the Exodus to the fourth year of Solomon's reign, or the year construction of the first temple began (1 Kings 6:1). Next, a meticulous study from the books of Kings and Chronicles finds 419 years from the beginning of temple construction until the beginning of the Babylonian captivity. These years are a bit challenging, however, the Bible provides two methods for validating them, and these will be expounded later.

The time periods thus far have all been from recorded biblical history, but our next block comes from prophecy: the Babylonian captivity would last 70 years (Jeremiah 25:11-12). The fulfillment of this prophecy was later confirmed by two additional prophets, Zechariah, and Daniel (Zechariah 1:12, Daniel 9:2), leaving only two unknowns in the entire chronology: 1) the age of Isaac at the time Abraham offered him as a sacrifice, and 2) the year Babylon fell to the Persians. Arranging the known data, we have the following:

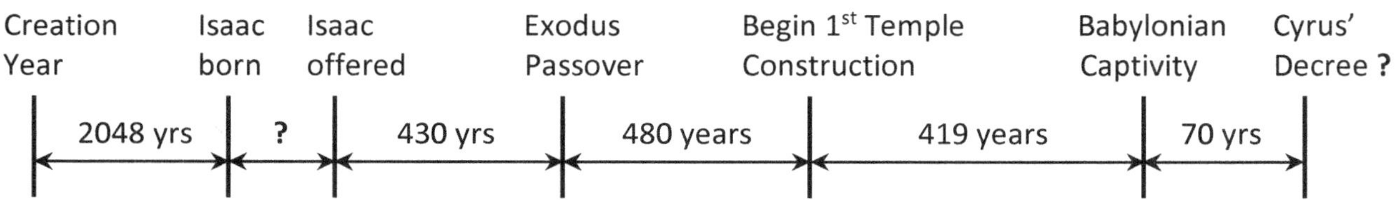

Biblical data arranged showing one unknown interval and no known dates.

The first judgment of the world was a worldwide flood 1656 years after creation. Noah was 599 years old when the flood began in his six-hundredth year. The flood lasted one year, and Noah lived 350 years after the flood, therefore, all the days of Noah's life were 950 years (Genesis 7:11, 8:13, 9:28-29). Noah lived twelve Jubilee cycles plus eleven years before the flood, one year during the flood, and seven Jubilee cycles plus seven years after the flood for a total of nineteen Jubilee cycles plus nineteen years.

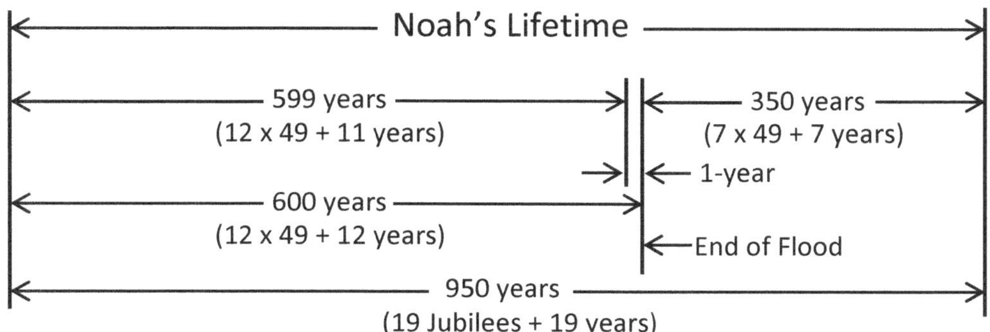

Noah's lifetime contains Jubilee patterns.

Separating Noah's lifetime into two parts, and using the end of the flood as the divider, he lived twelve Jubilee cycles plus twelve years in the first segment and seven Jubilees plus seven years in the second, giving the impressive numerical pattern:

12 x 7 x 7 + 12 years before the flood's end, **7 x 7 x 7 + 7** years afterwards, and **19 x 7 x 7 + 19** total years for Noah's life.

The forty-nine-year Jubilee period (i.e., 7x7 years) occurs throughout the lifetime of the famous biblical character, Noah. He fathered children at the age of five hundred years, making him by far the oldest man to ever do so. This miraculous begetting shows God's patience with man in that he supernaturally stretched the span of the last righteous generation to delay the inevitable flood. We will discuss Noah more in our chapter on the chronology's accuracy, but for now, the age of Isaac when offered remains one of only two unknowns. If we had his age and the exact date of any biblical incident, we could anchor the chronology and date everything.

> Note: The Jubilee cycles began after the children of Israel were in the Promised Land, but patterns of the Jubilee spans are found earlier. The Jubilee system was not in effect until the law was given, but multiples of those cycles are found in each period of Noah's life. If you are a reader who believes the Jubilee cycles are fifty years, rather than forty-nine, please consider the explanation at the end of this chapter.

Solomon's temple was destroyed in the eleventh year of the Babylonian captivity (2 Kings 25:2), and knowing this, these eleven years can be added to the 419-years derived earlier from the lineage of the kings to show the temple period lasted exactly 430 years as depicted below.

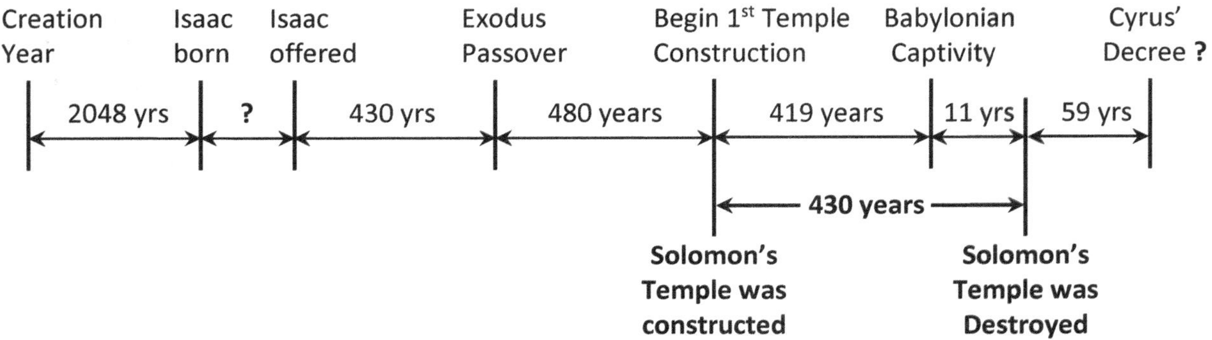

Biblical data arranged to show the temple was destroyed in the eleventh year of the Babylonian captivity, making the period from construction to destruction precisely 430 years.

Furthermore, being Jeroboam caused the house of Israel to begin worshipping the golden calves in Samaria three years after Solomon died (2 Chronicles 11:17), and being Solomon reigned 40 years until death (2 Chronicles 9:30-31) and did not begin construction of the temple until the fourth year of his reign (1 Kings 6:1), there were then forty years from the beginning of temple construction until the house of Israel began worshipping the golden calves. Simply put, this data compiles to reveal precisely 390 years transpired from the commencement of the golden calf worship until the first temple was destroyed, and these years were predicted by the prophet Ezekiel.

Ezekiel foretold a 390-year period of iniquity in the house of Israel that would conclude with the demise of Solomon's temple (Ezekiel 4:1-7), and when these are added to the forty-year interval from the start of temple construction until the worshipping of the golden calves, the result matches that of the lineage of the kings. The Bible has provided a cross-check that not only validates the period, but also helps explain the Ezekiel prophecy. Curiously, and almost as if to confirm an emerging pattern, these 430 years also match the much earlier and vital period spanning from Isaac being offered until the Exodus Passover.

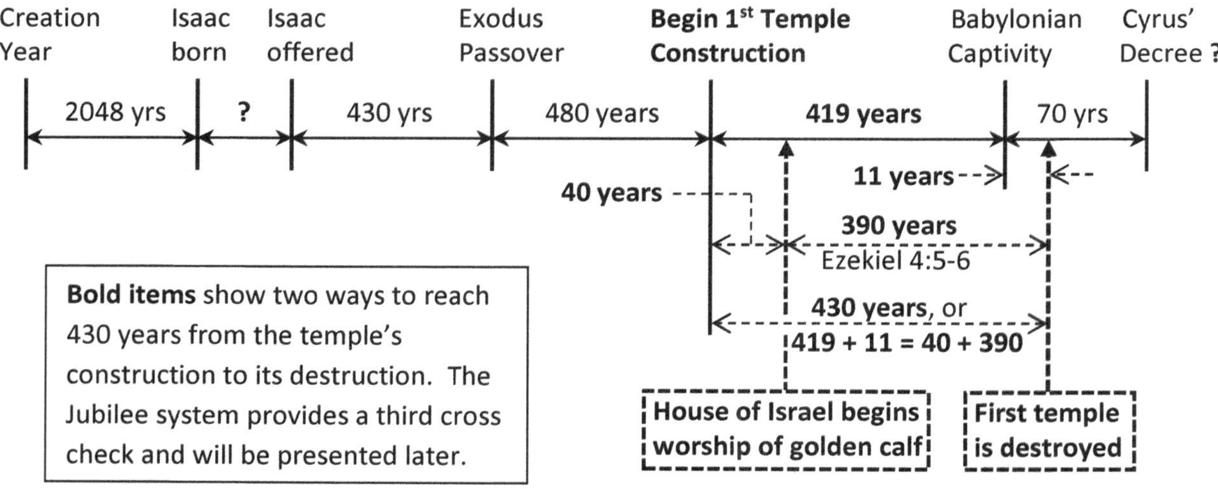

Biblical data depicting two ways to find the interval from the temple's construction to its destruction.

The 390-years iniquity in the house of Israel, displayed above, fulfilled half of Ezekiel's prophecy. The second half, the 40-year iniquity of the house of Judah, is not the one just presented, but rather a much later period, that being the interval from the resurrection of Jesus in 30 AD until the 70 AD destruction of the second temple. The prophetic details Ezekiel described for the destruction of the first temple likewise applied to the second – the second temple was again seized and destroyed (Ezekiel 4:1-7). This is the Christian view.

Our timeline still has two unknowns, but secular historians and biblical scholars agree on one of them, the date for Babylon's fall. Graciously preserved cuneiform inscriptions on the Nabonidus and Cyrus cylinders, artifacts discovered in the 1800s, date the fall of Babylon to October 12, 539 BC. Those findings show the initial takeover was by Darius the Mede (Daniel 5:31), the shorter horn on the ram from Daniel's vision (Daniel 8:3), and further agree with Daniel's writings stating Cyrus the Persian, the higher horn, arrived later.

After his triumphant entrance, Cyrus was busy setting up his reign over the Babylonians. With this occurring, his decree allowing the Jews to return and rebuild Jerusalem was probably not issued until early the following year, 538 BC. Cyrus issued the decree in his first year (Ezra 1:1), but the Jews were not settled in Jerusalem until the seventh month (Ezra 3:1), therefore, the captivity likely ended in 538 BC. Cyrus's decree concluded the 70-year Babylonian captivity as prophesied by Jeremiah, leaving just one unknown. Having the 538 BC date, every year up to and including the offering of Isaac is established: Isaac was offered in 1937 BC, but we do not know his age.

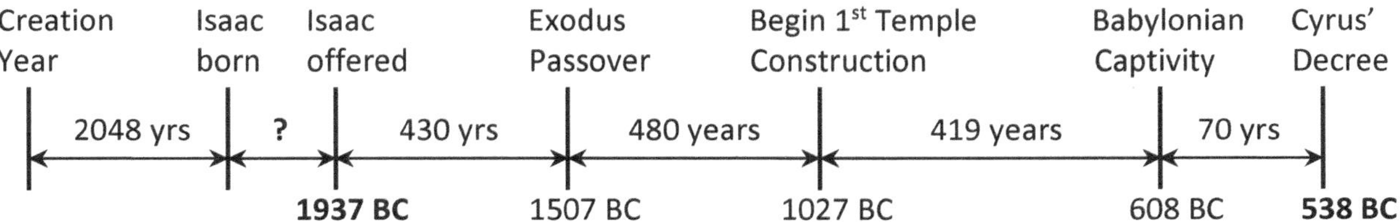

Biblical data showing only one unknown interval with most dates found.

With no secular sources to help, the age of Isaac must be conjectured, and the result checked for any notable evidence of authentication. The 539 BC date provided by archaeology for the fall of Babylon gives a hint:

$$539 = 11 \times 49$$

There are exactly eleven Jubilee cycles from 539 BC until One AD, the Year of Our LORD – One. Amazing! There are so many elevens in the Bible, here are some:

1. 11 generations from Adam to the flood generation (i.e., Shem's generation).

2. 11 post-flood generations, Shem to Isaac.

3. 11 years from the beginning of the Babylonian captivity until the temple is destroyed.

4. 11 years discrepancy between secular histories' dating of the first temple's destruction (586 BC) and the completed biblical chronology (597 BC). *

5. 11 Jubilee cycles makes up the year 539 BC, the year Babylon fell, as just shown.

6. 11 years + 12 Jubilee cycles are found in Noah's pre-flood life. This is interesting being Noah's Ark and Isaac's offering are both types of Jesus' salvation.

7. The monumental King David is born in 1100 BC. *

8. The ark of the covenant is captured and returned in 1111 BC. *

9. Samson and Eli both die in 1111 BC. *

10. The tribe of Benjamin is nearly annihilated by Israel in 1111 BC. *

11. Psalms 111 is the first of only three psalms in the Hebrew book of Psalms in which each line of the text is preceded by a Hebrew letter in its margin, each line of text begins with that letter, and continues in alphabetical order throughout the Hebrew alphabet for each line of text. The Psalmist intentionally did this beginning with Psalms 111 making it unique. Is there a message here?

* Indicates dates taken from the completed chronology

With so many elevens one can only imagine that God is trying to tell us something. Since Abraham was 100 when Isaac was born, he would have been 111 when Isaac was eleven. If our one unknown is eleven, then only the numeral one is found in the ages of both Abraham and Isaac on the day Abraham offered him. We can only proceed by using faith and reason, but faith (or hypothesis) supported by overwhelming numerical correlations to predictions is reason (theory), by a process that would have indisputably been called science 150 years ago, but today we might coin the name, *"math-science."* The chronology is completed using a hypothetical age of eleven for Isaac, and it produces FASCINATING results.

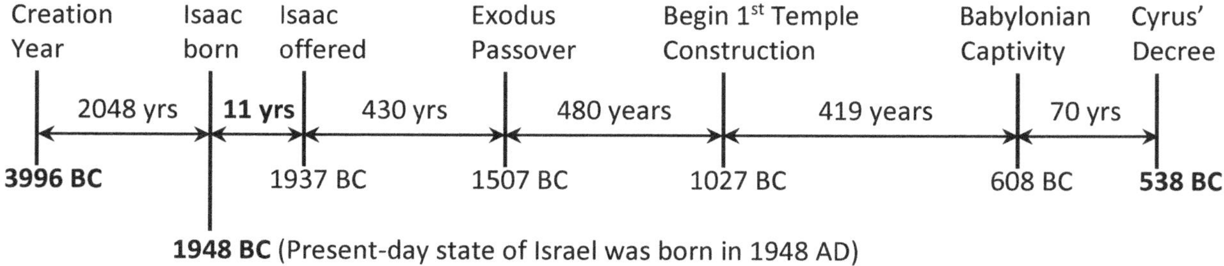

Biblical data arranged with the theoretical interval of eleven years inserted and all dates found.

From our hypothesis, Isaac was born in 1948 BC. He was offered at the age of eleven by Abraham who was then 111 and who was born in 2048 BC, or 1948 years after Adam. The year of Isaac's birth and the span from Adam to Abraham's birth both give a numerical relation to the 1948 AD birth of the modern-day nation of Israel. Also, Abraham is spelled אברהם in Hebrew, and his name has a numerical sum of 248 in Hebrew gematria, almost as if to confirm his birth year of 2048 BC. The chronology is solved: Adam was created in 3996 BC. Before presenting the finished timeline and pointing out its many amazing numerical correlations, the Jubilee period needs to be discussed.

The weekly Sabbath and Jubilee systems were biblical commandments involving cycles of rest for the people and farmland. The Jubilee was structured on the pattern of weeks, but instead of days, the entities were years. Just as the law required a day of rest for people every seventh day, or Sabbath day, it likewise required a year of rest for the land every seventh year or Sabbath year. Moses was instructed to count seven Sabbath years by the space of forty-nine years, and then blow the trumpet in the seventh month to signify the incoming Year of Jubilee. In the Jubilee year everyone would be restored their God-given possessions and slaves would be freed. (Leviticus chapter 25)

One major disagreement in the Christian world is the length of a Jubilee cycle; some believe the period is forty-nine years while others believe fifty, but who is right? To investigate, we must know that God is both consistent and logical. The instructions were to Moses who would begin the Jubilee system, and he was told they would observe a Sabbath-Year after entering the land (Leviticus 25:2).

Biblical years are grouped in spans of seven years, just as weeks are grouped in periods of seven days. The years were numbered, for example, there was a Year-One, Year-Two, Year-Three, etc. Moses was to count seven Year-Sevens, or Sabbath years, to the Jubilee, and he knew exactly how to do that. He would begin his count in a Year-Seven; therefore, the following year would be a Year-One, not a Year-Two. Make sure you understand this. Moses would number seven Sabbath years by the space of forty-nine years, but he would reach the seventh Sabbath year after just 43 years. Even so, he had to continue counting to the forty-ninth year, and then blow the trumpet to herald the incoming fiftieth year, or Jubilee. The Jubilee fell in a Year-Seven and was the fiftieth year of his count. This is consistent with the instructions Moses was given (Leviticus 25:8). It seems logical that if you were to count Sabbath-Years that you would start your count on a Sabbath-Year, a Year-Seven, rather than a Year-One, but this is confusing to many people being most counts begin at one, not seven. It is easier to grasp if you think in terms of names, rather than numbers. If you were going to count seven Saturdays, you would begin your count on a Saturday, not Sunday.

In this case the first-ever Jubilee, and all subsequent ones, would be both a fiftieth year and a Sabbath-Year, or Year-Seven, and would also be the first Sabbath-Year counted in the next group of seven such that forty-nine years later would again be a Year-Six. This means the trumpet of the Jubilee was blown near the end of a Year-Six to announce the incoming Sabbath-Year, or Year-Seven. The Jubilee cycle is a continuous forty-nine-year cycle (Leviticus 25:8). This explains why the Year-Sevens, and only the Year-Sevens, brought concerns about food: What will we eat in the year we are not planting and reaping (Leviticus 25:20)?

Weekdays are numbered one through seven with the seventh being a day of rest or Sabbath. On God's calendar there are never eight days in a week and the sequence never stops. The Jubilee cycle works the same way. Every seventh year, including the Jubilee year, is a year of rest. The sixth year provided food for three years, those being the sixth, seventh, and eighth years. The eighth year would also be a Year-One, and therefore they planted in the spring, or beginning of the year, and reaped in the fall. God is consistent.

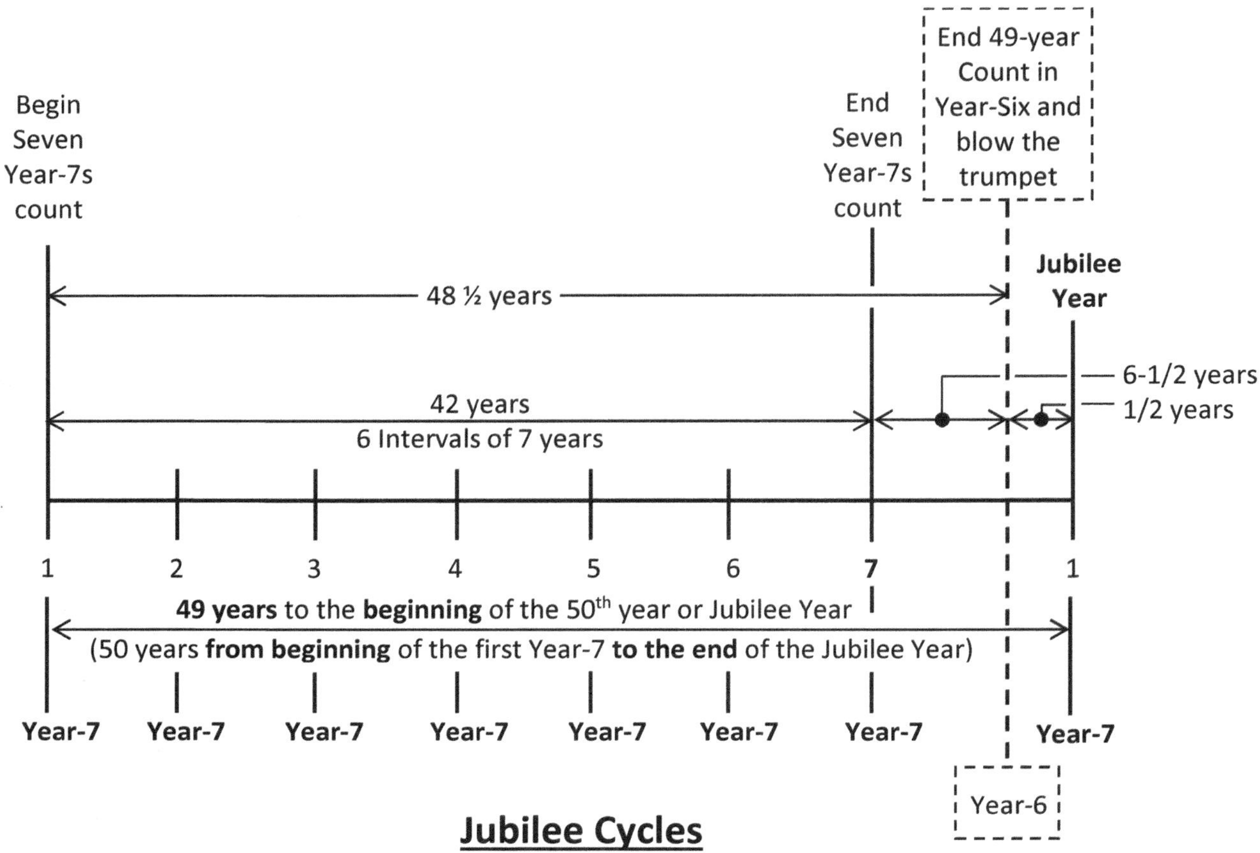

Jubilee Cycles

Counting the Omer was a similar process as the Jubilee count, except Sabbath days, rather than Sabbath years, were counted. The instructions were to number from the day after the Sabbath from which a wave offering had been made until the day after the seventh Sabbath. The day after the seventh Sabbath would be Day Fifty. Here the count is not from Sabbath-to-Sabbath, but rather from day-after-Sabbath-to-day-after-Sabbath, and the fiftieth day falls on a Day-One rather than a Day-Seven.

After this cumbersome explanation of Jubilees, the chronology should be relatively straight forward and will be presented soon, but first a few remarks about its content. In reviewing the chronology, a blatant pattern emerges. A pattern of the number six is found throughout the chronology, and might alarm some, being the number 666 is associated with determining the number of the beast's name in the New Testament book of Revelation. The number of years from Adam to the flood is made up of sixes, as is the year of the flood itself. The dividing of the languages at the tower of Babel occurred in the days of Peleg, the sixth post-flood progeny beginning from Noah, and interestingly, from Peleg's sixty-sixth year until the Exodus is exactly 666 years. Additionally, when the destruction of the first temple is placed correctly (i.e., in 597 BC verses the traditional 586 BC date), the interval to second temple's demise is exactly 666 years. Why all this? Man's number is six, and per the book of Revelation, man's number is also the variants, six hundred, sixty, and six.

We should expect to find the number of humans in the chronology of human history. Ironically, six-hundred-and-sixty-six divided by six solves the chronology, producing the age of Abraham when he offered Isaac. Furthermore, the resulting year of creation 3996 BC is found by multiplying 666 by six. How amazing that man's number six, and its variant 666, produces not only the one unknown, but also the solution to the chronology. Without any doubt, the Bible was written by men inspired by an Intelligent God who created and designed all of time. There are 66 books in the Christian Bible: Man's number times Isaac's age, or six times eleven. The number six is biblical, it is the number of a man.

The chronology is written to be concise, therefore some of the sentences may seem fragmented, but the purpose of the included text is simply to facilitate the chronology and not to replace the text of the Bible. The chronology is only a companion tool for Bible study. Not every story is included on the timeline, just those specific to the chronology, however, in reading the Bible every story can easily be traced to its location in time. All pertinent scriptural references are given in bold text, and most Jubilee years are displayed, while others omitted to maintain a concise and uncluttered layout.

Finally, one additional chance for confusion will be addressed. God told Abram his seed would wander in a land not theirs for 400 years, and many argue this to be a contradiction to the 430 years given from Isaac being offered until the Exodus from Egypt. This confusion is resolved by the completed chronology. Isaac married Rebecca 401 years before the Exodus, therefore, we conclude Isaac (Abraham's seed) left Abraham one year later to begin his new life with Rebecca and to begin their 400 years of wandering in a land not theirs (Genesis 15:13).

With this, welcome to the completed Biblical Chronology.

Biblical Chronology

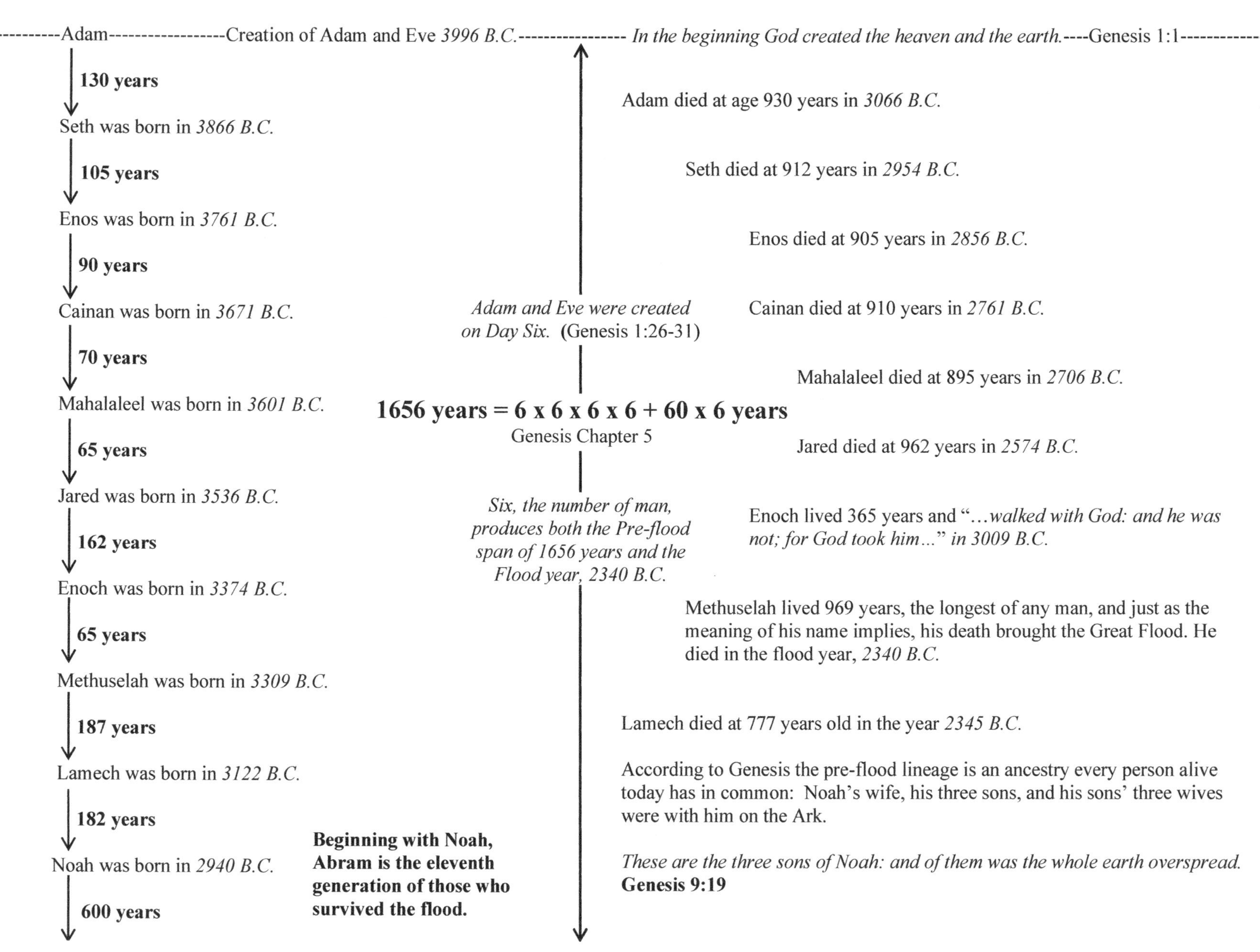

-------Shem was 98 years old at the flood's end------*The Great Flood ended in* **2340 B.C.** *2340 = (6 x 6 x 6 + 6 +6 +6) x 10; The Flood was the result of sin.*-----

2 years (Genesis 11:10)

Post-flood mankind descended through Noah and his three sons; our chronology follows the line of Shem.

Arphaxad (lived 438 years) *2338 B.C.*

35 years

Abram was born in *2048 B.C.*, 1948 years after Creation year, *3996 B.C.*, and *3996 years* before the end of 1948 A.D., the year Israel became a nation. He traveled from Ur with his father, Terah, his barren half-sister and wife, Sarai, and his nephew Lot towards Canaan. They settled in Haran. **Genesis 11:31**

Salah (lived 433 years) *2303 B.C.*

Noah died 350 years after the flood at the age of 950. *1990 B.C.* **Genesis 9:29**

30 years

Abram, Sarai, and Lot left Haran for the land of Canaan per a promise God made. They traveled to the plain of Moreh, where Canaanites were living then. God promised childless Abram that he would give his seed this land; Abram built an altar on a mountain east of Bethel. *1973 B.C.* **Genesis 12:1-8**

Eber (lived 464 years) *2273 B.C.*

34 years

Abram went to Egypt due to a famine and while there had Sarai present as being his sister. The Lord plagued Pharaoh because of Sarai, so he expelled them from Egypt. **Genesis 12:10-13 & 20**

292 years
Genesis
Chapter 11

Peleg (lived 239 years) *2239*

Abram, Sarai, and Lot returned to Bethel, then Abram and Lot separated because of strife between their herdsmen: they each had great wealth. Lot went east to Sodom, and Abram dwelt in Canaan for 10 years.

30 years

Reu (lived 239 years) *2209 B.C.*

While in Canaan, Abram heard Lot was taken captive in Sodom, so he assembled an army and went and rescued him. He gave tithes of the spoil to Melchizedek. Afterwards God told Abram his seed would be as numerous as the stars of heaven. *1973-1963 B.C.* **Genesis 14:18 & 15:5**

32 years

Serug (lived 230 years) *2177 B.C.*

After 10 years in Canaan, Sarai, who was barren, gave Hagar her maid to Abram, and Hagar gave birth to Ishmael. *1962 B.C.* **Genesis 16:16**

30 years

God changed Abram's and Sarai's names to Abraham and Sarah. Abraham, Ishmael, and all of Abraham's men were circumcised. *1949 B.C.* **Genesis 17**

Nahor (lived 148 years) *2147 B.C.*

God reigned fire and brimstone on Sodom and Gomorrah. *1949 B.C.* **Genesis 19**

29 years

Lot's two daughters gave him wine to get him drunk, and then both got pregnant by him. One gave birth to Moab and the other to Benammi; their descendants became the Moabites and the Ammonites.

Terah (lived 205 years, died in Haran) *2118 B.C.*

Isaac was born; Abraham was then 100 and Sarah was 90 years old. *1948 B.C.* **Genesis 21:5**

70 years

Isaac was weaned and Sarah made Abraham send Hagar and Ishmael away. *Approximately 1946 B.C.* **Genesis 21:8 & 10-11**

Abram, Nahor, & Haran *2048 B.C.* -----------

Abraham made a covenant with Abimelech concerning a water well at Beersheba. *1946 - 1937 B.C.* **Genesis 21**

(Note: The Flood generation, Shem, is the 11th generation of Adam, Abram is the 11th generation of Noah, and Isaac is the 11th generation of Shem.)

At age *111 years*, Abraham offered his *11-year-old* son, Isaac, as a sacrifice to God. His obedience established the covenant, and Isaac was passed over to a sacrificial ram (Continued on page 2)

Haran begat Lot and died in Ur; Nahor married Milcah, and Abram married Sarai his barren half-sister. Abram travels with Lot, Terah, and Sarai from Ur to the land of Canaan to live. The **chronology continues in the upper-middle region of this page** with the birth of Abram in *2048 B.C.*

caught in a thicket.   This *"Passover"* occurred exactly 430 years to the selfsame day before the lambs were sacrificed by Moses to begin the Exodus Passover. The Abrahamic covenant was confirmed when Isaac was offered. *1937 B.C.* **Genesis 22:16 and Exodus 12:41 -----------(1937 B.C.)----------------**

Abraham learned that his brother had a granddaughter, Rebekah. *1937-1911 B.C.* Later Sarah died and was buried in the cave of Machepelah. *1911 B.C.* **Genesis Chapters 22-23**

Isaac married Rebekah in *1908 B.C.* and Jacob and Esau were born in *1888 B.C.* Abraham remarried and had children but left all to Isaac. Abraham died when Jacob was 15 years old. *1873 B.C.* **Genesis 25:1-5, 20, 25, & 26.**

Noah's son, Shem from Noah's Ark, died at the age of 600 years, or 50 years after Jacob was born. *1838 B.C.*   **Genesis 11:11**

Jacob traveled to Padanaram (Syria) to the house of Laban and worked there 20 years. He married Leah and Rachel and his first 11 sons were born. *1815-1795 B.C.* **Genesis 31:38**

Rachel gave birth to Joseph when Jacob was 91 years old. *1797 B.C.* **Genesis 41:46-47, 45:6, & 47:9**

Jacob became aware that Laban had turned against him, so, with God's direction, he and family fled Laban for his homeland, but Laban soon followed and overtook them. They met in the mount of Gilead and Jacob made a heap out of stones that he called Galeed. They agreed to not pass over Galeed to each other for harm (i.e. boundary between them): Jacob swore by the fear of his father Isaac. Laban kissed his daughters and grandchildren and returned home. **Genesis 31:3, 17-25, & 48**

Jacob continued towards his home and the angels of God met him at Mahanaim. After this encounter, he sent messengers to his brother Esau in the land of Seir, or Edom.   Esau went out to meet Jacob with 400 men. For fear, Jacob divided his people into smaller groups to meet his brother, and afterwards, being left alone, he was visited by a man, either God or an angel, who face-to-face changed his name to Israel. Next, Jacob and Esau met, and the meeting went especially well. Jacob gave him a huge blessing of livestock, and Esau reluctantly accepted his brother's generous gift.

Jacob entered the city of Shalem in Shechem in the land of Canaan, bought a parcel of a field, spread his tents, and erected an altar he called El-el-o-he-Israel.   A man from Shechem apprehended Jacob's daughter Dinah, but Simeon and Levi rescued her, and as a result, they all had to leave Shechem. God instructed them to go to Luz in the land of Canaan, Bethel, the place God had appeared to Jacob when he fled from Esau years earlier. Jacob had everyone clean themselves, change their garments, and put away all the strange gods from among them; he hid their strange gods and their jewelry under an oak in Shechem before traveling to Luz where he erected an altar called El-beth-el. Deborah, Rebekah's nurse, died and was buried beneath Bethel under an oak. Next, God appeared to Jacob again, after he came out of Padanaram, and blessed him. **Genesis 35:1-9**

During this meeting God told Jacob his name would be called Israel from now on. He promised to give him and his seed after him the land he had given to Abraham and Isaac. Jacob set up a pillar of stone where God had spoken to him years earlier; he called it Bethel.

Rachel went into hard labor and died while giving birth to Jacob's last son. While dying she called his name Benoni, but Jacob called him Benjamin.   She was buried in the way near Bethlehem. Now the sons of Jacob were twelve, and all were born in Padanaram. (Note: Benjamin was born near Bethlehem, Judaea, not Syria, therefore the interpretation of Padanaram being a location must be wrong.) **Genesis 35:18-22 & 26**

Jacob dwelt in the land of Canaan where his father Isaac had been a stranger. While there, Joseph had a dream of his brothers bowing before him; he was 17 years old then, and his brothers despised him. *1780 B.C.* **Genesis 37:1-2**

Jacob sent Joseph to Shechem to check on his brothers who are feeding the flock there. They sell him to Ishmeelites for twenty pieces of silver, but God shows mercy to Joseph. He is taken to Egypt and placed in the house of Potiphar, an officer of Pharaoh, and is doing well until Potiphar's wife wants to have sex with him. He avoids her, and in revenge, she lies to her husband who in anger puts Joseph in the king's prison. In prison *(1769 B.C.)*, Joseph interprets two dreams that come to pass, and two years later Pharaoh has a dream that Joseph will soon interpret.

430 Years
Genesis 23:4

Meanwhile in Canaan, Jacob traveled to his father Isaac in Mamre, to the city of Arbah, or Hebron, where Abraham and Isaac sojourned. Isaac died at the age of 180 and Esau and Jacob buried him. *1768 B.C.* **Genesis 35:28**

Back in Egypt, Pharaoh learns Joseph can interpret dreams, so he brings him from the prison: Joseph reveals his dream is a soon to be famine, and as a result, Pharaoh sets him as second-in-command over all of Egypt to store up food. Joseph is currently 30 years old. *1767 B.C.* **Genesis 41:46**

Joseph stored up food for seven years, and at the end of these years, the seven years of famine began in *1760 B.C.* Ephraim and Manasseh were born in Egypt during that time. Soon Joseph's brothers will come to Egypt in search of food.

After going to Egypt for food, his brothers had to explain to their father that Joseph was still alive. Jacob, then 130 years old, went to Egypt to see his son, making a total of 70 souls from his loins, not counting his son's wives, who are now in Egypt. *1758 B.C.* **Genesis 45:6, 46:27, & 47:9**

Jacob lived 17 years in Egypt, and just before dying, he blessed his children. He also blessed Ephraim and Manasseh, Joseph's children, as his own; he set the younger Ephraim before Manasseh. He died in Egypt at the age of 147 years, and as Joseph had promised, he was carried to the cave of Machepelah and buried with Leah, Sarah and Abraham, and Rebekah and Isaac. Joseph was 56 years old then. *1741 B.C.* **Genesis 47:28**

Before dying at 110 years of age, Joseph requested the children of Israel keep his bones, and when leaving Egypt, to carry him to be buried in the Promised Land. *1687 B.C.* **Genesis 50:26**

Moses was born in Egypt in *1587 B.C.*, or *403 years* after the death of Noah, *100 years* after the death of Joseph, and *1656 years* (same exact interval as the pre-flood age) before destruction of the 2nd temple in 70 A.D. It was a tough time period of hard labor for the children of Israel. They had grown into a large multitude from the 70 souls who first entered Egypt. The present Pharaoh didn't know Joseph since he had now been dead *100 years*. Pharaoh has ordered the death of all Israelite males born to prevent them from growing any larger and taking up arms against him.

Moses was born to a Levite mother and father. When he was three months old his mother put him into a basket and placed it on a river to save his life. Pharaoh's daughter found the basket with baby inside and decided to save him. His sister who was watching, approached Pharaoh's daughter and convinced her to let Moses's mother raise the baby for her.

When Moses was grown, he saw an Egyptian beating an Israeli kinsman, and to stop him, he killed the Egyptian and hid his body in the sand. Soon Moses learned that people knew he had killed the man, so in fear for his life, he fled to the land of Midian. **Exodus 2:15**

In Midian, he married the daughter of Jethro, a priest of that land, and she gave birth to Moses's sons Gershom and Eliezer. While working in the field for Jethro, God visited Moses in a burning bush and explained He was the God of Abraham, Isaac, and Jacob, and He wanted Moses to lead the Israelites out of Egypt to a good land flowing with milk and honey. He told him to return to Egypt, assemble the elders of Israel, and tell them the God of their fathers, the God of Abraham, Isaac, and Jacob, had appeared to him and wants to free them from their bondage in Egypt. Next, God demonstrates the power He will use to free them: He turns Moses's rod into a serpent and then back into a rod, then causes Moses's hand to wither, and restores it. Moses responds that he can't speak well enough for the deliverance job, but God answers that Aaron, Moses's brother, whom God said speaks well, will help him.

At 80 years of age, Moses, along with Aaron who was age 83, went in before Pharaoh as the Lord had instructed them; they demanded Pharaoh let God's people go into the wilderness to worship him. During the meeting, Aaron cast down his rod and it turned into a serpent. Pharaoh called for his wise men, sorcerers, and magicians. They likewise cast down their rods, and they also turned into serpents, but Aaron's rod swallowed theirs. Even so, Pharaoh's heart was hardened, and he refused to let the Israelites go. *1507 B.C.* **Exodus Chapter 7**

Next, the Lord told Moses to take the rod that turned into a serpent and go meet Pharaoh as he goes out to the river in the morning. Moses was instructed to say, *"The Lord God of the Hebrews sent me to you, saying, Let my people go that they may serve me in the wilderness: and behold, up until now, you would not listen."* Then, the Lord told Moses to have Aaron hold his rod over the river; and when he did, it turned to blood. The Egyptians could not drink water in all of Egypt and the fish died. Even so, Pharaoh would not let them go.

Seven days later, God told Moses and Aaron to tell Pharaoh that if he didn't let His people go, He would plague the land with frogs, and He did, but still Pharaoh denied them. This pattern continued through the plagues of lice, flies, boils, hail, fire, and locusts. All the cattle in Egypt died, except for those of the children of Israel, none of theirs died. The locusts darkened the skies, so that the Egyptians had no light, but still, Pharaoh's heart was hardened, and he would not let them go. However, he did begin to negotiate.

Pharaoh proposed to let the Israelites go for a three-day journey into the wilderness to sacrifice to their God, but he wanted them to leave their children and livestock behind. Later in the plague process, he decided to let them take their children, but not their livestock. These compromises were all unacceptable to Moses since God didn't want to leave anyone or anything behind. **Exodus Chapters 8-10**

Finally, God told Moses to tell Pharaoh if he didn't let His people go, He would kill the firstborn of every Egyptian. This was harsh, but remember the situation, the Egyptians had been killing Israel's newborn babies.

God told Moses to have the Israelites sacrifice a lamb and to put its blood on their door posts; He explained He would pass over every house that had the blood token. Pharaoh was told this but still refused, so after midnight of the Passover every house in Egypt had a dead body, their firstborn. With this, Pharaoh immediately demanded they go for three days into the wilderness to perform their sacrifices to God. This was the first Passover, but could reasonably be counted as second, if Isaac being offered was counted as first: The Exodus from Egypt began exactly 430 years to the selfsame day after Isaac was offered. **Exodus 11:4-10, 12:29-33, & 40-41**

The children of Israel borrowed jewels of gold and silver, and raiment from the Egyptians according to the words of Moses, and they left Egypt to begin their journey to the Promised Land in the early morning just after the Passover. *1507 B.C.* **Exodus 12: 40-41 & 50-51--------*(1507 B.C.)*-----------**

The Lord led the children of Israel by day with a pillar of a cloud and by night with a pillar of fire. The Egyptians soon followed with horses and chariots and blocked them in at the Red Sea. God parted the Red Sea and brought the Israelites through on dry ground, but the waters overtook the pursuing Egyptians and they all drowned. *1507 B.C.* **Exodus 15**

After crossing the Red Sea, God fed the children of Israel with manna from heaven for 40 years while they were in the wilderness; He instructed Moses to smite the rock at Horeb, and it provided drinking water. Moses was disobedient, he struck the rock twice, as we learn from a second account of this story in the book of Numbers. (Note: Although not critical to the chronology, some believe the second account is a separate event, however both are called "the waters of Meribah." This is the same incident.) *1507 B.C.* **Exodus 16:35 & 17:6-7, Numbers 20:8-11 & 13**

The children of Israel fought with Amalek. Moses instructed Joshua to choose out men to go out and fight. Moses, Aaron, and Hur, Joshua's father, went up on top of a hill to watch the battle. When Moses held up his hands, Israel prevailed, but when he lowered them, Amalek prevailed. Aaron and Hur propped up Moses's arms with rocks and stayed them until sunset. Joshua prevailed. **Exodus 17:8-16**

Jethro, Moses's father-in-law, brought Moses's wife Zipporah and his two sons Gershom and Eliezer to visit Moses at Mount Sinai. Jethro helped Moses organize the children of Israel to reduce the workload on him. **Exodus 18**

Three months after crossing the Red Sea, the Lord gave Moses the Ten Commandments on Mt. Sinai, in addition to giving him many other laws and instructions. He wrote the commandments on two stone tablets and gave them to Moses while he was on the mount alone with God and fasting for 40 days. When returning from the mountain, Moses broke the tablets after finding the people worshipping a golden calf that Aaron had made. He destroyed the calf and told the people to choose sides, *"Who is on the Lord's side?"* The Levites stood with Moses and the Lord; they slew three thousand who chose otherwise. *(1507 B.C.)* **Exodus 32:26-35**

Next, Moses went for a second 40-days to the top of Mount Sinai to again get the Ten Commandments, and again he fasted 40 days. When he returned to the congregation his face shined so brightly that he had to wear a veil to speak to the people. During this period, the children of Israel were building the tabernacle, the temple furniture, the priestly garments, and the Ark of the Covenant. When Moses came down from the mountain this time, he put the new stone tablets inside the newly built ark. **Exodus 34:28-33, Exodus Chapters 19-39, and Deuteronomy 9:18**

On the first day of the first month in the second year after coming out of Egypt, the tabernacle was erected for the first time; when it was fully set up, each tribe gave an offering to dedicate it. Then, as Moses was instructed, they kept the Passover on the fourteenth day of the month. Also, the vow of the Nazarite was explained. *1506 B.C.* **Exodus 40:17-35, Numbers Chapters 6-7, and Numbers 9:1-5**

On the first day of the next month, or second month of this second year after leaving Egypt, the Lord commanded Moses to number by tribe, every male 20 years and older that was able to go forth to war in Israel. He also instructed that the head of each tribe would be with Moses. The total of all 20 years old and upward that were able to go forth to war was 603,550. *1506 B.C.* **Numbers Chapters 1-2, Numbers 1:46, and Exodus 38:26**

None of the tribe of Levi was numbered with the warriors: The Lord informed Moses He would take them as His in the place of all the firstborns in Israel *who had been spared during the Exodus Passover*. Moses was to number the children of Levi, every male from one month old and upward, to be the Lord's and to serve the tabernacle. The sons of Levi were Gershon, Kohath, and Merari: they would camp in the middle of the assembly with the tabernacle and only they would tend to it. Moses, Aaron, and Aaron's sons were to camp before the tabernacle toward the east, even before the tabernacle of the congregation eastward. All the numbered Levites were 22,000. **Numbers 1:47-53, 2:17, 3:11-16, & 38-39**

God gave additional laws concerning temple service for the priests and during one temple service Aaron's sons Nadab and Abihu performed activities God had not commanded: consequently, they both died. Aaron held his peace as Moses explained why it happened. God continued giving more detailed laws and instructions including laws concerning health, disputes, tithing, etc. The year of Jubilee was defined. He gave warnings for disobedience and explained the consequences in detail. The timing of Nadab's and Abihu's deaths is uncertain; it probably occurred in the first month of the second year, during the first Passover after the Exodus, but this is not definite. **Leviticus 7:38, 9:1 & 10:1-2**

On the twentieth day of this second month, having kept the Passover the previous month and having now numbered the warriors and Levites, the cloud was taken up from off the tabernacle of the testimony and it rested in the *wilderness* of Paran. (Note: Hebrew word מדבר being translated here as wilderness, doesn't consistently stand up to the scrutiny of a detailed chronology, as will be shown.) **Numbers 10:11**

The Glory of the Lord led the well-organized congregation of Israel onward from Mount Sinai after they had been there about one year; they were on their way to their Promised Land, but after leaving Mt. Sinai for three days, they complained, lusted, and doubted. The fire of the Lord fell in the outer parts of the camp and consumed them, but Moses prayed, and the fire was quenched. *1506 B.C.* **Numbers 10:33 & 11:1**

Moses was discouraged: the multitudes were divided, and his burden was heavy. God took Moses's spirit and put it on 70 elders to distribute his load. He also filled the lusting with their lusts until it came out their nostrils, yet even so, Moses's own siblings, Aaron and Miriam, also turned on him, as did the spies. Only Caleb and Joshua alone gave good reports: *they, like Moses, trusted God's promise.* The first journey to the Promised Land ended abruptly *in 1506 B.C.*; the next attempt would be 39 years later, and it would succeed, but only after learning faith through 40 years of hard trials in the desert. None of the doubters made it. **Numbers 11:11-20**

Note: Only Numbers Chapter 33 and Deuteronomy Chapter 10 give any specifics of these 39 years, and as translated, they contradict one another. For example, Numbers 33 supposedly gives every stop made along their journey from Egypt to the Promised Land, but the very first stop, the *wilderness (or מדבר)* of Paran is omitted? Why? Maybe the translators got this one wrong: מדבר might mean *"Who spoke,"* as it parses in Hebrew, rather than a location, translated *wilderness*. **God was speaking audibly in those days.** This translation possibility is expounded in later chapters. Another seeming contraction is the location of Aaron's death. Did he die on Mt. Hor or instead in Mosera? In Hebrew, *Mosera* can mean *"discipline,"* therefore, with this import, Numbers 33 and Deuteronomy 10 do agree. **Proper translations are important!**

Moses spoke to all Israel on the first day of the eleventh month in the fortieth year of the Exodus journey. He died soon after at the age of 120 years, and just before Israel entered the Promised Land. The children of Israel began taking possession of the Promised Land in the first month of forty-first year. Joshua led them across the Jordan River *in the Spring of 1466 B.C.* **Deuteronomy 1:1-3 & 34:7-9 and Joshua 1:1-2, 4:19**

Joshua gave Hebron to Caleb as Moses had promised. *1461-1460 B.C.* **Joshua 14:7-15**   Joshua probably died around *~1432 B.C.*

<u>After the death of Joshua there were still Canaanites and Amorites in the land; they became contributories.</u>   *~1432-1431 B.C.* **Judges Chapter 1**

8 years of children of Israel serving Chushanrishathaim king of Mesopotamia. **Judges 3:8**

Othniel begins to judge Israel *~1424 B.C.* **Judges 3:9-10**

40 years Judges 3:11   ** **1416 B.C. First-ever Jubilee Year**

Othniel dies *~1384 B.C.*

18 years serving Eglon, king of Moab **Judges 3:14**

Ehud subdued Moab *~1366 B.C.* **Judges 3:29**

80 years, Shamgar delivered Israel. **Judges 3:30-31**

The Lord sold Israel into hand of Jabin King of Canaan (Sisera was captain). *~1286 B.C.* **Judges 4:2**

20 years Judges 4:3

Deborah judges Israel *~1266 B.C.* **Judges 5:31**

40 years

The Lord delivers Israel into Midian's hands. *~1226 B.C.* **Judges 6:1**

7 years Judges 6:1

Gideon subdues Midian. *~1219 B.C.* **Judges 8:28**

40 years Judges 8:28   Eli is born *~1209 B.C.*

Abimelech (Gideon's son) reigned over Israel. *~1179 B.C.* **Judges 9:22**

3 years Judges 9:22

Tola defends and judges Israel. *~1176 B.C.* **Judges 10:1**

23 years Judges 10:2

Jair judges Israel *~1153 B.C.* **Judges 10:3**

Eli begins to Judge Israel. *~1151 B.C.* **1 Samuel 4:18**

22 years Judges 10:3

Nazarites⎯ Samson is born *~1151-1145 B.C.*
Samuel is born *~1150-1140 B.C.*

God speaks to the child Samuel about Eli. **1 Samuel 3**

480 Years
1 Kings 6:1

300 years Judges 11:26

Proverbs 28:28, *"When the wicked rise, men hide themselves; but when they perish, the righteous increase."*

--------------*~1131 B.C.*-------Israel is sold into the hand of the Philistines and Ammonites.------------- **Judges 10:7** ----------------*~1131 B.C.*------------------

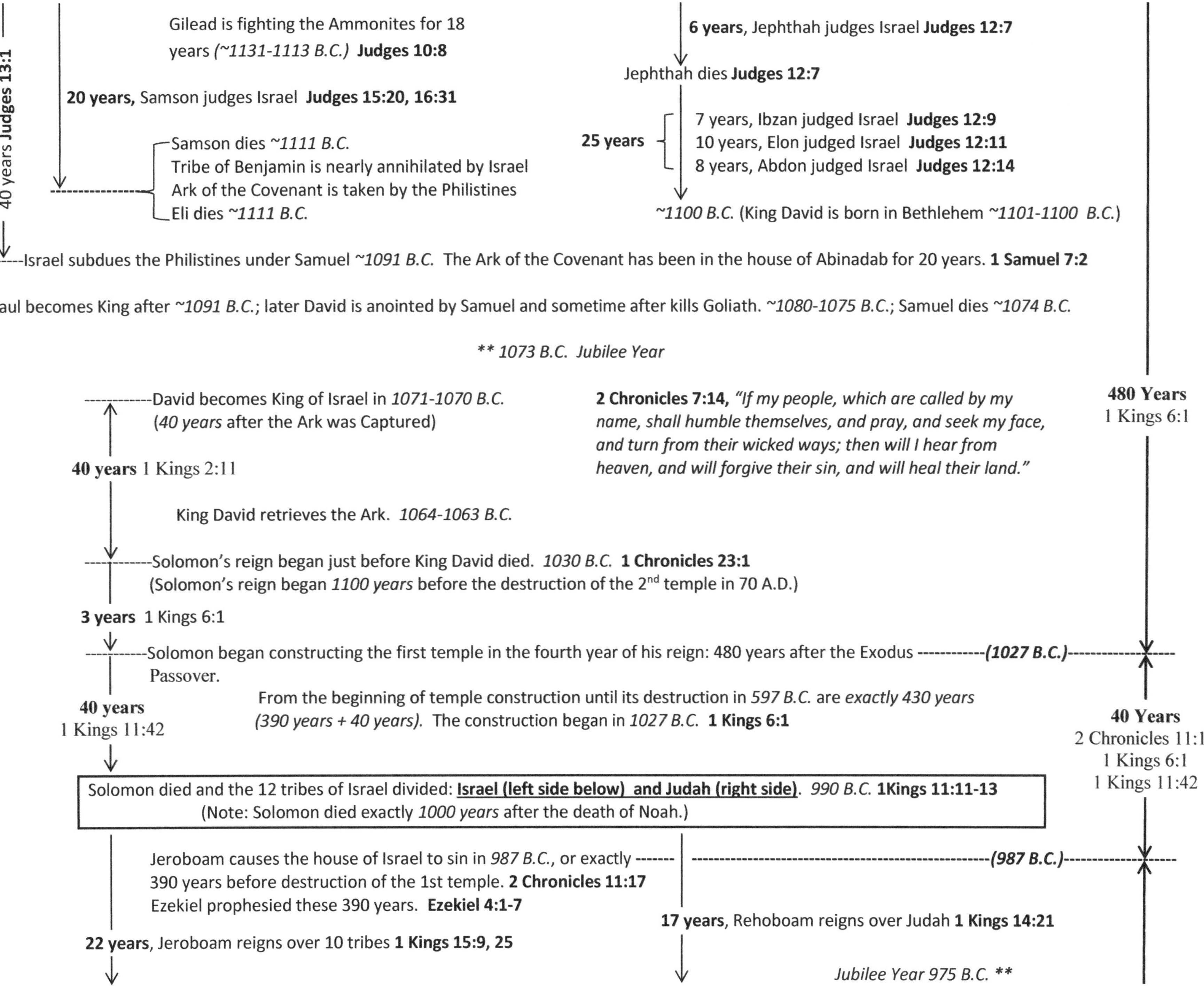

40 years Judges 13:1

Gilead is fighting the Ammonites for 18 years (~1131-1113 B.C.) Judges 10:8

20 years, Samson judges Israel Judges 15:20, 16:31

Samson dies ~1111 B.C.
Tribe of Benjamin is nearly annihilated by Israel
Ark of the Covenant is taken by the Philistines
Eli dies ~1111 B.C.

6 years, Jephthah judges Israel Judges 12:7

Jephthah dies Judges 12:7

25 years
7 years, Ibzan judged Israel Judges 12:9
10 years, Elon judged Israel Judges 12:11
8 years, Abdon judged Israel Judges 12:14

~1100 B.C. (King David is born in Bethlehem ~1101-1100 B.C.)

------Israel subdues the Philistines under Samuel ~1091 B.C. The Ark of the Covenant has been in the house of Abinadab for 20 years. 1 Samuel 7:2

Saul becomes King after ~1091 B.C.; later David is anointed by Samuel and sometime after kills Goliath. ~1080-1075 B.C.; Samuel dies ~1074 B.C.

** 1073 B.C. Jubilee Year

David becomes King of Israel in 1071-1070 B.C.
(40 years after the Ark was Captured)

40 years 1 Kings 2:11

2 Chronicles 7:14, "If my people, which are called by my name, shall humble themselves, and pray, and seek my face, and turn from their wicked ways; then will I hear from heaven, and will forgive their sin, and will heal their land."

480 Years
1 Kings 6:1

King David retrieves the Ark. 1064-1063 B.C.

Solomon's reign began just before King David died. 1030 B.C. 1 Chronicles 23:1
(Solomon's reign began 1100 years before the destruction of the 2nd temple in 70 A.D.)

3 years 1 Kings 6:1

Solomon began constructing the first temple in the fourth year of his reign: 480 years after the Exodus ------------(1027 B.C.)------------

40 years
1 Kings 11:42

Passover.

From the beginning of temple construction until its destruction in 597 B.C. are exactly 430 years (390 years + 40 years). The construction began in 1027 B.C. 1 Kings 6:1

40 Years
2 Chronicles 11:17
1 Kings 6:1
1 Kings 11:42

Solomon died and the 12 tribes of Israel divided: Israel (left side below) and Judah (right side). 990 B.C. 1Kings 11:11-13
(Note: Solomon died exactly 1000 years after the death of Noah.)

Jeroboam causes the house of Israel to sin in 987 B.C., or exactly ------- ---(987 B.C.)------------
390 years before destruction of the 1st temple. 2 Chronicles 11:17
Ezekiel prophesied these 390 years. Ezekiel 4:1-7

17 years, Rehoboam reigns over Judah 1 Kings 14:21

22 years, Jeroboam reigns over 10 tribes 1 Kings 15:9, 25

Jubilee Year 975 B.C. **

Nadab reigns over Israel in the 2nd year of Asa King of Judah ~968 B.C.

Abijam reigns over Judah 973 B.C. 18th year of Jeroboam

2 years 1Kings 15:25

Proverbs 29:23, *"A man's pride shall bring him low; but honour shall uphold the humble in spirit."*

3 years beginning **1 Kings 15:1-2**

Baasha King of Israel ~967 B.C.

Asa King of Judah, 20th year of Jeroboam ~969 B.C. **1 Kings 15:9**

24 years 1 Kings 15:33

Proverbs 28:13, *"He that covereth sins shall not prosper: but whoso confesseth and forsaketh them shall have mercy."*

Elah King of Israel ~944 B.C. 26th year of Asa **1 Kings 16:8**

2 years 1 Kings 16:8

Psalm 49:20, *"Man that is in honour, and understandeth it not, is like the beasts that perish."*

Zimri King of Israel ~943 B.C.

41 years 1 Kings 15:10

7 days 1 Kings 16:15

Tibni and Omri reign over Israel in 27th year of Asa king of Judah **1 Kings 16:15-23**

Note: Jeroboam ruled over 10 tribes while Rehoboam only ruled over 1 tribe (Judah only). This adds to just 11 tribes. The Priestly tribe of Levi was probably not included in this count.

Also, in the second book of Chronicles the tribe of Benjamin is included with Judah.

6 years (Tibni dies)

Omri King of Israel (worst yet) **1 Kings 16:25**

12 years 1 Kings 16:23

6 years

Ahab King of Israel (worse than Omri) **1 Kings 16:33**------------------------ ~ 931 B.C.
(38th year of Asa) **1Kings 16:29**

390 years
Ezekiel 4:1-7

3 years 1 Kings 22:41

22 years 1 Kings 16:29

------------928 B.C. Jehoshaphat made peace with the king of Israel **1 Kings 22:41**

Ahaziah King of Israel ~911 B.C., 17th year of Jehoshaphat

*926 B.C.**Jubilee Year*

2 years of Ahaziah's reign 1 Kings 22:51

25 years of Jehoshaphat's reign 1 Kings 22:42

Jehoram (Joram) King of Israel (son of Ahab, or rather son-in-law)
18th year of Jehoshaphat ~910 B.C. **2 Kings 3:1, 8:16-18**

Jehoshaphat has ties to Israel through his son, King Jehoram, king of Israel. ~910 B.C. **2 Chronicles 21:2**

Jehoram is the king of both Judah and Israel from *905 to 898 B.C.,* and likely a Judean co-ruler with his father

Jehoram King of Judah (son of Jehoshaphat) **1 Kings 22:50**
5th year of Joram King of Israel **2 Kings 8:16** ~905 B.C.

Jehoshaphat from *912-905 B.C.,* and with his son Ahaziah from *898-897 B.C.* **2 Kings 1:17, 8:18, 2 Chronicles 21:2**

8 years 2 Kings 8:17

12 years 2 Kings 3:1

*Ahaziah King of Judah 11th or 12th year of Joram *~898 B.C.* **2 Kings 8:25, 9:29**

Elijah went up in a whirlwind *~910-905 B.C.* **2 Kings Ch. 2**

1 years 2 Kings 8:26

Jehu becomes Israel's king *~897 B.C.* **2 Kings 10:36**

*Athaliah (Ahaziah's mother) reigned *~897 B.C.* **2 Kings 11:3**

28 years 2 Kings 10:36   *877 B.C.**Jubilee Year*

6 years 2 Kings 11:3

Jehoahaz becomes king of Israel in 23rd year Joash **2 Kings 13:1**

*Jehoash (Joash) King of Judah 7th year of Jehu *~891 B.C.* **2 Kings 12:1**

17 years beginning *~869 B.C.* 2 Kings 13:1

40 years 2 Kings 12:1

Jehoash (Joash) becomes king of Israel in 37th year Joash **2 Kings 13:10**
Elisha died. *~851-835 B.C.* **2 Kings 13:13-14**
16 years beginning *~852 B.C.* 2 Kings 13:10

*Amaziah king of Judah 2nd year of Joash **2 Kings 14:1**

29 years beginning *~850 B.C.* 2 Kings 14:2

Jeroboam becomes king of Israel
in 15th year of Amaziah *~835 B.C.* **2 Kings 14:23-25**
Jonah's prophecy is fulfilled
53 years 2 Kings 14:17, 14:23-25   *828 B.C.**Jubilee Year*
(likely 41 years as King plus 12 as co-ruler)

Azariah (Uzziah) king of Judah in 27th year of Jeroboam **2 Kings 15:1**
820 B.C.

Note: *820 B.C.* was the 16th year of Jeroboam, therefore Jeroboam was probably a co-regent before reigning from Samaria.

Zachariah becomes king of Israel 38th year of Azariah **2 Kings 14:29, 15:8**

52 years 2 Kings 15:2   *779 B.C. **Jubilee Year*

6 months beginning *~782 B.C.* 2 Kings 15:8

Jotham co-reigned four years with Uzziah at the end of his reign. **2 Kings 15:30**

Shallum king of Israel 39th year of Uzziah **2 Kings 15:13**

Jotham becomes king of Judah **2 Kings 15:7, 27, 31-32**
2nd year of Pekah *768 B.C.*

1 month 2 Kings 15:13

16 years in Jerusalem 2 Kings 15:33

Menahem king of Israel 39th year of Uzziah *781 B.C.* **2 Kings 15:17**

10 years 2 Kings 15:17   *779 B.C. **Jubilee Year*

Jotham co-reigned four years with Uzziah plus 16 years alone: total 20 years. **2 Kings 15:30-33**

Pekahiah king of Israel 50th year of Uzziah **2 Kings 15:23**

Ahaz becomes king of Judah 17th year of Pekah **2 Kings 15:38, 16:1**
752 B.C.

2 years beginning *~771 B.C.* 2 Kings 15:23

16 years 2 Kings 16:2

Note: Pekah and Rezin war against Jerusalem. **2 Kings 16:5**

390 years
Ezekiel 4:1-7

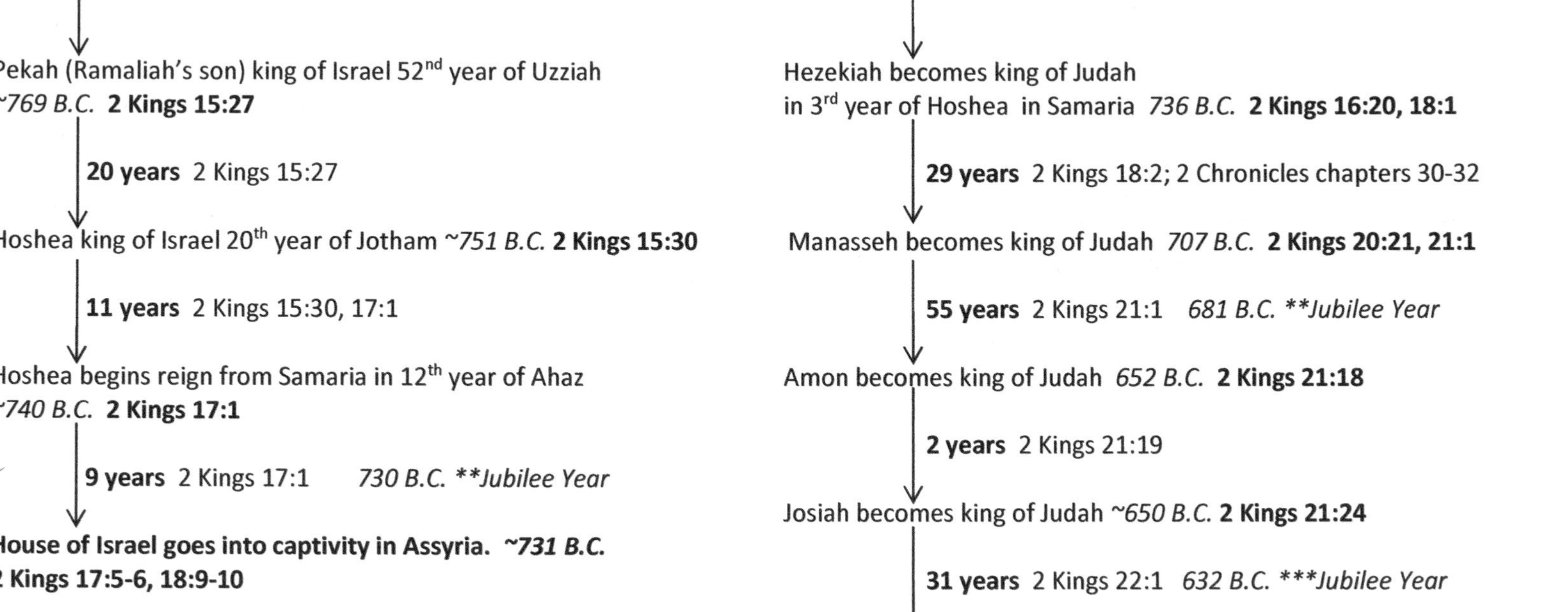

Pekah (Ramaliah's son) king of Israel 52nd year of Uzziah
~769 B.C. 2 Kings 15:27

20 years 2 Kings 15:27

Hoshea king of Israel 20th year of Jotham ~751 B.C. 2 Kings 15:30

11 years 2 Kings 15:30, 17:1

Hoshea begins reign from Samaria in 12th year of Ahaz
~740 B.C. 2 Kings 17:1

9 years 2 Kings 17:1   730 B.C. **Jubilee Year

House of Israel goes into captivity in Assyria. ~731 B.C.
2 Kings 17:5-6, 18:9-10

2 Kings 18:11-12, "And the king of Assyria did carry away Israel
unto Assyria, and put them in Halah and in Habor by the
river of Gozan, and in the cities of the Medes: Because they
obeyed not the voice of the Lord their God, but transgressed
his covenant, and all that Moses the servant of the Lord
commanded, and would not hear them, nor do them."

Hosea 13:9: "Oh Israel, thou hast destroyed thyself; but
in me is thine help."

Proverbs 25:2, "It is the glory of God to conceal a thing: but
the honor of kings is to search out a matter."

Hezekiah becomes king of Judah
in 3rd year of Hoshea in Samaria 736 B.C. 2 Kings 16:20, 18:1

29 years 2 Kings 18:2; 2 Chronicles chapters 30-32

Manasseh becomes king of Judah 707 B.C. 2 Kings 20:21, 21:1

55 years 2 Kings 21:1   681 B.C. **Jubilee Year

Amon becomes king of Judah 652 B.C. 2 Kings 21:18

2 years 2 Kings 21:19

Josiah becomes king of Judah ~650 B.C. 2 Kings 21:24

31 years 2 Kings 22:1   632 B.C. ***Jubilee Year

~619 B.C. Battle at Megiddo 2 Chronicles 35:20-23

*Jehoahaz becomes king of Judah 2 Kings 23:30

3 months 2 Kings 23:31

619 B.C. *Jehoiakim (Eliakim) becomes king of Judah 2 Kings 23:34

~615 B.C. Battle of Carchemish Jeremiah: 46:2

* Indicates kings not included in lineage of Jesus in Matthew chapter one.
   Also, Athaliah, mother of Ahaziah, was the only queen in the line.
  **Jubilee years (Note: not every Jubilee is shown)
***Jubilee and one of the largest Passover feasts ever. 2 Kings 23:22-23

616 B.C. Nebuchadnezzar becomes king in the 4th year of Jehoiakim Jeremiah 25:1 ---------------(616 B.C.)-----------------------------

Jehoiakim becomes the servant of Nebuchadnezzar, and Daniel, Hananiah, Mishael, and Azariah
are taken to Babylon for 3 years of training. 611 B.C. Daniel 1:5, 18

3 years with Jehoiakim serving Nebuchadnezzar and Daniel in training 2 Kings 24:1, Daniel 1:1, 5, 18

8 years
2 Kings 24:12

390 years
Ezekiel 4:1-7

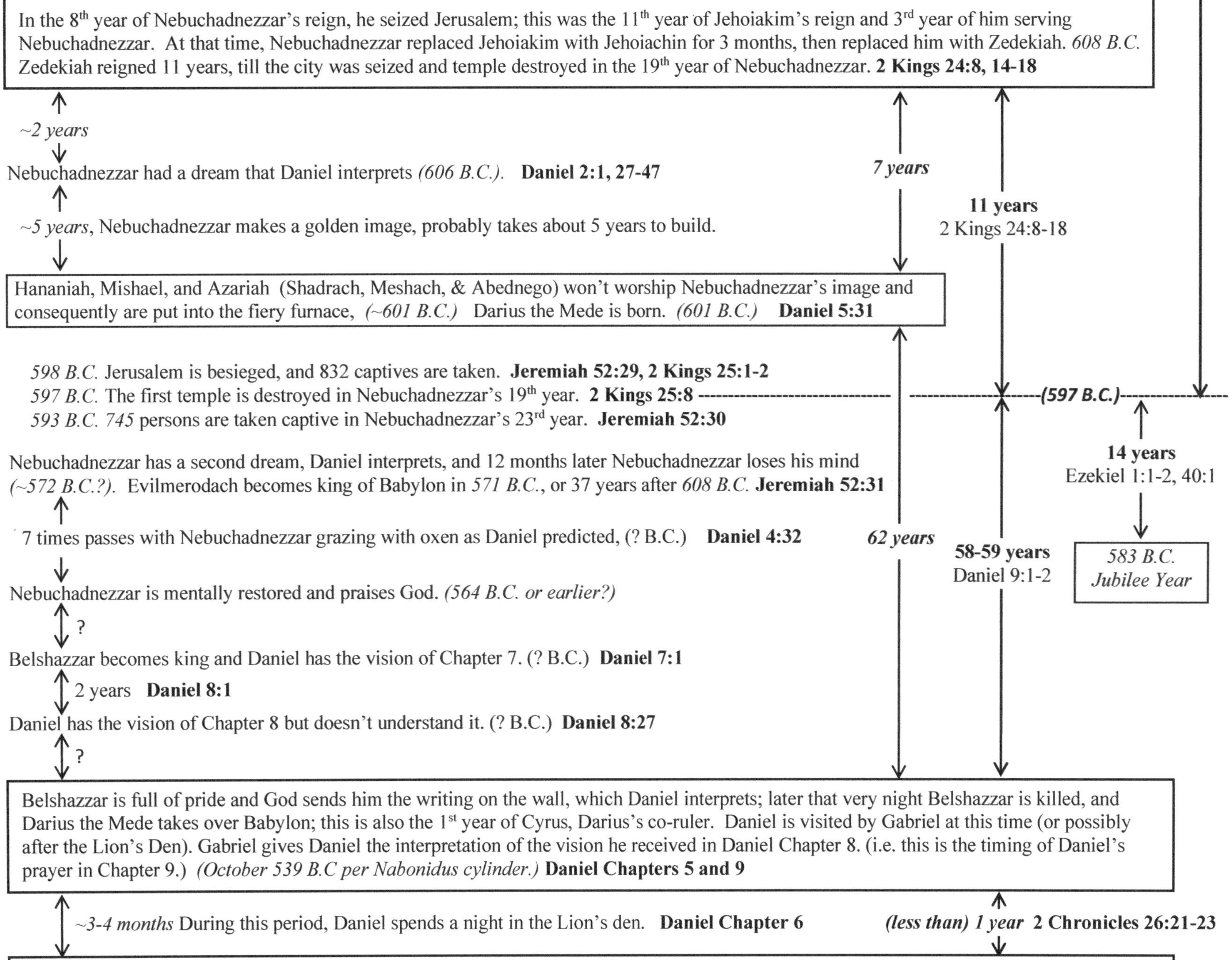

In the 8th year of Nebuchadnezzar's reign, he seized Jerusalem; this was the 11th year of Jehoiakim's reign and 3rd year of him serving Nebuchadnezzar. At that time, Nebuchadnezzar replaced Jehoiakim with Jehoiachin for 3 months, then replaced him with Zedekiah. 608 B.C. Zedekiah reigned 11 years, till the city was seized and temple destroyed in the 19th year of Nebuchadnezzar. 2 Kings 24:8, 14-18
~2 years
Nebuchadnezzar had a dream that Daniel interprets (606 B.C.). Daniel 2:1, 27-47
7 years
11 years
2 Kings 24:8-18
~5 years, Nebuchadnezzar makes a golden image, probably takes about 5 years to build.
Hananiah, Mishael, and Azariah (Shadrach, Meshach, & Abednego) won't worship Nebuchadnezzar's image and consequently are put into the fiery furnace, (~601 B.C.) Darius the Mede is born. (601 B.C.) Daniel 5:31
598 B.C. Jerusalem is besieged, and 832 captives are taken. Jeremiah 52:29, 2 Kings 25:1-2
597 B.C. The first temple is destroyed in Nebuchadnezzar's 19th year. 2 Kings 25:8 ----------------------------- ------------------(597 B.C.)-----------
593 B.C. 745 persons are taken captive in Nebuchadnezzar's 23rd year. Jeremiah 52:30
14 years
Ezekiel 1:1-2, 40:1
Nebuchadnezzar has a second dream, Daniel interprets, and 12 months later Nebuchadnezzar loses his mind (~572 B.C.?). Evilmerodach becomes king of Babylon in 571 B.C., or 37 years after 608 B.C. Jeremiah 52:31
62 years
58-59 years
Daniel 9:1-2
583 B.C.
Jubilee Year
7 times passes with Nebuchadnezzar grazing with oxen as Daniel predicted, (? B.C.) Daniel 4:32
Nebuchadnezzar is mentally restored and praises God. (564 B.C. or earlier?)
?
Belshazzar becomes king and Daniel has the vision of Chapter 7. (? B.C.) Daniel 7:1
2 years Daniel 8:1
Daniel has the vision of Chapter 8 but doesn't understand it. (? B.C.) Daniel 8:27
?
Belshazzar is full of pride and God sends him the writing on the wall, which Daniel interprets; later that very night Belshazzar is killed, and Darius the Mede takes over Babylon; this is also the 1st year of Cyrus, Darius's co-ruler. Daniel is visited by Gabriel at this time (or possibly after the Lion's Den). Gabriel gives Daniel the interpretation of the vision he received in Daniel Chapter 8. (i.e. this is the timing of Daniel's prayer in Chapter 9.) (October 539 B.C per Nabonidus cylinder.) Daniel Chapters 5 and 9
~3-4 months During this period, Daniel spends a night in the Lion's den. Daniel Chapter 6
(less than) 1 year 2 Chronicles 26:21-23
Cyrus issues the famous decree to rebuild Jerusalem in late winter or early spring, a few months after the fall of Babylon. 538 B.C.

CHAPTER THREE

THEORETICAL ELEVEN

The completed chronology displays all critical timeline dates including the creation of Adam, the flood year, Isaac's birth year and the year Abraham offered him, the Exodus, the construction of Solomon's temple and its destruction, and more. An abbreviated narrative of the entire Pentateuch is outlined, but not every exact year is known (e.g., we do not know the exact year Lot was taken captive in Sodom, but we know it was between 1973 and 1963 BC), but overall, all dates are presented. The timeline shows the Bible is not always written in chronological order, as can be seen by comparing the referenced verses, but the storyline is consistent.

Sarah conceived Isaac the same year Sodom and Gomorrah were destroyed. Genesis implies an explosion, maybe igniting hydrocarbons, released salt into the air. The salt caused the freshwater outflow from the Jordan water to become saline, and consequently the salt sea began forming, but more on that in a later chapter; for now, the takeaway is that Isaac and the Dead Sea are the same age.

This chapter will begin to show some of the resulting numerical correlations that support the chronology being genuine, rather than a product of random chance. Our theoretical age of eleven for Isaac has already been shown to be special, but there is more.

The Gregorian calendar, a twelve-month system well-known to most everyone, uses the acronym, AD, for Anno Domini, meaning "Year of the LORD." This designation is assigned for dates from the first century forward, for those following the birth of Jesus. The calendar was developed by Pope Gregory in the sixteenth century to replace the diverging Julian calendar of Rome. One curious oddity of the Gregorian calendar is the names of its months. December, from the prefix "deca" means tenth month, and likewise November means ninth, October is eighth as in Octagon, and September means seventh month; these are each off by two months from the meanings of their names. The simple explanation is an adjustment of two months was made to the ten-month Roman calendar to produce a twelve-month version in the early days of the Roman Empire. The Romans used a base-ten number system, so why the change? The official story is documented and detailed, but very strange.

History records Romulus inventing a ten-month calendar in 753 BC, but only one winter month was included, meaning sixty-one winter days were not on the calendar. In 700 BC, January and February were added to bring the total to twelve months, and some of the month names were displaced by two months from their meanings. Then, Julius Caesar created the Julian calendar in 46 BC to correct errors by incorporating a leap year system. By the year eight BC, the seventh month had been renamed July in honor of Julius Caesar and the eighth was renamed August in honor of Augustus. Centuries later, following the Protestant Reformation, the Catholic Church convened the Council of Trent to deal with the church revolt. The council, described as the embodiment of the Counter-Reformation, authorized the Gregorian calendar to be developed to replace the failing Julian calendar, and Pope Gregory XIII initiated its use in 1582. A reasonable question is, "How would a new calendar help quell the revolution?"

It is fascinating that so much history is known about the calendar, even as far back as 753 BC, including detailed explanations for the names of the months and how and when they changed, yet the birthdate the calendar is supposed to be based on is unknown. We know what Anno Domini means, but we do not even know what year Jesus was born. Why would the Julian calendar, a solar-based calendar that was supposedly invented before Jesus' birth, not be aligned with the sun? Why was the beginning of the year not set on the solstice or equinox? What is the origin based on? What is so special about January one? What is the true history? Jesus' birthday was well-known in the first century, the Jewish records were impeccable. Many discard the Bible, choosing rather to trust history without questioning, but truth is not resolved, and Jesus' true birthday is still unknown, or is it?

To reveal an amazing possibility, we now introduce a sideline hypothesis to accompany the chronology's validation. When and why did the Roman base-ten calendar really change? A possible answer is the first century AD with the advent of Christianity. The next two paragraphs conjecture a reasonable likelihood.

In the first century AD, Christianity began to grow throughout the Roman Empire, and by the fourth century, it was the state's religion. Early in those days, the Romans wanted to honor Jesus and therefore made a new calendar based on his birthday. The earliest Christians were comprised of Jewish members who knew the Hebrew calendar was based on the moon cycle, not the sun, so a need arose to change the base-ten calendar to match the twelve moons of the year. The year was renumbered to allow two new months to be added, and these months were named July and August in honor of the two Caesars, Julius, and Augustus. These new months were inserted into the middle of the first year of the new calendar, and the old remained in effect until the revision was completed. The change displaced the names of September through December by two months from the meanings of their names.

An easy way to go from one system to another would be to wait two months (i.e., 59 days) after the expiring ten-month calendar ended, then initiate the desired twelve-month calendar: the old January 1, 1 BC, would become the new November 3, 2 BC. The reference day, January first for the old ten-month calendar, was likely the true birthdate of the one the Romans were honoring with their calendar, the founder of their state's religion, Jesus Christ. The Romans had begun the initial ten-month calendar on 1-1-1 BC such that Jesus would be one year old on 1-1-1 AD (i.e., there is not a Year-Zero). On their original calendar, he would be one year old in the "Year of the Lord One," but on the new twelve-month calendar, he would be one year and two months old. There are two days separating the Gregorian and Julian dates in the first century, therefore, Jesus' true birthday is November 1, 2 BC on the modern Gregorian calendar. He would be just over one years old on January 1, 1 AD, giving real meaning to Anno Domini.

Enough hypotheses, now to the facts. The number of days on the present-day Gregorian calendar, extrapolated to the first century, have exactly **11,111 days** spanning from November 1, 2 BC to Jesus' crucifixion on the Passover, April 3, 30 AD. At the very least, this would have to be considered a major coincidence. A string of ones giving the number of days from the proposed true birthday of Jesus to his crucifixion. Surely the early Romans had honored Jesus by aligning their calendar to his birth. Again, November first is two months before January first, and this period matches the added two months.

From NASA studies, one of the longest total lunar eclipses ever sighted in the skies over Jerusalem began on January 10, 1 BC (Julian calendar), or sixty-eight days after our conjectured birthdate. Biblical days begin in the evening, meaning Jesus' birthday began the evening of November 2, 2 BC on the Julian calendar, therefore, this exceptional lunar eclipse occurred on the seventieth day of Jesus' life.

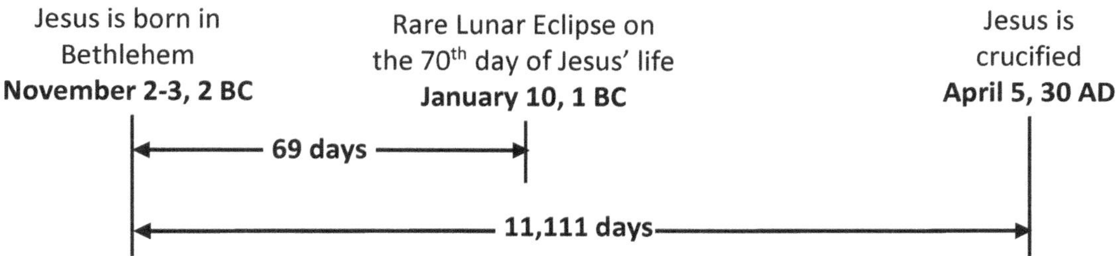

The life of Jesus spanned 11,111 days from birth to crucifixion. A long-duration lunar eclipse appeared over Jerusalem on the Seventieth day of his life. Note: The dates displayed are from the Julian calendar.

Again, the Gregorian and Julian calendars differ by two days in the first century, therefore, someone must have known the truth and adjusted for it when making the Gregorian Calendar: February is an unusual month of only 28 days.

The most logical way to divide the 365-day year into twelve months would be to use five 31-day months and seven 30-day months; this configuration would never require two 31-day months back-to-back, yet on the Gregorian it happens twice: July-August and December-January. For some reason, the configuration we have today was chosen to allow February to be only 28 days. Maybe Pope Gregory XIII shared these hypotheses and was adjusting the layout to make the eleventh month, November, begin on Jesus' true birthday as a step in quelling the Protestant revolt? As a side note, Halloween, a holiday with origin's beginning 2000 years ago, falls in a strange location, the eve of November first.

There is no reason for the Romans to have vacated their base-ten system before Christianity; they could have simply used five 36-day months and five 37-day months, after all, their calendar was a sun-based system. The hypotheses here conflicts with the recorded history of these calendars, yet logic supports upgrading our hypotheses to theory. The two months were added in the most reasonable place, the end of the year, and Jesus lived 11,111 days. This was just a short curiosity for consideration, especially being 11,111 days is related to the numbers for the theoretical ages, the eleven and one-hundred-and-eleven years of Isaac and Abraham when the Abrahamic Covenant was established. The comma even falls in the right place: 11,111.

Similarly, there is another interesting relationship from the theoretical ages of Abraham and Isaac: the ground distance between the Rock at Horeb struck by Moses and the crucifixion location is 1,111,111 feet. The striking by Moses was a foreshadow of Jesus being beaten and crucified, and according to the New Testament, Moses was in Arabia, rather the popularly held Sinai Peninsula, when he struck the rock. Google Earth shows the distance from the crucifixion location, Golgotha in Jerusalem (located behind the bus station in Jerusalem, just north of the Old City's Damascus Gate), to the Rock at Horeb in Saudi Arabia to be 1,111,111 feet on a heading of 180 degrees. Google Earth labels this site as "rock at Horeb", with Mt. Sinai being just eleven miles to its south. Why would there be correlations to distances across the Earth in present-day units? Sir Isaac Newton is reported to have thought the end days would bring out such concerning ground distances, and that report led your author to this discovery. Regardless of whether Newton said this or not, our finding is most interesting.

Another special biblical number, 2520, or 7 x 360, shows up throughout both the chronology and creation. Earth's average diameter, measured in the present-day unit of miles, is the product 2520 x π = 7916.8 miles, moon's diameter is 2520 - 360 = 2160 miles, and the sun's diameter is 2520 x 7 x 7 x 7 = 864,360 miles. Each are in miles, and each are based on 2520. Additionally, the surface elevation at Golgotha is 2520 feet. Man chose and made all measurement units, but it appears Almighty God foresaw his choice before the world was even created.

We have demonstrated the month of April 30 AD was the actual crucifixion month of Jesus. The end of that Hebrew month, or end of the moon cycle, was April 21, 30 AD on the first-century Julian calendar. Multiplying the first-century <u>month x day x year</u> of that dark-moon date, or 4 x 21 x 30 = 2520, produces the special biblical number 2520 and uncovers a hidden numerical template: the recurrence of <u>month x day x century x year</u> is found throughout human history. On the Gregorian calendar, Jesus died April 3, 30 AD, rose from the dead April 6, 30 AD, and first appeared to his disciples on April 7, 30 AD. Using our template, <u>month x day x year</u>, gives:

> Crucifixion, April 3, 30 AD (Gregorian): **4 x 3 x 30 = 360**. Jesus' ministry as the Lamb of God was one biblical year, or 360 days.

> Resurrection, April 6, 30 AD (Gregorian): **4 x 6 x 30 = 720**. Jesus was in the grave 72 hours. Jesus, the Lord of the Sabbath, rose from the dead on the Sabbath.

> First Appearance, April 7, 30 AD (Gregorian): **4 x 7 x 30 = 840**. Jesus first appeared to his disciples on the first day of the week, or Sunday. During his ministry, he had sent out two groups of disciples to minister: the first group was the 12 Apostles and the second was a group of 70 disciples. His first appearance to his disciples correlates its date calculation to the number of disciples in each group, **12 x 70 equals 840, as does 4 x 7 x 30**.

God foreknew not only man's length-measuring units, but also his calendars. Furthermore, number patterns from the Julian calendar's dark-moon date span all the way to present times:

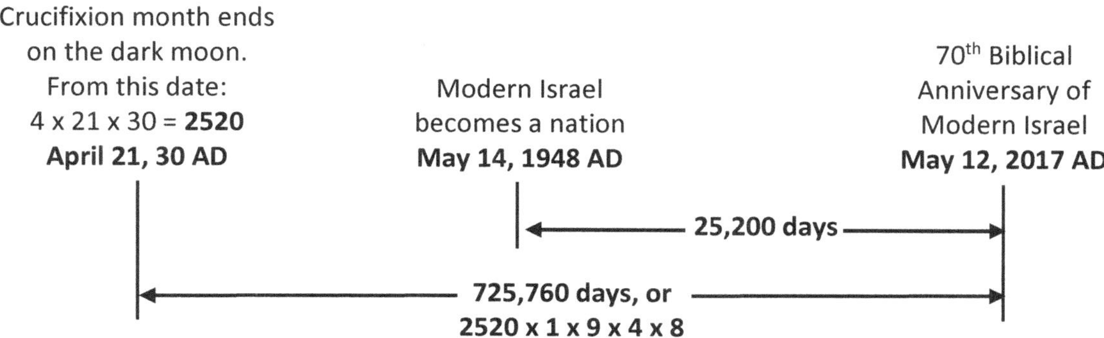

The exact number of days from the end of the passion month to the seventieth anniversary of Israel's statehood is found by calculations based on the first two dates (i.e., based on April 21, 30 AD and 1948). Also, the Seventieth Biblical Anniversary interval of 25,200 days is a multiple of the dark moon date result, or 2520 x 10. Note: The dark moon date is from the Julian calendar.

Abram was born 1948 years after Adam, Isaac was born in 1948 BC, and present-day Israel became a nation in 1948 AD. The product of numerals in 1948, or 1x9x4x8, and the multiplier of 2520 yields 725,760 days, or the precise span from the dark moon of the crucifixion month to the seventieth biblical anniversary of modern Israel. The term "biblical anniversary" refers to 360-day years, or the number of days in a year before Noah's flood. During the flood, Earth experienced unbalanced loads from its rotation, just like a washing machine sometimes does during an unbalanced spin cycle. The washing machine can walk across the floor, and similarly Earth shifted in its solar orbit, changing the length of our years and the orbit of our moon as well. Later chapters will reveal more amazing designs found throughout time, including wonders in present days.

CHAPTER FOUR

ACCURACY OF THE RESULT

In the six hundredth year of Noah's life, in the second month, the seventeenth day of the month, the same day were all the fountains of the great deep broken up, and the windows of heaven were opened. Genesis 7:11 KJV

A great flood destroyed the entire earth nearly 4400 years ago; only Noah, his wife, his three sons, and their wives, survived. The story is even older than the Bible itself, for example, *the story of Gilgamesh from ancient Sumerian tablets predates the Bible and records a world-wide flood.*

The Bible we have today was written in the days of, and after, Moses. Although written much later than the events of Genesis, the early biblical record is amazingly accurate, as our chronology testifies. Surely Noah had preflood records on the ark from which the Bible could be assembled years later. With God's guidance and oversight, primordial history has been preserved for us today. This author has not studied the Sumerian tablets, and cannot further comment on them, but certainly there would be other accounts of the flood, as there were eight survivors to recall it.

Nearly every religious culture has a flood story, yet most people today do not believe it ever happened. Earth is a water-filled planet, with nearly seventy percent of its surface covered in water, and many geologists estimate that there may be three to ten times more water below the ocean floors. According to the Bible, waters from the great depths of the earth were the source for much of the flood waters, *"the fountains of the great deep broke open."*

Was Noah six-hundred years old when the flood began? Many would say yes, but was he, or was he instead 599 years old when the flood began in his six-hundredth year? A fair and honest answer is, *"we don't know exactly, except that he was between 599 and six hundred years."*

For now, if the age of Noah at the time of the flood can vary up to a year, then the maximum accuracy the chronology can have is one year. Many skeptics will argue this problem propagates with each generation, requiring a one-year inaccuracy to be added for each generation, to give an accumulated error. However, this unlearned view degrades the ancient people's intelligence; look at the details written in the following verse:

And it came to pass in the six hundredth and first year, in the first month, the first day of the month, the waters were dried up from off the earth: and Noah removed the covering of the ark, and looked, and behold, the face of the ground was dry. Genesis 8:13 KJV

The ancients kept amazing records, but not the way we do today. Skeptics should realize that you cannot judge primitive metrics by modern ones. Comparing this verse with Genesis 7:11, we learn more about the precision of the chronology. In the first verse, the *"six hundredth year"* is referenced to Noah's life, *Noah's six hundredth year,* while in the second, the *"six hundredth and first year"* has no specific reference. The second did not need to say *six hundredth and first year of Noah's life,* that would be redundant, all previous references had perished in the flood. Make sure you get this point: the Bible is saying THIS IS *the six hundredth and first year,* creation year is no longer the reference, now Noah is! The Hebrew word בן is translated *"son"* and is from the root word בנה meaning *"builder".* Everyone after the flood were *sons of Noah,* or results of *"Noah's building",* and that includes us.

The second verse gives even further understanding. The six hundredth and first year began in the first month, in the first day of the month. Month comes from the Hebrew word for *new,* implying *new moon,* and years were recorded on the reliable cycle of the moon. New moons were correlated with the lights in the heavens (i.e., the constellations) to give seasons based on Earth's approximate position in its solar orbit. For specific dating, days were counted from new moon sightings, giving an exceptionally dependable and repeatable moon calendar.

And God said, let there be lights (sun, moon, and constellation) in the firmament of the heaven to divide the day from the night; and let them be for signs, and for seasons, and for days, and years: Genesis 1:14 KJV

The ancients did not celebrate birthdays when we do. They did not use a solar calendar. They would not have a birthday celebration for someone each day of the year. Their actual birthdays floated with the moon cycle, varying by up to a month from solar-year to solar-year, but they observed the constellations and related them to the moon cycle as God had commanded. They knew the moon cycle someone was born in, and day-count in that cycle, but not with reference to exact position in the solar orbit, but rather with approximations they could observe in the constellation.

From their writings, the antediluvians intended their records to be accurate to within one year but to neglect month and day. They kept accurate records over great spans of time (Exodus 12:41 and 1 Kings 6:1 are great examples). They were highly intelligent people! Many of the structures that remain are beyond our building capabilities today, just consider the Great Pyramids. They recorded the six hundredth and first year as a special marker in History, *the day the waters had dried off the earth.* God had indeed given them a new beginning on the very first day of the year on their moon calendar, their "New Year's Day."

The number correlations supporting the completed chronology strongly suggest this amazing tool is accurate to the year. All ages in antiquity are marked from one annually-repeating-day each year, a floating day on solar calendars being it is instead based on the moon cycle, but nonetheless, one specific marker in the yearly cycle.

Their "New Year's Day," or first day of the first new moon, was probably their annual reference, but whatever the marker, the time before this repeating day arrived was likely disregarded in counting age. A baby born two months before this special moon-day arrived would be considered zero years old when his first year began two months later. Likewise, the recorded age of the father at his child's birth would correspond to the father's age at this same point. If someone was born within six months of the reference, they may have opted to use the previous year but with adjustments to keep the accounting straight. We simply do not know the details, but we do know the results of the chronology and its supporting correlations. The flood-era data is straightforward and fits well, but what about later dates?

The chronology uses only two references, Exodus 12:40-41 and 1 Kings 6:1, to span 910 years from the offering of Isaac to the fourth year of Solomon's reign. In the previous chapter, we covered this in detail, but now add that these long spans used even decades. To accomplish this, the record keepers referenced the fourth year of Solomon's reign as an endpoint. The records after Solomon began a new reckoning system for the lineage of the kings.

Solomon reigned forty years until his death, and then, the Israelites divided into two houses: the house of Israel and the house of Judah. The records of the kings, like that of the antediluvians, neglected month and day, recording only years, but a major time-keeping difference began. The king period referenced the ascension years in terms of the reigning year of the king in the opposite house in addition to giving the length of their reigns. For example, King Nadab ascended the throne of Israel in the second year of Asa, king of Judah, and reigned two years. At first glance, this might seem to be only a superfluous detail, but unfortunately, it is not that simple.

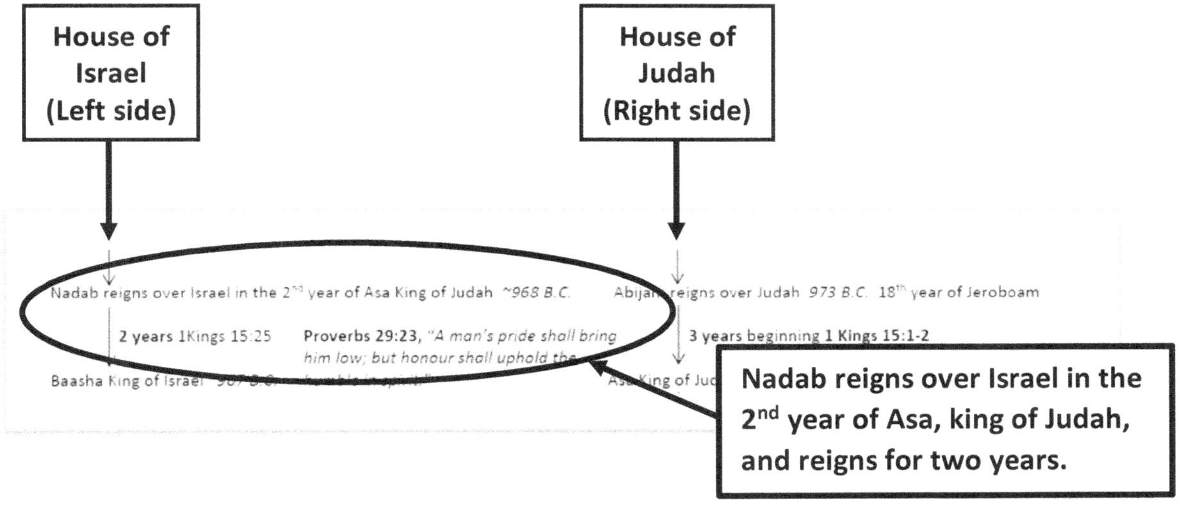

Excerpt from the chronology during the period of the kings.

The timeline of the kings is not as straightforward as that of Genesis. Early records are sequential and continuous from new year to new year, and the king lines also use the new year marker, but not necessarily in a continuous manner. By referencing one line to the other, years are sometimes added, and other times omitted from the actual reigns. The annual flag is still used, but sometimes new years are skipped, and sometimes counted, depending upon whether the king ascended before or after them. Equally problematic is the time of their deaths. Did the king die before or after the new year? Even by careful comparison of the record, we can only give approximate dates for the kings, but fortunately, the Bible provides two methods for verifying their overall span.

As expounded in the previous chapter, Ezekiel prophesied 390 years of iniquity in the house of Israel that concluded with the siege of Jerusalem and destruction of Solomon's temple. The pagan idol worship of the house of Israel infiltrated into the house of Judah and the destruction of Solomon's temple resulted. The completed chronology agrees that exactly 390 years after the house of Israel began worshipping the golden calves in Samaria, the temple in Jerusalem was destroyed.

The second overall verification of this period is the forty-nine-year Jubilee cycle. By comparing Ezekiel 1:1-2 with Ezekiel 40:1, scholars conclude that fourteen years after the temple's demise should be a Jubilee year, and on our chronology, it is, while on other chronologies, it is not. Most other chronologies use the secular 586 BC date for the temple's destruction, but that contradicts the Bible. There are eleven years from the beginning of the Babylonian captivity until the temple's destruction, therefore, the end of the seventy-year Babylonian captivity should be 59 years after the temple was destroyed. The Nabonidus and Cyrus cylinder artifacts assures the end of the captivity was 538 BC, therefore, per the scriptures, the temple was destroyed in 597 BC, not the secular 586 BC. Ironically, the span between the destruction of the first temple in 597 BC and the second in 70 AD is exactly 666 years.

The subject Jubilee, the one occurring fourteen years after the temple was destroyed, corresponds to 583 BC when using the artifacts in conjunction with the Bible. From this date, all other Jubilees, including some notable ones from the period of the kings and earlier can easily be dated:

1. The fifteenth Jubilee began in 730 BC and was exactly 777 years after the Exodus. The house of Israel went into captivity in Assyria either prior to or during that year.

2. The seventeenth Jubilee was 632 BC, and per our dating of the kings, was also the eighteenth year of Josiah's kingship. That year was the last Jubilee before the house of Judah went into captivity in Babylon and coincided with the largest Passover celebration in history. Josiah would likely agree that his eighteenth year was indeed a Jubilee, after all, he ordered a great celebration that year.

3. The Year 1122 BC was the seventh Jubilee, or the eleventh before our base Jubilee of 583 BC. Eleven years after this seventh Jubilee was the monumental Year 1111 BC, a year so special we devoted an entire chapter to it.

4. From the Jubilee count, the first Sabbath year in the promised land was 1465 BC, and the second one was 1458 BC. The resulting 3996 BC year of creation has a peculiar relation to the second Sabbath year, 3x9x9x6 = 1458. Surely God loves numbers.

This is just a scratch of the surface of the numerical congruencies and patterns revealed by the chronology. To facilitate an easy read of the book, many of the number relations are deferred to the Appendices.

The interval spanning the temple's construction-to-destruction was exactly 430 years, matching the length of another important span, the 430 years between Isaac's being offered and the Exodus Passover. The reoccurrence of this number is among many patterns that will be presented. The Biblical Chronology is exact, and time is designed.

The ancient record keepers intentionally excluded months and days, opting rather to preserve a chronological history with a precision of less than a year. Their documenting of ages, lineages, and intervals between major events was a most successful effort, accurate to the very year.

CHAPTER FIVE

DESIGNS IN TIME

Previous chapters have shown numerical designs, not only in biblical history, but also in creation. For example, the numbers making up the ground distance from the crucifixion site of Jesus to the rock at Horeb were only comprised of the numeral "one" like the ages of Abraham and Isaac at the time Abraham offered him. Abraham's and Isaac's ages were also shown to be related to the very number of days that Jesus lived. This chapter will continue to show astounding biblical patterns from the solved chronology. There are 2048 years from creation to the birth of Isaac and eleven years from his birth until he was offered:

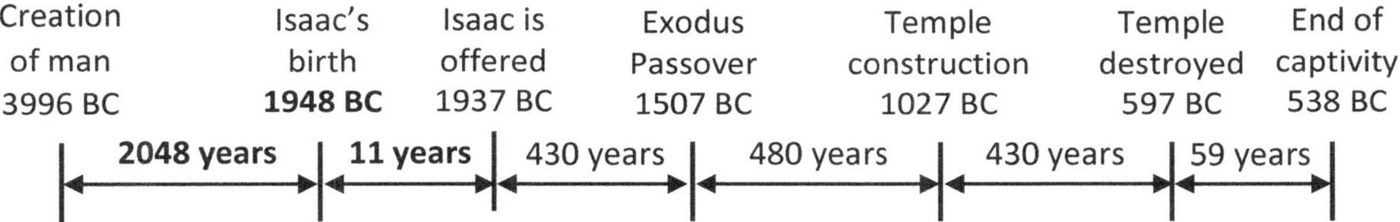

Solution based on Isaac's birth year and age when Abraham offered him.

Abraham was one hundred years older than Isaac, therefore, we can rearrange the graph above to present the solution based on Abraham's age and birth year, rather than Isaac's. One hundred years are subtracted from the interval from Adam's creation to Isaac's birth to find Abraham's birth year and then one hundred years are added to Isaac's age to find Abraham's age:

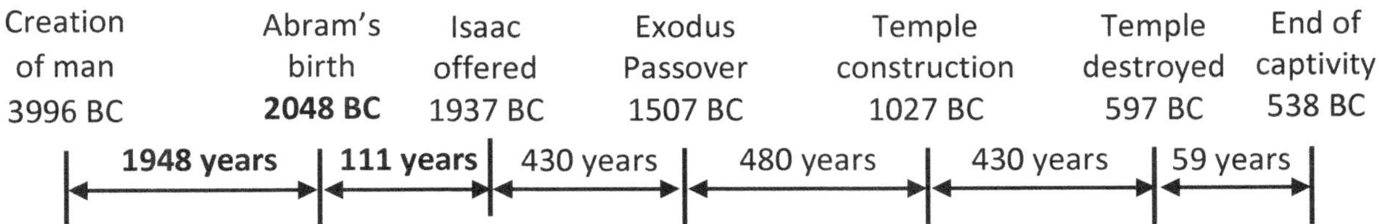

Solution based on Abraham's birth year and age when offering Isaac.

Comparing the above figures shows the birth years and spans from creation for both Abraham and Isaac are reciprocals of one another: Abraham was born 1948 years after Adam in the year 2048 BC, Isaac was born 2048 years after Adam in 1948 BC. Both approaches have a numerical relation to the year modern-day Israel formed in 1948 AD. Rearranging further reveals a pattern of Jubilees that span the entire chronological solution:

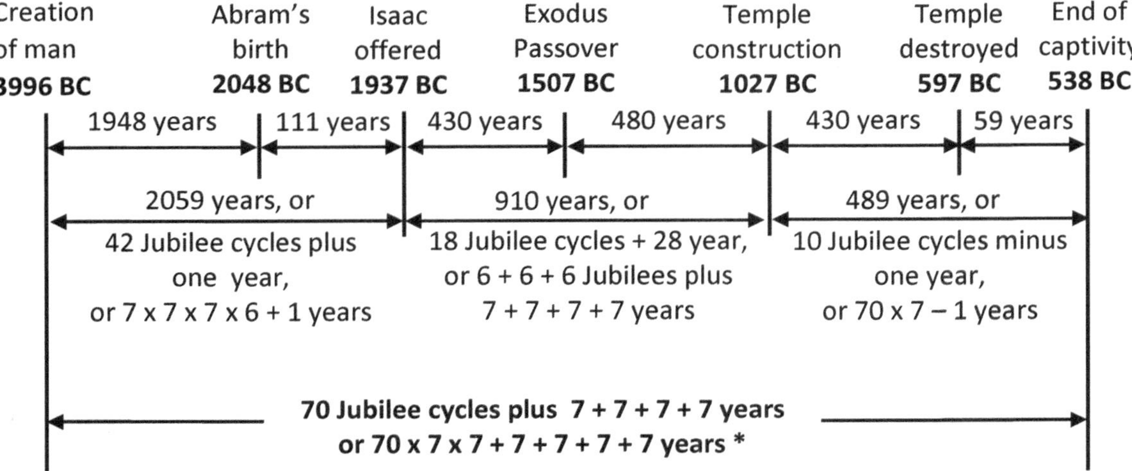

*The span of the completed chronology is comprised of seven numeral sevens.

The overall chronology is divided into three parts: the first and last divisions are each within one year of being even multiples of Jubilee cycles, while the middle division is four sabbath periods longer than even multiples. The overall span is 70 Jubilees cycles plus four sabbath cycles.

The overall span of the solved chronology can be expressed using seven occurrences of the biblical numeral seven. What could be more confirming? This is simply amazing and is such by design!

The intervals after Isaac is offered, up until the temple is destroyed, are each in even decades. The sum of the years before he was offered (i.e., 2059 years), and the years after the temple was destroyed (i.e., 59 years), both end with fifty-nine:

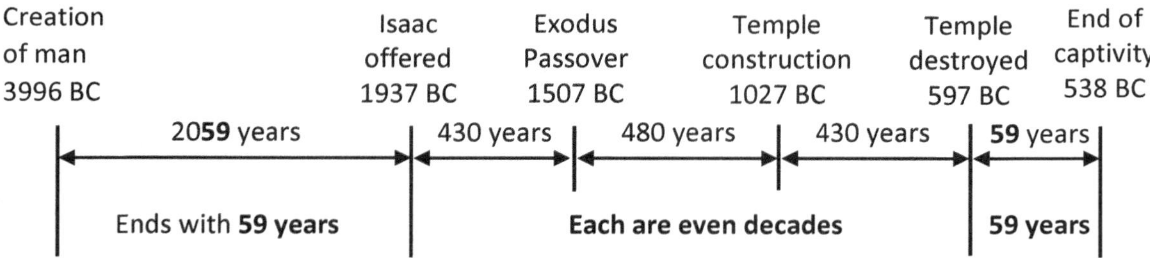

Solved chronology showing "End Periods" each contain fifty-nine years; all others are even decades.

Adding Isaac's theoretical age to the beginning and end periods makes them become even decades. The results are the even spans 2070 years and 70 years, both ending with the biblical generation, or seventy years. To balance the equations, eleven years are then subtracted from each 430-year span to make them a shortened 419 years, a length that was found earlier for the lineage of the kings, and almost as if to confirm that period:

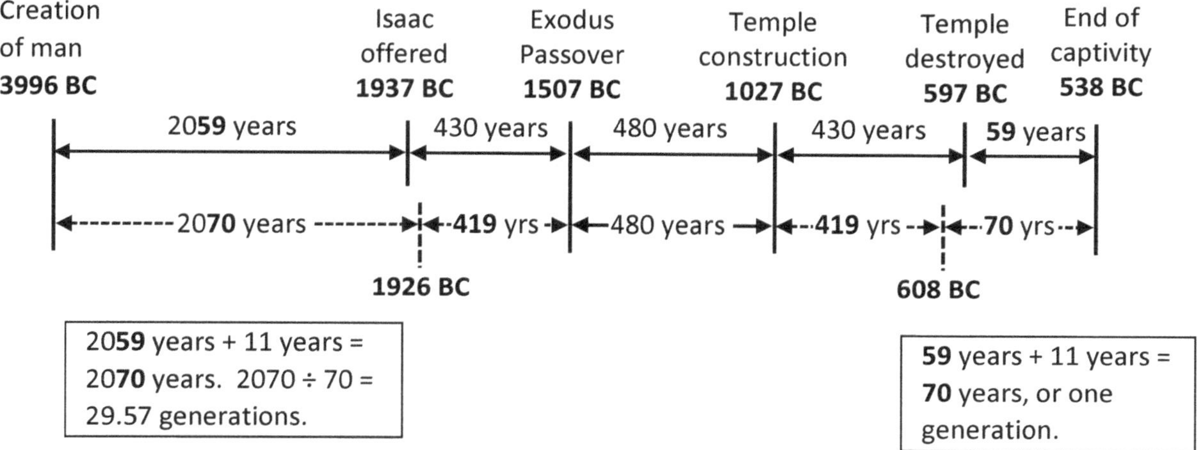

Isaac's age when offered is added to the first and last periods to make both end with seventy. This requires his eleven-years-age to also be subtracted from the two 430-year intervals.

Skeptics may ask, "Why are you adding the theoretical age to these end periods?" The answer is the patterns lead there. This is an intermediate step, like "completing the square in Algebra". This is a behind the scenes process that sometimes uncovers meaningful and provable results. We are not wildly manipulating numbers to create milestone dates, but rather adding our key interval, Isaac's theoretical age, to rearrange the timeline. The overall span is unchanged, and though 1926 BC is not known to be a meaningful date, 608 BC certainly was, it was the beginning of the Babylonian Captivity. The rearranged graph has symmetry. There are three periods of even decades, 2070 years, 480 years, and 70 years, and the remainder are duplicates and are both 419 years. Only the 480-year period was not affected by our adding of eleven years, but even it has a correlation with eleven. Adding eleven to 480 years would give 491 years, or the very beginning of an eleventh Jubilee cycle.

Our rearranged graph is a meaningful and balanced display of the solved chronology. The beginning and end periods both contain seventy, or explicitly 20**70** years and **70** years. A biblical generation is seventy years (Psalms 90:10), therefore these results, in generations, might hold a hidden pattern and mystery, further confirming the specialness of this chronology. The result on the right (on the above graph), is exactly one generation, while the one on the left is 29.57 generations. Like these numbers, Jesus' ministry as the Lamb of God began when he was almost thirty (Luke 3:23) and lasted one year (Luke 4:19). Adding the resulting generations together gives 30.57 generations, and although changing measuring units, 30.57 years is extremely near the exact number of years that Jesus was on Earth.

Considering a hidden message may be intended, years are converted to days: 30.57 x 365.24 = 11,165 days. In a previous chapter Jesus was shown to have lived exactly 11,111 days, and these additional 54 days extend to the day after the Holy Spirit was given on Pentecost, or May 29, 30 AD (Julian Calendar): Jesus ascended to heaven just before the Holy Spirit was given on May 28, 30 AD (Julian Calendar). With biblical days beginning in the evening, the 11,165 days could be the precise number of days from

Jesus' birth until Pentecost. Alternatively, his birthday could be reckoned as "Day One", making this Pentecost the 11,165[th] day since his birth.

There seems to be a hidden correlation from the solved chronology that relates the interval from Jesus' birth to Pentecost! For the skeptic who questions the method, or who insists the interval does not fall on Pentecost, but rather the day after, there is more: the terrorist's attacks on the United States occurred September 11, 2001, or exactly two thousand biblical years plus one day after this special Pentecost (i.e., 720,001 days), or exactly 720,000 days after May 29, 30 AD, the day that followed Pentecost:

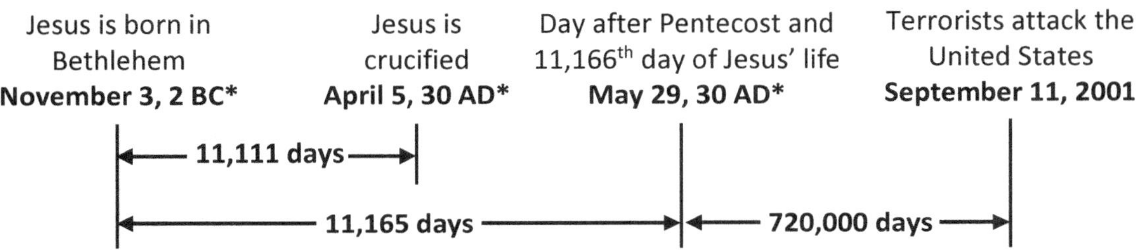

*** indicates Julian Calendar dates.**

Pentecost 30 AD was on the 11,165[th] day of Jesus' life (i.e. after his resurrection). The interval of 11,165 days ends the day after Pentecost, or the 11,166[th] day of his life. The day after Pentecost, or May 29, 30 AD, is exactly 2000 biblical years (i.e. 2000 x 360 days) before September 11, 2001.

Time patterns are found throughout history, including in our present day as shown on the next graph. All dates on the next display are exact, but bad theology mixed with those precise patterns can lead to bad conclusions. The graph displays major events and people's names; however, please do not jump to conclusions. **This author is not accusing any person of anything** but is rather presenting factual timelines. The number 666 appears in several key intervals on the graph, but the persons to which these spans point is not the intended message. The intervals are pointing to new eras rather than people, for example, the number of years from the crucifixion of Jesus to the first Sunday President Trump was in office is exactly 725,**666** days. On that Sunday, two days after his inauguration, President Trump had his first phone call with Prime Minister Benjamin Netanyahu of Israel, and that Sunday phone call also occurred precisely 103,**666** weeks after the Sunday of Jesus' first appearance after his crucifixion. This is a strange number combination being both intervals contain 666 in two separate units of measure, days, and weeks. There were two persons on the phone, so if the timeline is pointing to a single person, which one?

Again, your author believes these numbers are pointing to a period, not a person, and that much bad theology abounds with the topic of 666. The numbers probably point to a period of man trying to establish peace in the Middle East. It is most interesting to find these intervals, however, although not displayed on the graph, that Sunday was also exactly 736,**777** days after Jesus was born. The number of perfection is seven, therefore 777 is certainly not a bad number. Again, bad theology leads to bad conclusions.

The book of Revelations states the number 666 is the number of a man, or mankind, but contrary to popular and long-held opinions, it does not say this number is evil. The purpose of 666 is stated in the book of Revelation. It is to be used to calculate the number of the beast's name; therefore, the number of its name cannot be 666 itself. This is a bit tricky but hang in there and I will do my best to explain. In Revelation we find,

> *And that no man might buy or sell, save he that had the mark, or (i.e., which is) the name of the beast, or (i.e., which is) the **number of his name**. Revelation 13:17 KJV*

> *<u>Here is wisdom</u>. Let him that hath understanding count (i.e., pebble) the **number of the beast**: for it is the number of a man; and his number is Six hundred, threescore, and six. Revelation 13:18 KJV*

Man's number is six, and the variants, six-hundred, sixty, and six. The beast's number is six, the number of mankind. The number of the beast's name and the number of the beast are two different numbers: Revelations instructs the wise to count (or pebble, in Greek) the *number of the beast* to determine *the number of the name of the beast,* implying the beast has a name and that the name has a number.

> *<u>And here is the mind which hath wisdom</u>. The seven heads are seven mountains, on which the woman sitteth. Revelation 17:9 KJV*

> *And there are seven kings: **five are fallen, and one is**, and the other is not yet come; and when he cometh, he must continue a short space. Revelation 17:10 KJV*

Revelation brings up wisdom again, just as it did when introducing the method for calculating the number of the beast's name. This second mention of wisdom implies that the previous instructions needed additional information that is to be found in this second instance (i.e., Revelation 17:10 shows the number of the beast to be six).

The woman is riding a seven-headed beast, or seven different kingdoms at different points in history. In the days of John, the writer of Revelation, **five kings had fallen, *and one is***, therefore, the beast number was six, the number of mankind, and it was to be pebbled. The number of the beast's name likely being the number of times you pebble "six", or count by six, to reach 666. The number of the beast's name would then be one hundred and eleven. The following graph of modern times is for your consideration. All intervals and dates on it are precise to-the-day and match intervals found in the scriptures. More on that next.

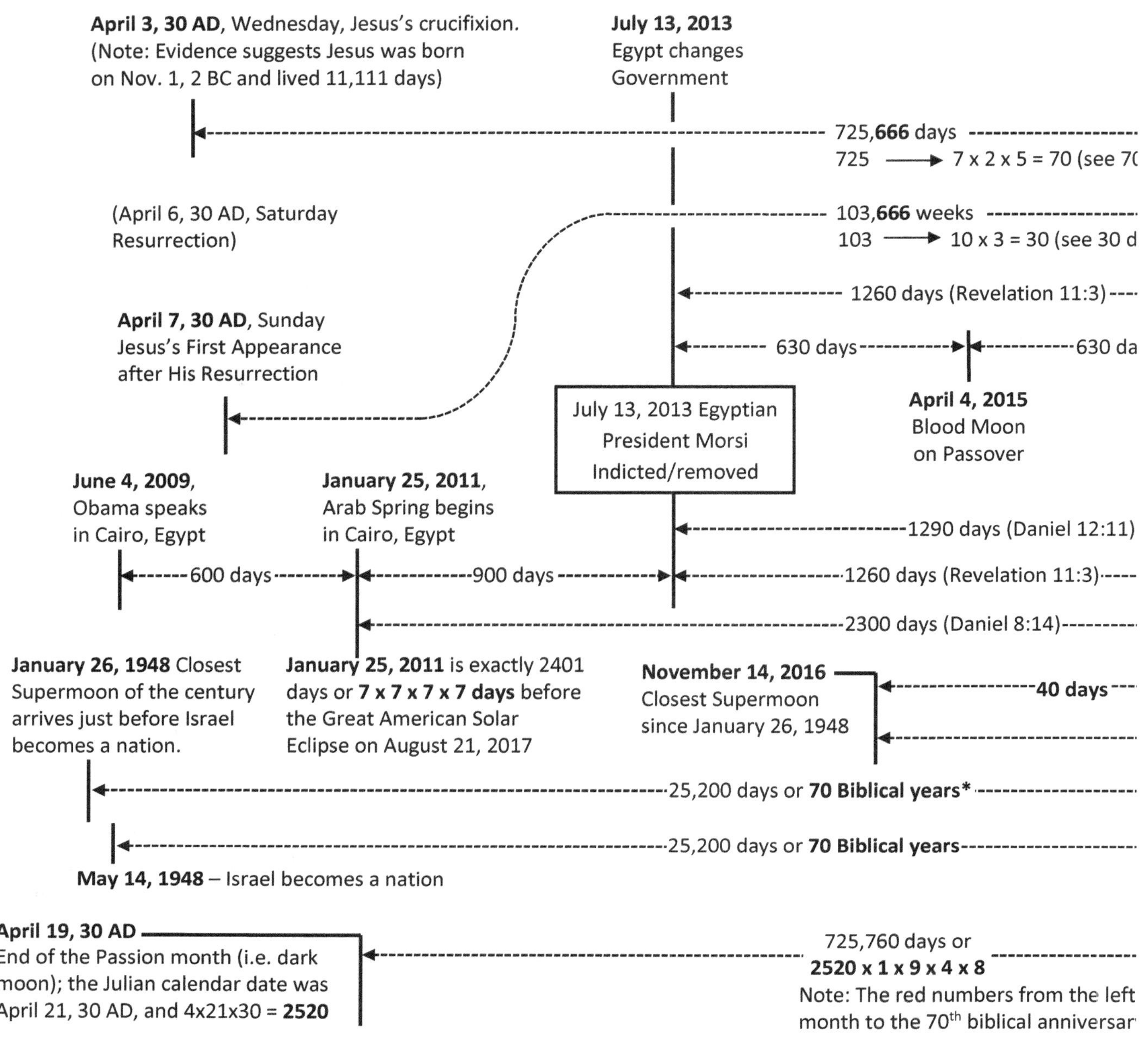

Book	No. Verses	Corresponding Date	Description
Exodus	1209	November 2, 2016	FBI releases case concerning Bill Clinton 6 days before the election.
Numbers	1288	January 20, 2017	Inauguration of Trump
Isaiah	1291	January 23, 2017	Trump's 1st Full business day; first-ever WTO amendment; 1st phone call with Netanyahu as day began in Israel (i.e. day begins at evening).
Jeremiah	1364	April 6, 2017	Jews sacrifice a lamb inside Old City for first time in 2000 years. USA attacks in Syria with 59 tomahawk missiles.
Samuel	1506	August 26, 2017	Most costly hurricane (Harvey) in world history following the Great American Solar Eclipse 5 days earlier.
Genesis	1534	September 23, 2017	Astronomical sign of Revelation 12
Kings	1534	September 23, 2017	Astronomical sign of Revelation 12
Chronicles	1765	May 12, 2018	Exact solar anniversary of May 12, 2017 (see timeline above) 5x12x20x18 = 6x6x6x100; US embassy moved on 5x14x20x18 = 25,200

In the Masoretic Hebrew Bible, the number of verses of each book is recorded as part of the biblical record. This table is produced by simply placing the verse-number counts from the Hebrew Bible on the proposed timeline above.

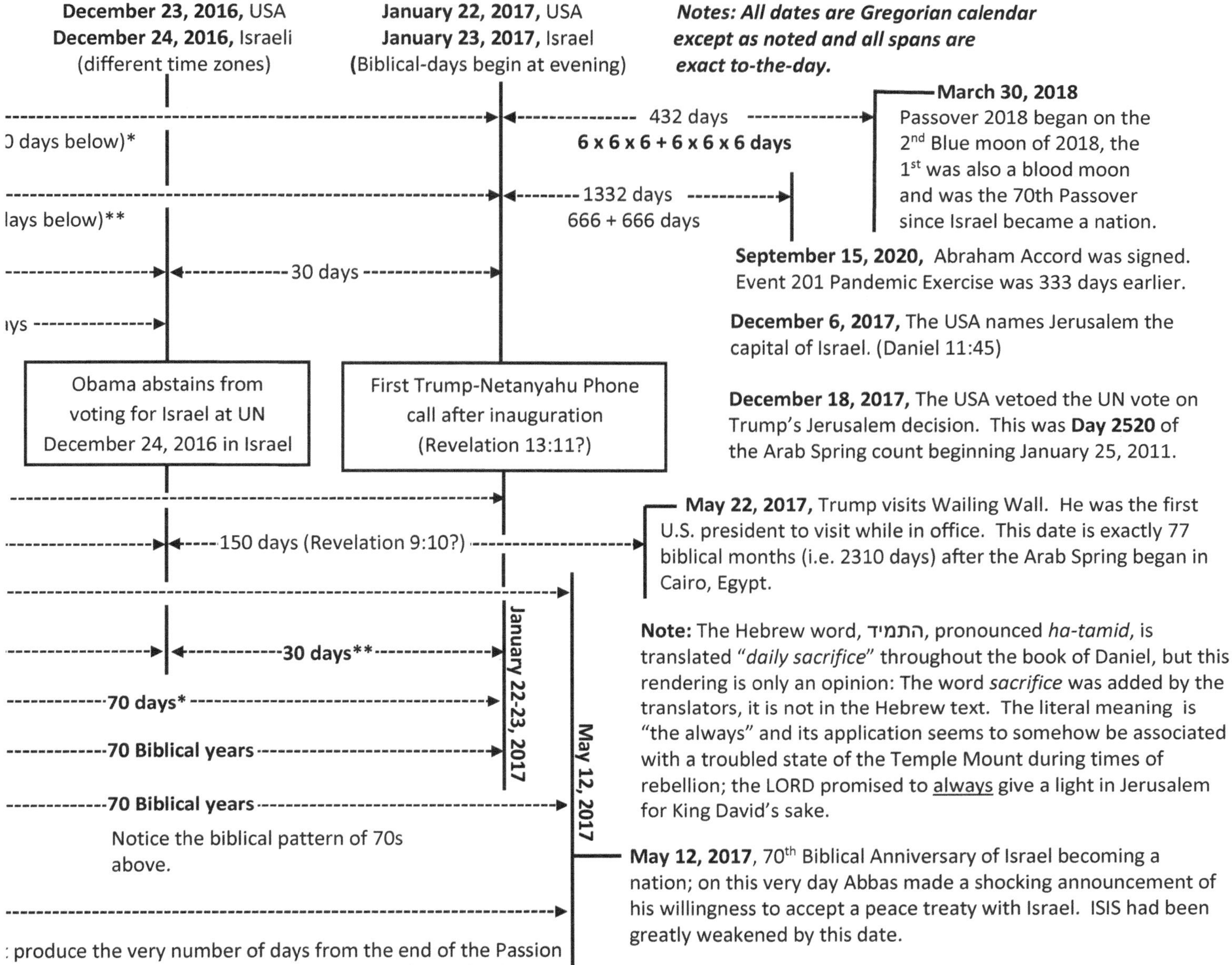

Moses and Elijah were prophets with qualities given in Revelation 11. They both ended their ministries in the same geographical area and at the lowest elevation on Earth (i.e., just east of the Jordan River at the entrance to the Promised Land.) Moses could only bring the Israelites up to the Promised Land, but not into it. Perhaps the witnesses in Revelation wore sackcloth to symbolize mourning. In the entire Bible, only Jesus, Moses, and Elijah fasted forty days and these three appeared together on the mount of Transfiguration. Could the forty days from the Supermoon of November 14, 2016, to the UN vote on December 23, 2016, be symbolically confirming Moses and Elijah as the two witnesses of Revelation?

On this timeline, the 1335-day given in Daniel 12:12 falls March 8, 2017, a Wednesday, and middle of the week in which David Freidman was confirmed as the US ambassador to Israel. During that week both Israel and the USA issued Muslim travel bans, a US Congressman toured Israel announcing Trump would fulfill his pledge to move the US embassy to Jerusalem, Trump ordered the 75th Ranger regiment to Syria, and a bill banning Muslim loudspeakers in the Old City received preliminary approval in the Israeli Knesset. The word "blessed" in Daniel chapter twelve could alternatively be translated as "happy" (Daniel 12:12): This indeed was the very center of a most happy week for Israel. Was this in-fact the 1335-day of Daniel 12:12? Was the first Trump-Netanyahu phone call the actual 1290-day of Daniel 12:11? If so, the evening of April 1, 2017, would begin the 1360-day, being biblical days start in the evening, and **4x01x20x17 = 1360**.

Again, to be clear, this author **is not saying** either Donald Trump or Benjamin Netanyahu is the Antichrist or any such accusations because this author does not think the Bible is saying that. However, these intervals contain 666 and 777 and that is quite peculiar and leads to a broad subject, much of which is beyond the scope of this work. The purpose of this book is to provide an accurate biblical chronology with supporting references and to report findings. Chronology is a backbone that gives structure to the body of ancient writings to help facilitate proper translations and gain understanding. The previous timeline is simply a finding to be considered when refining theological opinions.

This first phone call date, January 22, 2017, began a new policy in the United States' approach to the Middle East. The newly elected Donald Trump would bring huge changes including decimating ISIS and moving the U.S. Embassy to Jerusalem. His victory to become President was almost as surprising as the final year of his term that included the coronavirus pandemic, hurried vaccines, and chaos at the capitol. Exactly center of his presidency and peaking just twelve minutes after midnight, just as January 21, 2019, commenced, a lunar eclipse centered on the longitude of Washington DC illuminated its night skies. God was indeed making a statement in the heavens about this period just as he promised to do in Genesis chapter one. These were and are special times and nothing makes better sense now than to know the Bible.

The Abraham Accord peace treaty was reached during the final year of Trump's presidency, and whether that work-of-mankind will last is yet to be seen. The remainder of the book is a collection of interesting discoveries found by using the chronology and many of those are first-ever findings.

Abraham Accord commemorative coin minted after the peace treaty of September 2020.

CHAPTER SIX

THE MYSTERY OF ELIJAH

And after six days Jesus taketh Peter, James, and John his brother, and bringeth them up into an high mountain apart, And was transfigured before them: and his face did shine as the sun, and his raiment was white as light. And, behold, there appeared unto them Moses and Elias (Elijah) talking with him. Matthew 17:1-3 KJV

The New Testament transfiguration story is an intriguing account of Jesus being transformed on a *high mountain* before his disciples. His face shined as *the sun*, his raiment was *white as light*, and *Moses and Elijah appeared* and talked with him. The three disciples were terrified, and you can imagine why: Jesus's face was shining ***like the sun!*** What a description!

This remarkable event occurred only weeks, if not days, before Jesus died on the cross, and yet being so incredible, the disciples were required to keep it a secret until after the resurrection. Why? What does it mean? Where did it occur? Why were Moses and Elijah there? What is the relationship between these three, or further still, these six when including Peter, James, and John? This story is clothed in mystery!

These three amazing individuals, Jesus, Moses, and Elijah have a unique commonality. They are the only persons in the Bible that ever fasted 40 days and Moses even did so twice, but what else did they share, other than a relationship with God?

Considering them two at a time, they had much in common but with the third always being totally in contrast. For example, Jesus and Moses both died, but Elijah did not. Of the three, only Jesus has an empty tomb. Jesus and Elijah both publicly ascended into heaven, while Moses instead has a grave. Moses never raised the dead, but both Jesus and Elijah did. Furthermore, much is known about the ancestry of Jesus and Moses, but not so for Elijah. Who were his parents? We do not know. He was said to be a *Tishbite*, but there are no other *Tishbites* in the Bible? What is a *Tishbite*? We were never told Elijah had parents, nor that he was even human. Consider the following:

> ***And no man hath ascended up to heaven,*** *but he that came down from heaven, even the Son of man which is in heaven.* John 3:13 KJV

*And it came to pass, as they still went on, and talked, that, behold, there appeared a chariot of fire, and horses of fire, and parted them asunder; and **Elijah went up by a whirlwind into heaven**.* 2 Kings 2:11 KJV

Jesus said no man has ascended to heaven, but the Old Testament says Elijah did. Therefore, if we believe Jesus, we must believe Elijah was not a man. Elijah referred to his fathers, but only once, and he never said who they were. Were they the watchers that came down on Mount Herman? The evidence is an astounding, yes! The Bible's first mention of Elijah is found in the following verse:

And Elijah the Tishbite, who was of the inhabitants of Gilead, said unto Ahab, As the LORD God of Israel liveth, before whom I stand, there shall not be dew nor rain these years, but according to my word. 1 Kings 17:1 KJV

Elijah appears for the first time in the Bible with a dramatic introduction: Elijah the Tishbite from Gilead stands before the LORD God of Israel, and he is going to control the weather. Interestingly, the name Israel was given to Jacob right after the Galeed (same Hebrew spelling as Gilead) covenant was made in Genesis 31, and the names, *Israel,* and *Gilead*, are both found in this introductory verse. More on that later, but for now, we will consider the word *"Tishbite."*

The words translated, *"...the Tishbite, who was of the inhabitants...",* are taken entirely from two consecutive Hebrew words, and written right to left, are, התשבי מתשבי. These two sequential words, without the prefixes, or the bolded letters in each, leaves the identical base, תשבי, or *Tishbite* in English.

The prefix ה is translated *"the"*, and the leftover תשבי is translated *"Tishbite"*, giving *"the Tishbite"*. The second word, מתשבי, has the prefix מ meaning either *"who"* or *"from"*, and here has been translated *"who was of the"* with the residual, תשבי (or Tishbite), in this instance being translated *"inhabitants of"*. Without the prefixes, the remaining letters are again identical, *"Tishbite"*, or תשבי. *"Tishbite"* means either *dweller of,* or *inhabitant of,* therefore, Elijah could be considered *a dweller from the dwellers of Gilead*: Elijah's often title, *"Elijah the Tishbite"*, is literally the unusual, *"Elijah the dweller"*.

With this, we next investigate *"Gilead"*, and it has the same Hebrew spelling as *Galeed*, or גלעד, an agreement made between Jacob and Laban in Mount Herman (Genesis 31: 44-48). *Galeed* was to be a memorial of a covenant that God would watch between them and they would not pass over its location to harm one another. Jacob would occupy the land south of Galeed and Laban the land north.

*And Moses went up from the plains of Moab unto the mountain of Nebo, to the top of Pisgah, that is over against Jericho. And the LORD shewed him all the land of **Gilead**, unto Dan,* Deuteronomy 34:1 KJV

In this verse, Moses was near Jericho looking north towards Dan's inheritance. The tribe of Dan inherited the northernmost part of the Promised Land near Mount Herman. The passage implies all the land south of Dan was *Gilead*, and the northernmost part would be Galeed in Mount Herman, the northern boundary of Israel established by Jacob's agreement. Jacob's name was changed to Israel just after the Galeed covenant was made. (Genesis 31:44-48, 32:28.)

Many believe that Enoch, like Elijah, never died, but Jesus said, *"No man has ascended up to heaven..."* (John 3:13). Enoch, who preached (or prophesied) about the fallen sons of God (see Jude 14), was *translated (or moved) so that he would not die*, implying, **not die at that time** since his audience would probably have killed him for his testimony of faith.

The book of Hebrews does not say Enoch was translated to heaven, nor does it say he never died, but rather, *"He was translated (or moved) so that he was **not found**."* He was translated for his testimony, *his faith;* faith is the subject of Hebrews chapter eleven, and that chapter says, *"these all died in faith..."* Enoch certainly died, but we do not know when since God had *taken him* (or moved him) *from the location* of those recording the Genesis scriptures. We are not told where God *took him*; the record keepers probably did not know either.

Although not in the biblical canon, the ancient book of Enoch associated Mount Herman with the "watchers", as being their portal to heaven, and Elijah dwelt with the inhabitants of Gilead located near Mount Herman. Elijah, unlike Enoch, was a *divine being* from heaven, and this explains why he could raise the dead. In the Old Testament, no one raised the dead until Elijah, and after him only Elisha, the man whom Elijah anointed to take his place. Elijah was a son of God, like the ones in Genesis Six. Elijah is the only *being* in the Bible who never died.

> Note: In the New Testament, Jesus was comparing John the Baptist to Elijah, and during his dialogue, said, *"For I say unto you, **Among those that are born of women** there is not a greater prophet than John the Baptist: but he that is least in the kingdom of God is greater than he."* (Luke 7:28 KJV), implying some men are not born of women and strengthening the case that Elijah was not human.

On the Mount of Transfiguration, we find a distinctive relation between Moses, Elijah, and Jesus: Moses was a son of man (i.e., human), Elijah was a son of God (i.e., divine), and Jesus was both – the Son of man and the Son of God. Again, these three, two at a time, had much in common, with the third always being in contrast. Jesus and Elijah were divine, and Moses was not; Moses and Jesus were men, and Elijah was not.

What was the location of the high mountain of the transfiguration? There is no higher mountain in Israel than Mount Herman, and Jesus, Peter, John, and James were in this geographical location just before the Transfiguration story. Mount Herman is a strong candidate for being the Mount of Transfiguration.

Elijah and Elisha are unquestionably two of the most fascinating individuals in the Bible. They lived during the period of Solomon's temple when the Israelites had divided into two houses, the house of Israel and the house of Judah. Their lives were mysterious and exceptional. They both worked miracles; they both raised the dead. Elisha even raised the dead while dead. An unnamed dead man was put into his grave, and upon touching the bones of Elisha, the man revived. The irrefutable identity of this mysterious man will be disclosed in the next chapter.

CHAPTER SEVEN

BONES OF ELISHA

The time periods of Elijah and Elisha are among the most difficult to reconcile in the biblical record, and scholars have attributed much of the difficulties to scribal error, rather than unsolved and misunderstood dates, ages, and methods in the succession of the kings. In this article we will examine these problems and offer solutions while proving who resurrected by touching the bones of Elisha.

Sixty years after the death of Solomon the house of Israel was totally given to the idolatries of its neighbors. They had exchanged the worship of the God of their ancestors in Jerusalem for the worship of their own golden calves in Samaria. They warred with their Jewish kinsmen and were defeated by Judean armies half their size (2 Chronicles 13), but this changed with the ascension of King Jehoshaphat. Jehoshaphat made peace with Ahab, the king of Israel (2 Kings 22:44). The two houses, Judah and Israel, would seek to reunite, but the house of Israel was practicing the pagan religions of those north of Galeed, and this seems to have invoked the Galeed covenant (Genesis 31:44), thereby bringing Elijah into the world.

The days of Elijah and Elisha are the only days in biblical history in which both houses had coexisting kings with the same names, and this fact provides a clue for resolving the narrative and unlocking the mystery and identity of the man resurrected by touching the bones of Elisha (2 Kings 13:21). Some of these same-name kings were in fact the same men.

Jehoram (also spelled Joram) was the son of Ahab by marriage and the son of Jehoshaphat by birth as found by comparing 2 Kings 1:17, 3:1, and 8:18. Jehoram king of Israel will be shown to be the same person as Jehoram king of Judah, proving son and son-in-law are synonymous terms in the Bible.

> *So he died according to the word of the LORD which Elijah had spoken. And Jehoram reigned in his stead in the second year of Jehoram the son of Jehoshaphat king of Judah; because he had no son.* 2 Kings 1:17 KJV

Scholars have assumed two Jehoram(s) in this verse, two distinct individuals: Jehoram king of Israel and Jehoram king of Judah. However, a detailed chronology shows they reigned and died at the same time. Prevailing scholarly opinion allows a second Jehoram to begin reign over Israel when King Jehoshaphat's son Jehoram was either two years old, or alternatively when he had co-reigned two years with his father Jehoshaphat, and with this, they attribute the age difficulties to scribal error. The usual logic goes as follows:

> Since Jehoram did not succeed his father as king until the fifth year of the reign of Jehoram king of Israel, he would have only been fourteen years old when his 42-year-old son succeeded him at his death, so the scribes must have miscopied the numbers.

Obviously, a son cannot be 42 years old when his father is fourteen, so it is easy to see why the scholars turn to copyist's mistakes to explain the anomalies, but before consenting too quickly, another perspective will be considered.

The Hebrew word, בן, translated "son", is from the root word, בנה, meaning "builder." 2 Kings 1:17 is stating Jehoram began to reign in *the second year of the building of the son(s) of Jehoshaphat in the house of Israel*, implying that Ahaziah was a "builder", and probably either the birth-brother or even birth-son of Jehoram. Later Jehoram king of Judah will be succeeded by his son, a second, Ahaziah, who is also son-in-law to the house of Ahab (2 Kings 8:25-27). These two Ahaziah(s) will soon be pointed out in an excerpt from the chronology that will help clarify.

The two houses, Judah, and Israel, were becoming intertwined by marriage. Shortly before Jehoram died, Ahaziah went to visit him in Jezreel because he was sick (2 Kings 8:29), and this leads to an interesting peculiarity with the name Jezreel worth mentioning.

The Hebrew words, *Israel* and *Jezreel,* or ישראל and יזרעאל, are remarkably similar in structure. Replacing שר meaning "prince" with זרע meaning "seed" changes the word from *Israel* to *Jezreel.* In Genesis 32:28 where the name *Israel* first appears, Jacob was given the name because *he had power as a **prince** with both God and man.* Is it too big of a stretch then, to believe Jezreel means *having power as a **seed** of both God and man*? Were these kings trying to become divine? If so, it sounds like the original lie from Satan, *"You'll become like God."*

The name Jezreel might be intended to be prophetic with respect to Jesus becoming the seed of both God and man. If so, this reveals much about the heart of God when studying the Jezreel of Hosea chapter one: Jesus would not die in a religious system considered a whore; therefore, John the Baptist had to come first and turn the people back to faith as predicted by Malachi 4:5-6.

The New Testament lineage of Jesus Christ listed in Matthew chapter one skips over four successive Jewish monarchs from the period of Elijah and Elisha. These four, Ahaziah, Athaliah, Jehoash (or Joash), and Amaziah are not listed in the genealogy of Jesus but are found on the chronology as shown below:

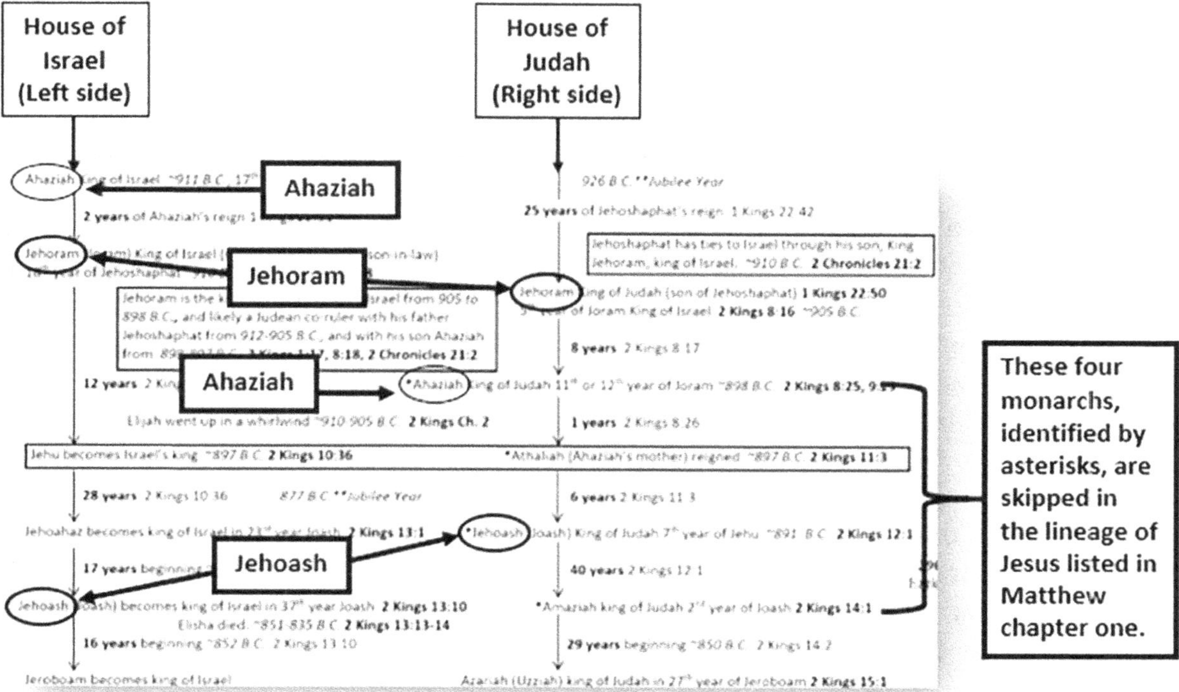

Excerpt from the chronology showing the lineage of the kings of the house of Israel on the left and house of Judah on the right. These were the days of Elijah and Elisha, occurring approximately 110 years after Solomon constructed the first temple. The heavy ovals indicate contemporary kings with the same names and the light ovals indicate kings that are not co-reigning but have the same names.

Again, this is the only time in biblical history where both sides had same-name kings; those that coexisted are identified here by heavy ovals and the noncontemporary ones are identified by light ovals. During this period, the house of Israel was trying to bring their pagan worship of gods from north of Galeed into the house of Judah, and this is likely why the four consecutive monarchs are skipped in the lineage of Jesus recorded in Matthew. Without those skipped, is it possible to trace a continuous lineage from Adam to Jesus? To answer, we must first prove Jehoram king of Judah, the last in the lineage before the skip, is in fact, the same man, Jehoram (also spelled Joram), king of Israel.

Comparing 1 Kings 22:51 with 2 Kings 3:1 shows that Ahaziah reigned for less than two years. Jehoram succeeding Ahaziah in the second year of Jehoram, implying he also had reigned less than two years then (2 Kings 1:17). Your author contends these two years are the building years of the sons of Jehoshaphat in the house of Israel: Jehoram was the son-in-law, not birth-son of Ahab (2 Kings 8:18).

From the chronology, both Jehoram(s) died within one year of each other, yet, the ascension year of Ahaziah is problematic when comparing the following:

> *In the **twelfth year** of Joram the son of Ahab king of Israel did Ahaziah the son of Jehoram king of Judah begin to reign.* 2 Kings 8:25 KJV

> *And in the **eleventh year** of Joram the son of Ahab began Ahaziah to reign over Judah.* 2 Kings 9:29 KJV

These verses have two dissimilarities: *Jehoram* king of Judah is spelled differently from *Joram* the son of Ahab, and secondly, the years are different. Regardless, focus is needed to stay on track. We are comparing the ascension year of Ahaziah based on the reigning year of Joram (on the left in the excerpt), not Jehoram (on the right), so the Bible is intending two different ordinal numbers here, eleventh and twelfth. The Hebrew words eleventh and twelfth are spelled quite differently, therefore we can rule out copyist's error. The Bible is using two distinct reckonings, but why?

In Hebrew, the meaning of a word changes by adding prefixes, suffixes, and infixes. Here the infix letter ה has been added to יורם (Joram), to give the name יהורם (Jehoram) for the king of Judah at the time of his death. There may be a specific reason for this, or otherwise these are simply two spellings of the same name. These two spellings were used for both the king of Israel and the king of Judah at different points, so we cannot rule out these being the same persons.

The ancient Hebrew letter ה (English letters **eh**) means "breath", and the writer included it in Joram's name in this instance, and others. The difference in spelling might be associated with their concept of the afterlife and their understanding of *Jezreel*, the location where Jehoram died (2 Kings 8:29). Otherwise, if Joram and Jehoram are the same person, it could be used to distinguish the active reference (e.g., referring to him as king of Judah instead of him as king of Israel).

In these verses, the difference in years could simply be that Jehoram died at the end of the year, when Ahaziah ascended the throne, or instead have something to do with their concept of *Jezreel*. Alternatively, the difference might be related to the timing of Ahaziah marrying into Jehoram's family, that being the twelfth year of Jehoram. Royal bloodline was required for kingship, and in the eleventh year Ahaziah might have only had right to the throne through Ahab, king of Israel, but later also through Jehoram, the son of Jehoshaphat, king of Judah. Eleventh or twelfth year is not contradictory when you understand who *Joram* and *Jehoram* are. *Joram* is certainly *Jehoram*, the same man reigning over both the house of Israel and the house of Judah in the days of Elijah. He is the last in the lineage of Jesus before the four-monarch skip.

The final two same-name kings, Ahaziah and Joash (also spelled Jehoash), refers to a minimum of three persons. There were obviously two separate Ahaziah(s), but possibly only one Joash. Joash king of Judah is the third omitted in Matthew chapter one, with his son being the fourth. The four were skipped due to the infiltration of the pagan practices from the house of Israel into Judah. Again, Israel was worshipping the pagan gods of those north of Galeed, and the line of Jesus had to be kept pure. Therefore, the missions of Elijah and Elisha ensued to ensure that happened, but through whom did the line continue while the four monarchs were being skipped?

Joash king of Israel (on the left) ascended around 852 BC before the death of Elisha. Joash visited Elisha just before he died (2 Kings 13:14-20), and this is extremely interesting, being earlier, Elisha did not have any respect for the kings of Israel:

> *And Elisha said unto the king of Israel, What have I to do with thee? get thee to the prophets of thy father, and to the prophets of thy mother. And the king of Israel said unto him, Nay: for the LORD hath called these three kings together, to deliver them into the hand of Moab.* 2 Kings 3:13 KJV

> *And Elisha said, As the LORD of hosts liveth, before whom I stand, **surely, were it not that I regard the presence of Jehoshaphat the king of Judah, I would not look toward thee, nor see thee.*** 2 Kings 3:14 KJV

What changed? Why would Elisha now be willing to visit with the king of Israel? Could it be that Joash was also the king of Judah? Again, considering the excerpt, Joash ascended the throne of Israel three years prior to the death of Joash king of Judah, and before Elisha died.

Was Joash king of both Israel and Judah for three years before dying and resurrecting by touching the bones of Elisha? Does the Bible say little about this, or does it instead say much? Did this KING OF THE JEWS also become the king of Israel, and then die and resurrect to continue as the king of Israel? The following verses are remarkably similar, except for the underlined differences:

> *And Jehoash king of Israel took **Amaziah king of Judah, the son of Jehoash, <u>the son of Ahaziah,</u>** at Beth-she-mesh, and came to Jerusalem, and brake down the wall of Jerusalem from the gate of Ephraim unto the corner gate, four hundred cubits.* 2 Kings 14:13 KJV

> *And Joash the king of Israel took **Amaziah king of Judah, the son of Joash, <u>the son of Jehoahaz,</u>** at Beth-she-mesh, and brought him to Jerusalem, and brake down the wall of Jerusalem from the gate of Ephraim to the corner gate, four hundred cubits.* 2 Chronicles 25:23 KJV

Amaziah's father was the king of Israel, the son, or rather son-in-law, of Jehoahaz (left side in the chronology); Amaziah's father had previously been the king of Judah. Amaziah's father was Joash, or Jehoash, the birth-son of Ahaziah, the king of Judah (right side in the chronology), and at his death, his first death, his son Amaziah became king of Judah. Joash touched the bones of Elisha and resurrected. The above verse from Second Chronicles is proceeded a few verses earlier with a very strange response from father to son:

> *And Joash king of Israel sent to Amaziah king of Judah, saying, The thistle that was in Lebanon sent to the cedar that was in Lebanon, saying, **Give thy daughter to my son to wife**: and there passed by a wild beast that was in Lebanon, and trode down the thistle.* 2 Chronicles 25:18 KJV

This verse provides even more insight into their ideas about *Jezreel* and who would carry the seed of God and man. The remainder of this chapter in Second Chronicles explains that Joash prevailed against his son, so likely the tables turned: Joash's son would be given Amaziah's daughter, rather than the way Amaziah had envisioned. As a result, the child Azariah was born, and the lineage of Jesus Christ continued with this grandson-and-great-grandson of the resurrected Joash.

The lineage of Jesus was unbroken through the resurrected Joash, who as a child was hidden to escape death at the hands of his grandmother, the monarch Athaliah. The skipped ancestry of Jesus resumed with the resurrected Jehoash's grandson, Azariah, also called Uzziah, who was also his great-grandson through Amaziah's daughter, Jehoash's granddaughter.

Joash (or Jehoash) was a righteous king until the death of the high priest, but later had the high priest's son killed, and then he himself was killed by conspirators. We are told he was buried in the city of David with his fathers (2 Kings 12:21), but not with the kings of Judah (2 Chronicles 24:25).

How fitting that an ancient story, revealed now in 2021, would so foretell the story of the Savior Jesus Christ, the King of Israel: Joash, the ancient king of both Israel and Judah, died and resurrected as king of Israel! Even through an imperfect king such as Joash, God worked a miracle to continue his plan of salvation!

> *For Jozachar the son of Shimeath, and Jehozabad the son of Shomer, his servants, smote him, and he died; and they **buried him with his fathers in the city of David**: and Amaziah his son reigned in his stead.* 2 Kings 12:21 KJV

> *Now **Elisha** was fallen sick of his sickness whereof he died. And Joash the king of Israel came down unto him, and wept over his face, and said, O **my father, my father**, the chariot of Israel, and the horsemen thereof.* 2 Kings 13:14 KJV

> *And when they were departed from him, (for they left him in great diseases,) his own servants conspired against him for the blood of the sons of Jehoiada the priest, and slew him on his bed, and he died: and **they buried him in the city of David, but they buried him not in the sepulchers of the kings.*** 2 Chronicles 24:25 KJV

> *And Joash slept with his fathers; and Jeroboam sat upon his throne: and Joash was buried in Samaria with the kings of Israel.* 2 Kings 13:13 KJV

Joash, king of Judah, was buried with his fathers, including Elisha whom he called father (2 Kings 13:14). His first burial was in the city of David, not in the graves of the kings, but rather in Elisha's tomb. Years later, he was buried again, but that time in Samaria with the kings of Israel. This timely 2021 discovery is hidden in the Jewish Bible: the King of the Jews died and resurrected by touching the bones of Elisha!

As a final confirmation of Joash's resurrection, the following incongruency with the chronology needs to be explained. Jehoahaz ascended the throne of Israel in the twenty-third year of Joash, king of Judah, and reigned 17 years (2 Kings 13:1). At Jehoahaz's death, Joash became king of Israel, however, he had already become king of Israel in the thirty-seventh year of Joash, king of Judah. As recorded, and without the aid of a chronology, this is confusing.

Math proves a span from the twenty-third year to the thirty-seventh year would be a maximum of fifteen years, and certainly not seventeen. However, Joash reigned forty years as king of Judah, therefore he must have co-reigned as king of Israel with Jehoahaz from his thirty-seventh year until his first death two to three years later. These two to three years account for the difference between the stated fourteen and seventeen years, and apparently Jehoahaz also died at Joash's first death during an invasion of the Syrians (2 Chronicles 24:24). The chronology was developed as the story appears from a straightforward read, and therefore, to avoid confusion, its configuration was not changed. However, a further study using the chronology reveals the following updated outline:

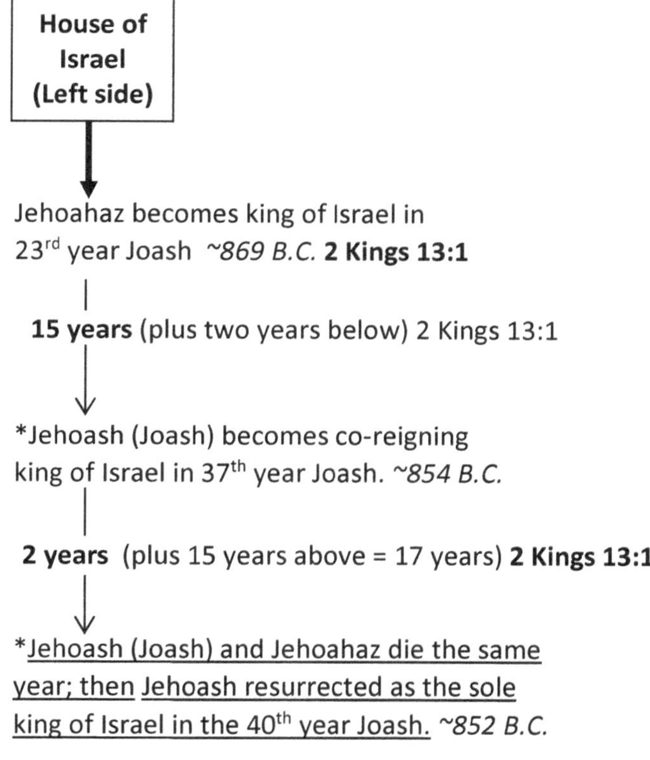

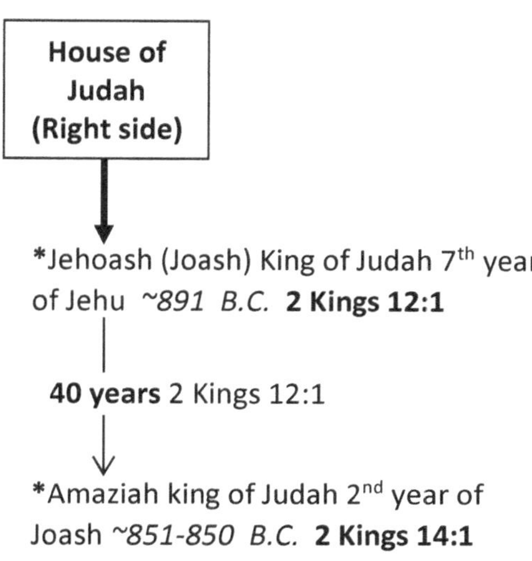

Notes: Amaziah's ascension is based on the reign of Joash that began with his resurrection in ~852 B.C.

Asterisks are kings skipped in the ancestry of Jesus.

Underlined item are derived conclusions not explicitly stated in the Bible.

The seventeen-years reign of Joash as king of Israel is broken into the actual configuration of fifteen-years and two-years intervals (2 Kings 13:1).

CHAPTER EIGHT

VALLEY OF DECISION

At 1380 feet below sea level, the shoreline of the Dead Sea is the lowest dry ground elevation on the surface of the entire earth, and with a salinity greater than nine-and-a-half times that of the world's oceans, it is one of the saltiest bodies on Earth. Only rare bacteria can live in the Dead Sea. Its main tributary is the freshwater supplied by the Jordan River and it has no outlets.

Just upstream of its mouth, the Jordan River was miraculously dried three times in the Bible. The first of these happened when Joshua brought the Israelites into the Promised Land in 1466 BC:

> _That the waters which came down from above stood and rose up upon an heap_ very far from the city Adam, that is beside Zaretan: and those that came down toward the sea of the plain, even the salt sea, failed, and were cut off: and the people passed over right against Jericho. Joshua 3:16 KJV

> And the priests that bare the ark of the covenant of the LORD stood firm on dry ground in the midst of Jordan, and all the Israelites passed over on dry ground, until all the people were passed clean over Jordan. Joshua 3:17 KJV

The underlined words show the upstream waters were cutoff and the river downstream dried up. This could only happen if the downstream elevation were lower, otherwise, the waters would need to divide as they did some 550 years later, when Elisha and Elijah crossed the Jordan on dry ground:

> And Elijah took his mantle, and wrapped it together, and smote the waters, and they were _divided hither and thither_, so that they two _went over on dry ground._ 2 Kings 2:8 KJV

Elijah ascended to heaven in a whirlwind and his mantle fell to the earth. Elisha picked up the mantle and returned through the Jordan River on dry ground:

> And he took the mantle of Elijah that fell from him, and smote the waters, and said, Where is the LORD God of Elijah? and when he also had smitten the waters, _they parted hither and thither:_ and Elisha went over. 2 Kings 2:14 KJV

These three miracles occurred at the same location and the last two uncovered a record for the lowest dry-ground elevation on Earth, or at least for that point in time. According to Genesis, the Dead Sea did not exist in Abram's day being battles were fought there (Genesis 14:3). This researcher believes the destruction of Sodom and Gomorrah caused deep salt mines containing hydrocarbons to explode and bring salt to the surface. Even in present times, it is reported that chunks of bitumen (i.e., hydrocarbons) sometimes float to the surface of the Dead Sea. Lot's wife, who was behind him and therefore closer to the explosion, was covered in salt:

> *But his wife looked back from behind him, and she became a pillar of salt.* Genesis 19:26 KJV

Again, there are no outlets on the Dead Sea, only freshwater tributaries. Water can only leave by evaporation, but with it being far below mean sea-level, the atmosphere at the Dead Sea's surface is hot and prime for that process. Just as temperatures decrease when ascending mountains, they also increase when descending. Before Sodom and Gomorrah were destroyed, the freshwater from the Jordan River descended one thousand feet lower than they do today. The water outflew to the hotter elevation that is now the Dead Sea's floor and evaporated.

The destruction of Sodom and Gomorrah released salt and thereby slowed the evaporation rate of the Jordan River's runoff being it was now becoming salty. The evaporation rate for freshwater is much greater than for saltwater, and especially when descending another one thousand feet to hotter elevation, that is now, the Dead Sea's floor. The saltwater levels began rising in 1949 BC, the same year Isaac was conceived by Sarah (Genesis 17-20): Isaac and the Dead Sea are the same age.

The three water-drying miracles of Joshua, Elijah, and Elisha were separated by a considerable length of time. Joshua led the children of Israel on dry ground 483 years after the Dead Sea began forming, compared to Elijah and Elisha who crossed there 550 years after that. In Joshua's day the levels were still rising, in Elijah and Elisha's time, the waters had finished their rise. These stories are simply eyewitness accounts of what they saw. The early account saw the upstream *waters standing on a heap*, while in the later story, they divided, *hither and thither.*

The site of these three miracles was just east of Jericho on the Jordan River at Earth's lowest surface elevation. Jesus would later be baptized by John the Baptist at this same spot. When the Bible was written, its elevation simply could not have been known, thereby providing a remarkable distinctiveness of Jesus's baptism site – a biblical claim with a global uniqueness unknowable before modern science, but now known to be fact. Jesus was baptized at the lowest place on Earth, and it was even lower than that three times prior.

> *For, behold, in those days, and in that time, when I shall bring again the captivity of Judah and Jerusalem,* Joel 3:1 KJV

> *I will also gather all nations, and will bring them down into the **valley of Jehoshaphat**, and will plead with them there for my people and for my heritage Israel, whom they have scattered among the nations, and parted my land.* Joel 3:2 KJV

The valley of Jehoshaphat in the book of Joel is a reference to the valley where King Jehoshaphat took a large spoil from his enemy without a fight (2 Chronicles 20). The people of Ammon, Moab, and Mount

Seir, people God had instructed Moses to not harm when he led the Israelites out of Egypt, were now ganging up to fight against Judah and King Jehoshaphat. Knowing this, Jehoshaphat ordered his entire nation to fast and pray. He reminded God these nations were not destroyed by Moses when they were a larger nation of twelve tribes leaving Egypt, and now the much smaller Judah was being rewarded by having them as an invading enemy. God answered Jehoshaphat's prayer through his prophet Jahaziel:

And he said, Harken ye, all Judah, and all ye inhabitants of Jerusalem, and thou King Jehoshaphat, Thus sayeth the LORD unto you, Be not afraid nor dismayed by reason of this great multitude; for the battle is not yours, but God's. 2 Chronicles 20:15 KJV

To-morrow go ye down against them: behold, they come up by the cliff of Ziz; and ye shall find them at the end of the brook, before the wilderness of Jeruel. 2 Chronicles 20:16 KJV

Ye shall not need to fight in this battle: set yourselves, stand ye still, and see the salvation of the LORD with you, O Judah and Jerusalem: fear not, nor be dismayed; to-morrow go out against them: for the LORD will be with you. 2 Chronicles 20:17 KJV

Jehoshaphat responded by commanding the people to believe the LORD and his prophet. He set singers before his army to sing praises to God for his mercy, and as they began to sing, the invaders began to fight internally and ultimately destroyed themselves. Judah's army went out but only to find dead bodies. They spent three days gathering spoils from the fallen, and on the fourth day they assembled in the valley with a collection of precious jewels taken from their enemy. They called the valley, Berachah, or Hebrew ברכה, meaning blessing (2 Chronicles 20:25-26).

The valley of Jehoshaphat mentioned by the Prophet Joel is the *valley of Blessing* for God's people. Many scholars believe it is between the Temple Mount and Mount of Olives in Jerusalem, but this cannot be. Jehoshaphat did not re-enter Jerusalem until after leaving the *"valley of Blessing"*, and he was gone from Jerusalem four days (2 Chronicles 20:26-27). Additionally, *the cliff of Ziz*, or במעלה הציץ (2 Chronicles 20:16), could instead be *ascent of blooms,* and could be describing the northern Dead Sea area. In the humble of opinion of this novice Hebrew reader, the following could be intended:

Tomorrow you will go down upon them and they will be ascending the ascent of blooms (במעלה הציץ) and you will find them by the end of the river (or valley, נחל) facing the thing spoken and instructed by God (פני מדבר ירואל). 2 Chronicles 20:16

Note: The Hebrew word, מדבר, or *midbar*, is usually translated *"desert"* or *"wilderness"* but rules of constructing Hebrew words should allow this possibility. This idea of translating *midbar* in the sense of *"from-word"* or *"who spoke"* will be discussed in more detail in the next chapters. For now, understand the original language of the Bible's record was not the biblical Hebrew we read today. Written Hebrew records are only traceable to at most 1000 BC; the original language of this verse was probably Paleo-Hebrew, or pictographs, and then translated into biblical Hebrew after the Babylonian captivity.

Not being a trained scholar in ancient languages, your author can only offer insight from reading this Hebrew in context. In subsequent chapters, specific reasons for questioning *midbar's* true import in some incidences will be given. If you are a language expert, please consider those occurrences and concerns. God spoke audibly during the days of Moses but had quit doing so by the period of the judges, or even earlier; perhaps the meaning of *midbar* evolved over time from *"who spoke"*, to the latter definition, *"the wilderness"*, the place where the word had been spoken.

The Numbers chapter thirty-three account of the Exodus has the Israelites going through several wildernesses during their short journey from the Red Sea to Mount Sinai: Would every grain of sand in that small region be named, or instead, does midbar sometimes mean *"who spoke"*?

The valley of Jehoshaphat is likely just east of Jericho near Jesus' baptism site. The end of the Jordan River at the Dead Sea would allow a one-day walk from Jerusalem, as the text suggests they made, and the dead bodies in the valley could then be seen from the mountains west of the Dead Sea. The prophet Joel had even more to say about the valley:

*Let the heathen (nations) be wakened, and come up to the **valley of Jehoshaphat**: for there will I sit to judge all the heathen (nations) round about.* Joel 3:12 KJV

Put ye in the sickle, for the harvest is ripe: come, get you down; for the press is full, the vats overflow; for their wickedness is great. Joel 3:13 KJV

*Multitudes, multitudes in the **valley of decision**: for the (a) day of the LORD is near in the valley of decision.* Joel 3:14 KJV

*And it shall come to pass in that day, that the mountains shall drop down new wine, and the hills shall flow with milk, and all the rivers of Judah shall flow with waters, and a fountain shall come forth out of the house of the LORD, and shall water the **valley of Shittim**.* Joel 3:18 KJV

This valley at the lowest elevation on Earth has many names: *Valley of Jehoshaphat, Valley of Berachah, Valley of Shittim, and Valley of Decision.* Joel was prophesying that God would one day bring all the nations of the world to the lowest place on Earth to contend with them for his people Israel, a prophesy with *multitudes, multitudes in the valley of decision.*

CHAPTER NINE

THE EXODUS

Our Exodus story begins with the baby Moses floating in a basket on the Nile River. Pharaoh had ordered the death of all infant Israeli males to prevent Israel from becoming a larger people and challenging his reign. Moses' mother hid him in the basket to save his life and Pharaoh's daughter found the basket and immediately adored him. Moses' sister was watching as he was found, and she courageously approached this powerful Egyptian girl and convinced her to let Moses' mother raise the baby for her. Moses was raised in Pharaoh's house and enjoyed all the advantages that went along with being a child of the rich Pharaoh, much unlike the fate of his Israelite kinsmen who were under hard labor as slaves.

One day Moses saw an Egyptian beating an Israeli and went to his brother's aid. He killed the Egyptian and hid his body in the sand. The next day, fearing this had become known, Moses fled Egypt to Midian and lived there about forty years. He married the daughter of a priest in Midian and worked for him tending his flocks. While out with the flock, God appeared in a burning bush and spoke audibly with Moses, telling him to return to Egypt and lead the Israelites out. He returned to Egypt, and with the help of God, and with the help of his brother Aaron, who was fluent in their language, he led the Israelites to freedom. The Exodus is one of the most amazing stories ever told. Moses was eighty years old when they left Egypt, Aaron was eighty-three.

The above overview gives several key background points needed in this chapter: Moses' sister and brother were older than him, he was raised in Pharaoh's house by his birth mother, not as an Israeli, but rather as a wealthy child of Pharaoh, and finally, his wealth was in stark contrast to his Israeli kinsmen who were slaves. Aaron and Miriam were not the rich-and-famous Hebrew child of Pharaoh that Moses was. His well-known fortune was surely resented among the many Israelites who were suffering at the hands of Pharaoh. During his years before fleeing to Midian, Moses was conceivably the most hated Hebrew man on Earth. Most Israelites probably considered him to be an Egyptian enemy even though he was compassionate towards them.

The Bible never mentions Moses having other siblings, so it is assumed that Miriam is his only sister and Aaron his only brother. His family probably had some privileges from Pharaoh on account of Moses, although this is only speculation, however, his brother and sister surely had more influence over the Israelites at the time of the Exodus, and arguably much more so, than did Moses: people had not forgotten this privileged "Hebrew-Egyptian" from forty years earlier. Furthermore, Aaron and Miriam spoke the Israeli's language fluently, while the Bible implies that Moses did not.

The Exodus journey contains several references to the city Kadesh, a name meaning *"holy"* or *"set apart."* Moses spoke of Kadesh as being a city on the boundary of Edom (Numbers 20:16), thereby defining it as a city with a location, however, Kadesh could be a traveling city: it is also found in the wilderness of Paran (Numbers 13:26) and in the wilderness of Zin (Numbers 20:1, 33:36-38).

Numbers chapter thirty-three supposedly gives the entire Exodus path from Rameses in Egypt to the plains of Moab near Jordan Jericho, the entrance to the Promised Land. Curiously, the wilderness of Paran is not mentioned even though Moses sent spies from the wilderness of Paran (Numbers 13: 1-3, 26) and they returned from spying to Kadesh in the wilderness of Paran. The omission of the wilderness of Paran is a mystery that we will begin to investigate in this chapter.

Deuteronomy 10:6 tells that Aaron died and was buried in Mosera, but Numbers chapter thirty-three says he died on Mount Hor. Many atheists question, "Did Aaron die in Mosera or Mount Hor? The Bible says both!" This is a legitimate point and deserves an answer, but unfortunately, Deuteronomy chapter ten and Numbers thirty-three, as translated, seem to have even more chronological and geographical disagreements making matters worse.

Deuteronomy 10:7 states the Israelites journeyed from Mosera to Gudgodah and from there to Jotbath, *"a land of rivers of waters"*. The scriptures of Numbers 33:30-33 do agree with the stops mentioned in Deuteronomy 10:6-7, although it might not be obvious to English readers unless the following clarifications are known: Benejaakan in Numbers 33:31 should be translated *"children of Jaakan"* as found in Deuteronomy, and Horhagidgad should be *"the Gudgodah Mountain"*, but that only resolves some of the problems. Again, Deuteronomy says Aaron died in Mosera, the station given as Moseroth (the plural of Mosera) in Numbers 33:30, while Numbers 33:38 says he died on Mount Hor, seven stops later. Which is right? Where did Aaron die?

> Note: In the Deuteronomy account Israel departs from Beeroth, or water wells, of the children of Jaakan and not from Jaakan. This is simply a more detailed record and not a contradiction. Also, Jaakan is mentioned only one other time in the Bible: Jaakan is son of Ezer, a Horite in the land of Seir. The Horites were confederate with the Edomites, and this important point will be needed later.

The book of Numbers presents another key dilemma: Miriam died in the desert of Zin in the first month (Numbers 20:1). The question here is obviously not what month it is, that is given, the question is, what year is it? **This is the only time detail in the entire Exodus story that does not specify the year.** Many scholars believe this is the beginning of the fortieth year based on Numbers chapter thirty-three, but we simply do not know for sure as will be shown. Beginning with the assumption that it means what it says, *"THE FIRST MONTH"*, the whole congregation of Israel has then already entered the desert of Zin in the first month and first year of the Exodus, but how could that be? Also, Miriam became a leper in the second year, so this would this rule out her dying in the first year, right?

More specifically, Numbers chapter twenty tells that she died in *Kadesh in the desert of Zin*, perhaps intending that she died at a certain location rather than at a certain time. Supporting this argument is the fact that the word *"then"* was added to the verse by the translators, it does not appear in the Hebrew. The translators are implying chapter twenty occurs after chapter nineteen and is therefore written chronologically, but the Hebrew text does not necessarily support this. So, now more questions are added to the list of mysteries: When and where did Miriam die? Did she die in the first month, and if so, what year? Did she die in Kadesh in the desert of Zin, or Kadesh in the first month, or both? The death of Miriam in the desert of Zin is a mystery, but hopefully this chapter can shed more light on it.

Biblical records can stand up to scrutiny, but in some cases only if they are thoroughly understood and properly translated. Perceptions affect translations, and translating ancient texts is difficult enough without opinions influencing the process, but a chronology can help. The first incongruency, the location of Aaron's death, can be resolved by considering when he died. Aaron was 83 years old at their departure from Egypt (Exodus 7:7) and was 123 years old at his death forty years later (Numbers 33:38), however, Deuteronomy also seems to contradict these details:

> *And the children of Israel took their journey from Beeroth (i.e., water wells) of the children of Jaakan* **to Mosera: there Aaron died, and there he was buried**; *and Eleazer his son ministered in the priest's office in his stead.* Deuteronomy 10:6 KJV

> *From thence they journeyed unto Gudgodah; and from Gudgodah to Jotbath, a land of rivers of waters.* Deuteronomy 10:7 KJV

> **At that time the LORD separated the tribe of Levi, to bear the ark of the covenant** *of the LORD, to stand before the LORD to minister unto him, and to bless in his name, unto this day.* Deuteronomy 10:8 KJV

The tribe of Levi was separated in the second year (Numbers 1:1, 47-51), not the fortieth, yet Deuteronomy is saying Aaron died at the time they were separated, so how can these be reconciled? The answer is found by considering the timing of this speech in Deuteronomy.

Moses was addressing a second generation of Israelites and retelling of events that began forty years earlier. The timing of Deuteronomy is not just after Aaron died in Mosera. The entire audience knew when and where Aaron had physically died (i.e., Mount Hor), they had just buried him five months earlier. Mosera is not a location but instead an action or condition: Mosera, or מוסרה, can mean *"discipline"*, *"correction"*, or even *"bondage"*. Moses is telling the Israelites that Aaron died in *discipline* or *correction* from events occurring in the first year of the Exodus. He uses *"at that time"* in a relative manner to describe it being near the second year when the Levites were ordained. His speaking of Aaron's death in discipline at the beginning of the Exodus is a metaphor, but the mention of him being buried there may or may not be symbolic as will soon be shown.

> *And the children of Israel took their journey from Beeroth of the children of Jaakan to* **Mosera (i.e. discipline): there Aaron died, and there he was buried**; *and Eleazer his son ministered in the priest's office in his stead.* Deuteronomy 10:6 KJV

> *From thence they journeyed unto Gudgodah; and from Gudgodah to **Jotbath (i.e., goodness or pleasantness), a land of rivers of waters**.* Deuteronomy 10:7 KJV

Jotbath, or יטבתה, means *"goodness"* or *"pleasantness"* and is a *"land of rivers of waters."* The true Exodus trip crossed the Gulf of Aqaba to Mount Horeb located in present-day Saudi Arabia. There are no rivers there today, and neither were there in Moses' day, until he struck the rock at Horeb with his rod and a mighty river gushed out. Jotbath is the land of Horeb near Mount Sinai. Aaron died on Mount Hor, or הר ההר, likely meaning *"mountains of mountains,"* or tallest mountain in the area and matching the aspects of Mount Sinai (i.e., Jabal al Lawz in Saudi Arabia). The same name, *"Mount Hor"*, or הר ההר, is also used in the book of Numbers to describe a mountain at Israel's northern boundary. The northern *"Mount Hor"* is probably Mount Hermon, as can be discerned by comparing Numbers 34:8 with Joshua 13:5 and considering the description, *"entrance of Hamath"* that is used in each. Like Mount Sinai, Mount Hermon, located some 330 miles north of Mount Sinai, is the tallest mountain in its region, making these the two tallest mountains in the writings of Moses: one at the northern boundary of the Promised Land and the other at the southernmost part of the Exodus route. The following is a conjecture:

> Contrary to popular opinion, the Bible does not have two mountains by the proper name, Mount Hor. The intended meaning is highest mountain in the region. Aaron died on Mount Sinai, the *"mountain of mountains"*, in the fortieth year of the Exodus. The children of Israel stayed at Mount Sinai most of their forty years in the wilderness, and their journeys recorded in Numbers chapter thirty-three were not simply physical travels, but rather were mostly spiritual wanderings. The only water source they had was the river coming from the rock that Moses struck, and they stayed near that river for forty years.

The first three months of the Exodus are filled with concerns about water, but for the next forty years of the story, no mention of water is made again until they traveled north towards Mount Seir (Deuteronomy 2:1-8). Early during the Exodus, Moses struck the rock at Horeb, and a river emerged to satisfy water demands. Some contend a second similar event happened again forty years later, but this will be proven to be wrong. There was just one rock-striking episode in the Exodus journey. Christians should accept this easily, being the story predicts Jesus, the one-and-only spirit-giving Rock, being beaten and crucified. Would God have two water-giving rocks?

After they arrived at Horeb, Moses struck the rock twice, and next they fought the Amalekites (Exodus 17:1-8), or children of Amalek, the grandson of Esau (Genesis 36:12). Although the book of Exodus does not give the same details as the book of Numbers, the Amalekites (or Edomites) came and fought them because Moses had sent messengers requesting passage through their country (Numbers 20:13-20). Esau is also known as Edom (Genesis 36:8) and his descendants are Edomites. The Amalekites descended from Esau (Genesis 36:12); therefore, the Amalekites are Edomites and are the same people that fought against Israel in both accounts of Moses striking the rock. The book of Numbers' account, like Deuteronomy, is a recalling of events from years earlier. In the fortieth year, Esau did not fight with Israel, they instead sold them water (Deuteronomy 2:1-8).

Numbers chapter twenty could be explaining that Miriam died in the first month of the Exodus, and if so, her death was probably metaphorical, like that of Aaron in Deuteronomy (i.e., she was still alive when she became a leper in the second year). Otherwise, the reference to her death is not to when, but rather to where, that being Kadesh (Numbers 12:1). The Israelites could have been in Kadesh in the first month of the Exodus: they were "set apart in singleness of purpose." They were in the traveling city "Kadesh" on their journey to the Promised Land but were probably following Miriam and Aaron much more so than they were Moses at that time.

Miriam and Aaron were older than Moses and were much closer to the slavery hardships of the Israelites at the beginning of the Exodus. The people trusted them as leaders, and they must have agreed being they challenged Moses. In the second year during his first attempt to lead the Israelites from Mount Sinai (Numbers 10:11-13, 12:1-2), Miriam and Aaron questioned Moses' authority. God intervened though, Moses was his leader and their powers had to die (Numbers 12:5-15). Maybe Miriam and Aaron died together, figuratively, and with this, their younger brother Moses became more empowered.

The first time the Israelites left Mount Sinai, the cloud was taken up from the tabernacle and rested in the wilderness of Paran, but the wilderness of Paran is not listed in the chronicle of Numbers chapter thirty-three. The timing of Miriam's death and the omission of Paran have one similarity, their stories both include a *"wilderness"*, or מדבר, pronounced *midbar*. Does the Hebrew word *"midbar"* always mean *"wilderness"*? The following is a brief background on biblical Hebrew to help answer.

The earliest writings of Moses would have been written in Paleo-Hebrew. This ancient language, as well as later Hebrew, only used consonants (i.e., no vowels), and in the older writings, these consonants were in the form of pictographs. The pictographs were later replaced with letters assigned from the Phoenician alphabet to give the biblical Hebrew we have today. Hebrew words are generally based on roots each containing three letters, with a few exceptions. Hebrew root words can be modified using prefixes, suffixes, and infixes to change meaning, object of verbs, tense, etc. Without getting too elaborate, we state this to examine the word *"midbar"*, not to criticize the translators, they have done an excellent job, but rather to consider a possible alternative that solves all the inconsistencies in the narratives.

The Hebrew word, דבר, generally means *"to speak"*. It is comprised of the root consonants דבר, or DBR. These three consonants can vary to give the words: spoke, speak, spoken, declare, tell, word, thing, etc. The three root consonants plus the prefix מ, or M, the Paleo pictograph representing water, form the Hebrew word *"midbar"* (i.e., MDBR or מדבר). Without being an expert in ancient Hebrew, this is simply pointed out to offer that the ancient word *"midbar"* might somehow be associated with a word or command to *"find water"*. In journeying across a desert country with two million people, water would certainly be a necessity. Could it be that adding the prefix M (water) to DBR (word, declare, or spoken) was meant to produce the primitive word MDBR having the meaning *"spoken directions to water"* rather than the present renderings, *"desert"* or *"wilderness"*?

Your author is an engineer rather than a language expert, however, in his opinion the numbers and the journey records point to problems with the translation of *midbar*. As said in the last chapter, this would be a great topic for an expert to address.

The route from Rameses to the Promised Land recorded in Exodus through Deuteronomy includes five wildernesses: Etham, Sin, Zin, Paran, and Sinai. Except for the wilderness of Paran, the remainder are all listed in the supposedly complete journey-record of Numbers chapter thirty-three. The omission of Paran is resolved by realizing Numbers thirty-three is primarily a spiritual journey, although some of their physical travels are mentioned. They wondered forty years while their children were learning that God had not lied but instead was faithful (Numbers 14:33-34). Their spiritual departures are listed, and these partings are based on *"whose word"*, or *"midbar"*, they were listening to. The words of the One they were rebelling against were omitted in Numbers chapter thirty-three because that was not their path.

The Exodus story from the books of Exodus through Deuteronomy contains a detailed record of only two to three years of the entire forty-year journey, those primarily being the first and last years. Prior to the Exodus Passover, God performed many miracles in Egypt to build faith in the Israelites before beginning their risky trip across the desert. They needed to be united in a state-of-holiness and togetherness (i.e., Kadesh). They needed God's presence and his provision, especially water. They needed to stick together by faith in God and Moses, and the exhibition of miracles in Egypt initiated the process.

The Exodus party was an extremely large group, probably over two million people, and they needed lots of water. When they left Egypt, they were united. After crossing the Red Sea, they first found bitter water that Moses miraculously cured, and later found twelve water wells. These waters replenished the supplies they had taken from Egypt. The twelve water wells were likely those of the descendants of Jaakan, a people who lived among the Amalekites. Based on modern discoveries, the wells were geographically only a few miles from Horeb and Mount Sinai. Water was a huge topic during the first year.

Forty years later and just before his own death, Moses addressed the masses of Israelites who would enter and possess the Promised Land. During his speech he recalled making a second trip to the top of Mount Sinai forty years earlier, that being just after the allegorical death of Aaron in Mosera. He associated Mosera with the geographical region of Mount Sinai making it clear that the wells of Jaakan, Gudgodah, and Jotbath, *the land of rivers of waters*, were all remarkably nearby. (Deuteronomy 10:10)

Summarizing, water was a main topic in the early days of the Exodus, but after they arrived at Horeb and Moses stuck the rock twice, and after he sent messengers to Esau and fought the Edomites, or Amalekites, no further mention of water is made again until the fortieth year. In the fortieth year they were united and continued their journey to the Promised Land, and from what they recorded, it appears Esau then peacefully allowed their passage without a fight (Deuteronomy 2:6-8). Based on what we know, and the 37-38 years that are unknown, the following is a reasonable theory:

Kadesh was the congregation of Israel when united in purpose (i.e., Holy). They were in Kadesh when leaving Egypt but later rebelled against God and wandered from him, although not far geographically from Moses, the tabernacle, and the water supply. They stayed forty years near the river God had given at Horeb, but occasionally some of them wandered off to nearby places such as *the wells of Jaakan* and even to *Ebronah* (Numbers 33:34-35), the site of the Red Sea crossing: the rebellious generation tried to go back to Egypt, but they could not. They wandered and died while their children observed God's provision for forty years. Their children learned to trust the God of Moses.

Kadesh likewise applied to that next generation, the children who united with God and Moses and who finally entered the Promised Land. *Midbar* is not a location, or at least not in all cases, but is a *"spoken word"*, usually audible, or alternatively, a location where an audible word had been given. We do not know when Miriam died, but she died in Kadesh in the *"midbar Zin"*, or *"spoken-word Zin"*.

The story of the Exodus is a major part of biblical history. It was included in this book because it is so fundamental to the Bible, but much is left to be learned. These opinions might have some flaws, but overall, it seems reasonable that they remained at the water-giving Rock for forty years, because there was no other water. Again, the Rock is a foretelling of the story of Jesus Christ, the one-and-only Rock, there is no other.

The next chapter is a short exposition on *Paran* that further investigates its absence in Numbers chapter thirty-three.

CHAPTER TEN

PARAN

The previous chapter showed the children of Israel remained at Mount Sinai for forty years. This short chapter is a continuation to explain the omission of the wilderness of Paran in Numbers chapter thirty-three. The reason for making this chapter separate is to ease the explanation being this really is a stand-alone topic. The previous chapter is needed for background.

The Hebrew word, פארן, is translated *"Paran"* eleven times in ten verses of the King James Bible, and a similar word containing *Paran* is found even earlier than those: the translators combined the very first occurrence of Paran with its adjacent word, El, to give *"Elparan"* (Genesis 14:6). This is interesting being the first time the ark of the covenant ever moved, it moved to the *wilderness of Paran* (Numbers 10:11-12). This would have been approximately 49-50 days after Moses erected the tabernacle for the first time. Understanding Paran is instrumental in understanding the Exodus period and more.

פארן is translated *"Paran"*

ארן, pronounced *"Aaron,"* is translated *"ark"* (as in ark of the covenant)

אהרן, pronounced *"A-ha-ron,"* is translated *"Aaron"* (i.e., Moses' brother's name)

In the above, the middle Hebrew word is the root, ארן, meaning *"ark,"* and is found in each of the other words. In the top word, the prefix, פ, or *pey,* yields, *Paran,* and in the third the infix, ה, or *hey,* gives the proper name *"Aaron"*. Each Hebrew letter has a meaning: the letter *pey* means *"mouth"* and the letter *hey* means *"spirit"*, or *"breath"*. It is interesting that the spirit letter ה (*hey*) was inserted inside the ancient word for the non-living ark, ארן , to produce the living high priest אהרן, or *Aaron*, and that the prefix פ (*pey*) meaning *"mouth"* was added to *"ark"* to generate *Paran*. Following this early logic and considering the importance and timing of the only *"Elparan"* in the Bible, Paran is conjectured to mean *"speaking ark"* (Genesis 14:7).

"Elparan" is derived from two words, "איל פארן", and based on Paleo-Hebrew pictographs might mean *"strong-leader Paran"* or possibly even *"God Paran."* In Genesis chapter fourteen, the ark of the covenant had not yet been built (i.e., it was built some 500 years later), yet the writer could be referring to it. In the very next verse (Genesis 14:7) the Amalekites are mentioned, but they too had not yet existed; the Amalekites were descendants of Esau the grandson of Abraham and much later than the storyline

in Genesis. Therefore, the first true occurrence of *"Paran"* could have happened much later in history and could be related to the root word, ארן, or *"ark"*, as in *"ark of the covenant."*

Tradition holds that Moses wrote the first five books of the Bible and it seems reasonable to find his experiences in his writing: Moses would refer to the God who spoke to him audibly from the mercy seat of the ark (Numbers 7:89), and we find the word *Paran* in his earliest writings.

Does adding a *pey* (meaning mouth) to *ark* produce a word meaning – *speaking-ark*? God spoke audibly to Moses from the ark of the covenant and from a burning bush, and he also spoke audibly to all the Israelites at Mount Sinai. *"Paran"* likely means *"speaking-ark"*, and the first two actual occurrences are both found in Genesis. Genesis was written, or perhaps rewritten, years after its events and after the ark of the covenant had gained fame in its association with God's power.

The first true-occurrence of *"Paran"* and the first-ever mention of the *"Amalekites"* are not the only firsts found in the early scriptures of Genesis chapter fourteen: our featured word, *"midbar"*, also debuts there (Genesis 14:6-7). As explained in the previous chapter, *midbar* could have been intended to be *"Who speaks"* rather than *"wilderness"*, but later evolved to become *"wilderness."*

Did Moses write *"Who speaks"* in the ancient texts or did he instead write the present rendering *"wilderness"*? The meaning of words commonly changes over time for various reasons, and God quit speaking audibly after the days of Moses. Numbers chapter thirty-three likely omitted *"the wilderness of Paran"*, or *"midbar Paran"*, because it was recording those who wandered from God, not those who followed him; therefore, the true import of the *"wilderness of Paran"* should be, *"Who speaks from the Speaking Ark."*

> *And when Moses was gone into the tabernacle of the congregation to speak with him,*
> *then he heard the voice of one speaking unto him from off the mercy seat that was upon*
> *the ark of the testimony, from between the two cherubims: and he spake unto him.*
> Numbers 7:89 KJV

CHAPTER ELEVEN

GALEED

Galeed was the name given to a monument Jacob and his father-in-law Laban built to mark their boundaries (Genesis 31:48). Jacob had fled secretly from Laban who pursued and overtook him in the mountains, near or on Mount Hermon, and there they built Galeed. They made an oath that Jacob would not cross north and Laban would not cross south of Galeed to harm one another. Jacob swore by the God of his fathers, by the God of Abraham and Isaac, and Laban swore by his gods. Additionally, Rachel, Laban's daughter who was married to Jacob, had stolen her father's pagan idols, and Laban searched for them at this meeting but did not find them.

Galeed became the northern boundary of the Promised Land after Joshua began conquering the land three-hundred years later, although the very region of Galeed was never dominated by Israel. As explained in the chapter entitled, The Mystery of Elijah, the Galeed agreement seems to have had spiritual significance that brought Elijah into the world. Jacob and Laban had agreed nearly one-thousand years earlier that Laban would not cross over Galeed to the south to harm Jacob: the harmful idolatry had to stay north of Galeed. Just before Elijah's arrival, the pagan practices of Syria had infiltrated the house of Israel and were beginning to creep into the house of Judah, as Jehoshaphat, king of Judah, made peace with Ahab, king of Israel.

This chapter will demonstrate the effectiveness of the chronology as a tool for unlocking mysteries and increasing learning. Overall, the ancient stories of the Bible have been well preserved and translated, but this accurate timeline can reveal even more, and sometimes, much more. Fascinating discoveries await the Bible's diligent students.

Soon after Galeed was established, Jacob and family continued migrating towards Canaan. Jacob sent messengers ahead to his brother Esau, from whom he had fled Canaan in fear twenty years earlier. The messengers returned with word that Esau was coming to meet him with four-hundred men. Fearing the worst, Jacob divided his family and livestock into two groups to meet Esau in stages. He was hoping to make the best of the horror he expected, a fight with his brother. The night before Esau arrived, an angel met Jacob and told him his new name would be "Israel"; this was the first mention of "Israel" in the Bible (Genesis 32:28). The next day he met Esau and the meeting went much better than anticipated. Jacob offered his brother gifts of livestock that he had gained in Syria and Esau reluctantly accepted his generous offering.

After the encounter, Esau returned to Seir and Jacob proceeded to Shalem, a city of Shechem in the land of Canaan. He bought land and settled there. Shalem was the Israelites first home after leaving Padanaram, and Jacob erected an altar there he called El-el-o-he-Israel. Jacob's daughter Dinah went into the city of Shalem to meet other young girls, and while there, she was abducted by Shechem, the son of the Hamor the Hivite, a prince of that land. Jacob's sons soon found out and they were livid. They wanted revenge. Meanwhile, Shechem was in love and wanted to marry Dinah. He had his father Hamor meet with Jacob to ask permission for her to marry him. Hamor offered Jacob's sons their women in exchange for Dinah and other Israeli women. The furious sons played along, insisting they all first be circumcised, which they agreed to do.

While the men of Shalem were healing from their circumcisions, Jacob's sons Simeon and Levi went into the city with swords and slew all the males. The slaughter greatly troubled Jacob and strained his relations with these two sons. Worried there would be more violence to follow, he had all his family and workers put away their strange gods, or idols, and to travel with him to Bethel to pray and seek the God who had appeared to him there years earlier when he had first fled to Syria. They gave Jacob their idols and he hid (or buried) them under *"an oak which was by Shechem"*, or alternatively from Hebrew, this could be rendered, *"curse with Shechem"*, implying *"curse of Shechem"*. This alternative translation fits the narrative well: *Shechem* was the man who raped Dinah, whereas *Shalem* was a city or location. If *"oak"* was intended, it would have been located near a place rather than a person (i.e., near Shalem, not Shechem).

After he buried their idols, they all proceeded to Bethel where Deborah, Rebekah's nurse, died and was buried under an oak beneath Bethel. Curiously, Deborah had not been mentioned prior nor was she ever mentioned again in the Bible. More on this as we proceed with the story.

Immediately after Deborah died and was buried, God appeared to Jacob and informed him that his name would be called *"Israel"* from then onward. The following two verses join the continuing storyline:

> *And God appeared unto Jacob again, when he came out of Padanaram, and blessed him.* Genesis 35:9 KJV

> *And God said unto him, Thy name is Jacob: thy name shall not be called any more Jacob, but Israel shall be thy name: and he called his name Israel.* Genesis 35:10 KJV

After coming out of Padanaram, Jacob was supernaturally met for the second time concerning the name *"Israel."* Again, the first time he was told his name would be *"Israel"* was just after he and Laban had established Galeed. Now, after removing the pagan gods from his company, and burying the mysterious Deborah, he is again visited and told his name would henceforth be *"Israel"*. There seems to be a connection between Padanaram, Deborah, and the name Israel. We will now investigate this relationship beginning with the following verse:

> *And Isaac was forty years old when he took Rebekah to wife, the daughter of Bethuel* **the Syrian of Padanaram, the sister to Laban the Syrian.** Genesis 25:20 KJV

This verse is from a much earlier time when Jacob's father Isaac had married his mother, Rebekah. The King James' rendering *"Padanaram"* is found multiple times and those are translated from two different Hebrew spellings, פדנה ארם and פדן ארם. In both spellings, the last letter of Padan is a Hebrew final form, requiring these to always be translated as two individual words, *"Padan Aram"*, never the combined, *"Padanaram"*. This is important being the second word, *"Aram"*, is the proper name for Syria, but Padanaram is not just in Syria, as will be explained. For now, the word *"Padan"* should be a single word having a meaning, and its timely uncovering might be intended for the days in which it is being made known, our days!

With the birth of Benjamin, Jacob then had a total of twelve sons. Genesis lists each son by their mothers: Leah's sons are recorded first, then Benjamin and Joseph who were born to Rachel, next the sons of the handmaid Bilhah, and finally the sons of the handmaid Zilpah (Genesis 35:22-26):

> *And the sons of Zilpah, Leah's handmaid; Gad and Asher:* **these are the sons of Jacob, which were born to him in Padanaram.** Genesis 35:26 KJV

The Bible is saying all twelve sons were born in *"Padanaram"*, but Rachel died while giving birth to Benjamin near Bethlehem in the land of Canaan (Genesis 35:19). From this, Padanaram cannot be a location in Syria. Again, Padanaram should be two words, *"Padan Aram"*, or *"Padan Syria"*, or further still, *"Padan of Syria"*. Padan appears only once in the Bible without the accompanying Aram, so it is difficult to discern its meaning, but not impossible.

> *And as for me, when I came* **from Padan**, *Rachel died by me in the land of Canaan in the way, when yet there was but a little way to come unto Ephrath: and I buried her there in the way of Ephrath; the same is Bethlehem.* Genesis 48:7 KJV

This verse contains the only stand-alone-occurrence of Padan in the Bible. Being Jacob had left Syria, it would be easy to believe that Padan was in Syria, however, knowing Benjamin was one of the twelve sons born in Padanaram, in the land of Canaan, things are not so simple. The following are known:

1. Abram was called out of Haran, or Syria.

2. Jacob went to Syria per his mother Rebekah's words. (Genesis 27:43)

3. Rachel stole Laban's Syrian idols. (Genesis 31:32)

4. God changed Jacob's name to Israel on their journey home from Syria.

5. Jacob destroyed all the idols before going to Bethel, and Deborah, Rebekah's nurse, (מינקת רבקה דברה) who had never been mentioned prior, nor afterwards, died, and was buried like the idols. (Genesis 35:4-8)

6. God blessed Jacob after he came out of *"Padan Aram"* and told him his name would be called *"Israel"* forevermore. (Genesis 35:9-10)

Hebrew readers might see the argument being made more easily: Padan is idolatry, or Syrian idolatry, or alternatively, Padan is a "curse". Jacob had practiced idolatry in Syria by placing rods before the livestock to determine their offspring's skin features. Laban had agreed to give Jacob livestock born with certain skin colors and patterns, and Jacob had used this superstitious method to gain wealth. He left idolatry, or Padan Aram, and when he did, God immediately changed his name to the Abrahamic covenant name, *"Israel"*.

One final point from the six knowns. English translations have Deborah, Rebekah's nurse, dying and being buried under an oak similarly as the idols were hidden (or buried, יטמן). Furthermore, *"Deborah, Rebekah's nurse"* could feasibly be, *"nursing words of Rebekah."* This possibility resolves the otherwise rhetorical questions: When did Rebekah's nurse join Jacob on the trip home from his twenty-year stay in Syria? Why is Deborah even mentioned? She had never been mentioned prior to her death and burial, nor was she ever mentioned again? We do not know how much younger Benjamin was than Joseph, so perhaps they stayed in Shalem several years. If so, and if Deborah was a person, she could have joined them then, but her importance at her death remains unknown. Again, why would she be mentioned only once, and that being at death? Deborah might not be a person but instead, *"words of Rebekah"*, the words that sent Jacob to Syria, to the land of idols, or curses.

The Galeed covenant divided between two beliefs, Laban's idolatry, and Jacob's belief in the God who visited him on his journey to Syria. Rachel was unwilling to let go of her childhood idolatry, she stole and kept Laban's idols. She died giving birth to Benjamin in Padan Aram, and perhaps her death was a consequence of her Syrian idolatry or curses.

Your author has read the entire Bible in Hebrew nearly seven times, but his skills in ancient Hebrew are still limited. These points were discovered by studying the sequence of events and are being reported because they are valid, but a language expert should investigate further.

In previous chapters the Hebrew word, *midbar*, was considered as possibly having a meaning other than wilderness or desert, or at least in the earliest biblical records. It was explained that the original meaning might have been *"God-given word"* or *"spoken word"* that later evolved to be a name for the place where a word had been spoken by God. When the land of Canaan was inherited by casting lots, Joshua used *"midbar"* five times. In each case it appears at either the beginning or at the end of the inheritance description. In two instances, it is found in the very same sentence with the lot being cast (Joshua 15:1, 16:1), and in two others (Joshua 15:61, 18:11-12) it seems to be associated with the location where the lot was cast. The fifth occurrence of *midbar* is used in choosing Bezer as a city of refuge (Joshua 20:8).

This fifth case could mean *"God-given-word"*, implying Bezer was chosen by divine guidance. Bezer only appears four times in the Bible, three times with *midbar* (Deuteronomy 4:43, Joshua 20:8, and 1 Chronicles 6:78) and once without (Joshua 21:36). Each time *midbar* is present the city is referred to as being chosen as a city of refuge, however in Joshua chapter twenty-one, Bezer is the only city of refuge not being selected as a city of refuge and *midbar* is not in the text. Bezer was likely selected by the *midbar* (spoken word) given to Moses in the plains east of Jordan Jericho (Deuteronomy 4:43) and not by Joshua in the land of Canaan, strongly supporting *midbar* as *"God-given-word"* instead of wilderness.

Before crossing the Jordan River into the Promised Land, Jehovah (YHWH) described to Joshua the land they would be possessing:

> *Every place that the soul of your foot shall tread upon, that have I given unto you, as I **said** unto Moses.* Joshua 1:3 KJV

> *From the **wilderness** and this Lebanon even unto the great river, the river Euphrates, all the land of the Hittites, and unto the great sea toward the going down of the sun, shall be your coast.* Joshua 1:4 KJV

The bolded word, ***"said"*** is the Hebrew, דבר , or English DBR, and at the beginning of the very next verse, ***"wilderness"*** is translated from *midbar*, or MDBR. The King James Version translates DBR as *"said"* and MDBR as *"wilderness"*, but *midbar* might have instead been intended to read, *"from that spoken"*. Oddly and immediately following *midbar* are the words, *"and this Lebanon"*? Joshua is at the entrance to the Promised Land near Jordan Jericho, many miles from Lebanon: *"This Lebanon"* is geographically out of place unless *midbar* was the spoken instructions given to Moses a month or two earlier:

> *Every place whereon the soles of your feet shall tread shall be yours: **from the wilderness and Lebanon**, from the river, the river **Euphrates**, even unto the uttermost sea shall your coast be.* Deuteronomy 11:24 KJV

Moses was told every place their feet treaded would be theirs. The mention of Euphrates brings questions being they never went near the Euphrates, and furthermore, the first verse in Deuteronomy raises more questions:

> *THESE be the words which Moses spake unto all Israel on this side Jordan in the wilderness (midbar), in the plain over against the Red **sea**, between Paran, and Tophel, and Laban, and Hazeroth, and Dizahab.* Deuteronomy 1:1 KJV

In this verse Moses is commencing his final speech to the Israelites just before his death. The bolded word *"sea"* was highlighted to point out that it was added by the translators, **it is not in the Hebrew text.** Secondly, *"between"* comes from בין, that can also mean *"understanding"*, and if that is the true import here, the entire translation is in question. The locations, Laban, Tophel, and Dizahab, each only appear once in the entire Bible and that being in this instance, therefore writing them as location references adds nothing for the reader. Furthermore, Moses' location is repeated in verse five: he is in the land of Moab, on this side Jordan, near the Jordan River. Moab's boundary did not extend far northward because Ammon's land began at the Jabbok River, therefore, Moses' location did not need a detailed description, bringing further doubt on the translation.

Additionally, the rendering *"Red"* could instead be *"end"*, another of its Hebrew meanings, and would fit the context of Moses' life ending. In the previous chapter, Paran was conjectured to mean, *"speaking ark"*, and God certainly did speak audibly from the ark of the covenant (Numbers 7:89). Assuming our theoretical meaning of Paran is correct, and logic suggests it is, the following translation might be closer to the intended message:

> *These are the words Moses spoke to all Israel on the side of Jordan with that Who spoke in the plains, facing the end, and understanding the speaking ark, and understanding the foolish, and Laban, and the settlements with plenty of gold (or Dizahab).* Deuteronomy 1:1
> (Your author)

The Israelites were preparing to cross the Jordan River and possess the Promised Land. Moses knew the cities they would be conquering contained idols of gold and silver. God had instructed him earlier to address the fact that golden idols were going to be in the land and that they were to be destroyed (Numbers 33:51-52, and Deuteronomy 7:25). Moses was concerned that some of the more foolish people might keep them, and he was addressing this concern.

One misunderstood word like *midbar* can have a ripple impact, but fortunately, the Bible's overall message is intact. The purpose here is not to rewrite the Bible, the King James translation is quite good, but the goal is instead to learn and improve the text where problems are found. Some people warn that bringing out inconsistencies could hurt people's faith; however, their faith should be in God rather than in translations: King James is not the savior, and his translation has a copywrite for a reason, it is an opinion. The translations were made many centuries after the life of Jesus and simply do not affect the plan of salvation. However, truth should always prevail, and these few irregularities should be pointed out.

From Paleo-Hebrew pictographs, Lebanon appears to mean "Laban-and-seed" or "Laban and his descendants" – Lebanon (LBNFN). The *midbar* associated with Lebanon is a treaty, not a wilderness, and is referring to *"Galeed"*, the spoken agreement between Jacob and Laban. Galeed was established only a short period before Jacob went to Egypt and it was still in effect after the Exodus. Moses knew about Galeed.

"Gilead" is a word with the same Hebrew spelling as *"Galeed"* but pronounced differently; Gilead was all the land south of Mount Hermon on the east side of the Jordan River. Moses called the land west of the Jordan River, *"the Land of Canaan"*, (Exodus 6:4, 16:35 and Deuteronomy 32:49) and the land east of the Jordan River, *"Gilead."* Maps of the area show Gilead as only part of the land east of the Jordan, however Joshua tells a different story (Joshua 12:2-5, 17:1).

Most maps show the northern boundary of Israel in the days of Joshua to be Mount Hermon (i.e., Galeed). Laban (and Lebanon) would possess the land to the Euphrates River, not Israel. Israel never treaded land to the Euphrates River, so by God's instructions to Moses, and Joshua, it was not theirs: it was not trodden under their feet, so it was not part of their land. The Bible's use of Euphrates in the Promised Land description might not be intended to be a proper noun, but rather to be the meaning of its name, *"bursting forth of sweet water"*: Euphrates might be referring to the river that burst forth from the rock that Moses struck. The northern and southern boundaries of Israel then being Mount Herman and Mount Sinai, the two tallest mountains in land they had been promised.

During his farewell speech, Moses prayed he could cross the Jordan and see the goodly mountain and Lebanon (Deuteronomy 3:25). He wanted to see the covenant mountain of Galeed that Jacob had agreed would be the northern boundary with Laban. Moses could not see Mount Hermon from the plains of Moab. The goodly mountain could not be Mt. Zion because Jehovah had not yet chosen a location to place his name (Deuteronomy 12:5).

Moses was denied passage to the Promised Land and to seeing the goodly mountain and Lebanon, although some 1500 years later he finally got there: Moses was on the Mount of Transfiguration with Jesus and Elijah in the New Testament, and that tall mountain, close to Caesarea Philippi, is surely the *goodly mountain* he wanted to see.

The Promised Land boundaries were established long before Israel crossed the Jordan River: they would be father-in-law Laban on the north, twin brother Esau on the south, cousins Moab and Ammon on the east, to be later joined by Jacob's sons Reuben, Gad, and Manasseh, to half of the tribe, to Machir the firstborn of Manasseh as they received their inheritance in the east. In inheriting the land of Canaan, the first lot came out to the tribe of Judah and the last to the tribe of Dan. The first and last lots of the inheritance might be connected to the New Testament words of Jesus, *"the first will be last and the last first".*

After casting the first two lots, those for Judah and Joseph, there were seven tribes who had not yet inherited in Canaan (Joshua 18:2). For them, Joshua sent out scouts to survey the remaining land, to divide it into seven parts, and to write descriptions of the divisions. He then cast lots and the first went to Jacob's youngest son Benjamin, maybe correlating again to the words of Jesus, *"the first will be last and the last first."* At that time Jehovah had not yet chosen the city for his name, but later chose Jerusalem in Jacob's youngest-son Benjamin's inheritance (Joshua 18:28). Benjamin means, *"son of the right hand."*

Dan's allotment was too small for him, so he conquered the city of Leshem, meaning "precious stone", that was in the northern boundary of the Promised Land. Dan renamed Leshem to match his own name, Dan, a name meaning "Judge"; the city of Dan was located within two miles of Caesarea Philippi where Jesus traveled before going to the Mount of Transfiguration. Dan is not listed among the tribes of Israel in the New Testament's book of Revelation; they were replaced by the Levites who previously had not been numbered among the tribes. The exchange of Levi for Dan likely alludes to a transfiguration of the priesthood to a new relationship between God and man: one based not on judgment and the law but instead on salvation by grace (Hebrews 7:12, and Revelation 7:4-8). Also, the book of Joshua appears to have prophetic implications to the New Jerusalem descending at the end of this age (Joshua 19:49-50, and Revelation 21:2-3).

We have demonstrated how a detailed chronological study can reveal translation anomalies and give new understandings. The stand-alone word *Padan* was found to be associated with the pagan idols of Syria, or their curses from the land north of Galeed. As mentioned, the lone Padan is only found once in the entire Bible, but a variant form, also found only once, occurs in the prophetic book of Daniel. Padan's meaning, revealed now in present times, helps to gain understanding of those prophecies as they relate to our day.

Note: The translation anomaly of *midbar* appears to have crept in during the Babylonian Captivity period or even earlier. By the first century, *midbar* was commonly accepted as being *"wilderness"* as seen in the New Testament reference to John the Baptist (Matthew 3:3). Perhaps the earliest translations from Paleo-Hebrew were made by people who did not believe God was speaking audibly in the days prior to them, so rather than translate it as *"spoken word"*, or something similar, they instead chose *"wilderness"*, the location where God had spoken. This is one possibility.

CHAPTER TWELVE

THE YEAR 1111 BC

The solved chronology has identified every Jubilee year in biblical history. The seventh Jubilee occurred in 1122 BC, or exactly eleven years before a most-eventful year, that being the Year 1111 BC. This chapter delves into specifics of the period of the judges before the times of the kings of Israel.

> *"In those days there was no king in Israel: every man did that which was right in his own eyes."* Judges 21:25 KJV

In the days of the judges God delivered Israel seven times through the first seven judges: Othniel, Ehud, Shamgar, Deborah, Gideon, Tola, and Jair, but he only delivered seven times, perhaps he thought, "enough is enough". This is interesting because seven is a key biblical number. God said he would no longer deliver Israel because they had forsaken him (Judges 10:13-14). Furthermore, he told Samuel that Israel had not rejected him but rather they had rejected God from reigning over them (1 Samuel 8:6-7).

A meticulous chronology of this time shows both Samson and Samuel were born during the time of Jair judging Israel. Their births were under remarkably similar circumstances as their mothers were both barren and conceived only through divine intervention. They were consecrated to God prior to conception; they were both Nazarites from birth (Judges 13:5 and 1 Samuel 1:11) and were both born just prior to Israel's seventh rejection of God's sovereignty.

During this period Israel was given into the hands of the Ammonites and the Philistines, and they called on Jephthah to deliver them from the Ammonites (Judges 10:7-8). Jephthah, being promised that he would become their leader, agreed to fight for them, and he made an oath to sacrifice the first one he saw coming from his house if he won the battle. Unfortunately, after delivering Israel, the first one who came from his house was his only child, his daughter, who he sadly sacrificed as a burnt offering.

This incident is especially revealing in two ways: first, it shows Israel was practicing human sacrifices during this period, and second, God had informed them not to call on him anymore because he would not deliver them. Jephthah had obviously not called on the true and loving God when making his vow or his daughter would certainly not have been sacrificed. God was fed up with Israel's vain and pagan practices, such as that of Jephthah and his vow, and consequently they were without a king.

The Israelites were on their own, however, the chronology shows God was still their God, because he was working another plan in the background: the Nazarites, Samson, and Samuel, would be born and would be anointed from birth to deliver Israel. God would work through special men but not through superstitions.

Samson was a Nazarite from birth who began to deliver Israel from the Philistines. He was a Nazarite in the power of a law that had been given to Moses: the Nazarite's hair was not to be cut during the sanctified period. In the story, Delilah convinced Samson to tell her the source of his supernatural strength. He told her his power came from his hair, so she shaved his head while he slept, and his strength departed. She then sold him for eleven hundred pieces of silver to the Philistines who took him prisoner and put out his eyes.

In captivity, Samson's hair began to regrow, and during that time, he was forced to put on a humiliating show for all the high-ranking Philistines. When Samson was brought into the arena to be belittled and mocked, he prayed to have his strength restored, and he was answered. The blind Samson then asked his young assistant, who was assigned as his seeing guide, to help him find the pillars of the building. Samson put his hands on these columns and pushed them, causing the building to fall and thereby killing both himself and over three thousand of the ruling-class Philistines. Although Samson died then, there is more to his story in the scriptures.

In the following chapter Micah stole eleven hundred pieces of silver from his mother. This was a huge sum of money as proven by the fact that Micah later employed a Levite priest for a whole year for only ten pieces of silver. This same fortune was surely the very same money awarded to Delilah for betraying Samson: Delilah was likely Micah's mother, but regardless, the enormous amount of silver and the timing of events support this being the same money. Micah later returned the eleven hundred pieces of silver to his mother who then had molten and graven images made for him.

Micah set up a graven image for worship in the city of Dan, a city of the tribe to which Samson had belonged. With this, we are told a critical timeline detail: the ark of the covenant was in Shiloh at the time the image was set up (Judges 18:31). We are not told how long Samson was in prison before his death but are told his hair began to regrow. It is likely Micah's image was set up before he died. The ark was later captured by the Philistines at the time of Eli's death and remained in their possession seven months. Per the known timeline, the Philistines probably captured the ark in a battle-of-revenge for Samson having killed their leaders. After Samson died, the Prophet Samuel, the second Nazarite born to help Israel, rose to his purpose in God's plan.

The Philistines had the ark of the covenant in their possession seven months, but consequently, while it was there, they were plagued. They soon decided to return it to the Israelites. They put the ark on a cart to be pulled by two unmanned milk cows who brought it to the field of Joshua, a field in or near the tribe of Benjamin's inheritance. From there the ark was taken to Kirjathjearim where it remained for twenty years while the Philistines were subdued by Samuel (1 Samuel 7:2, 7:13-14).

Connecting the dots, Samson likely died prior to the Philistines capturing the ark, or shortly thereafter, being it was still in Shiloh when Micah's image was set up. The ark could not have been taken to its twenty-year home in Kirjathjearim until after Micah's image was set up since that happened after Samson was taken captive. Furthermore, Micah's image was likely setup with the betrayal money that led to Samson's death. This chronological sequence, though complex and requiring diligence to follow, leads to many intriguing conclusions about the Year 1111 BC.

Israel was delivered into the hand of the Philistines for forty years (Judges 13:1) and Samson judged Israel for twenty of those years (Judges 16:31). The ark was taken captive around the time of Samson's death at the midpoint of the Philistine's domination. At that time Samuel rose to his role as Nazarite for the next twenty years. These details, plus those of the overall chronology, show the Philistine's capturing of the ark and the deaths of Samson and Eli, all occurred approximately the same year, that being 1111 BC. Also, that year, the tribe of Benjamin was decimated in a civil war against Israel and its timing proves much happened in 1111 BC.

The overall chronology reveals that Israel rejected God around 1131 BC and Samuel finished subduing the Philistines in 1091 BC to conclude their forty years of domination. Saul became Israel's first king sometime after 1091 BC and David became king in 1071 BC, or sixty years after Israel had rejected God as King. Israel's first man-king, King Saul, ascended after the Nazarites, Samson, and Samuel, had judged Israel.

> Notes: King Saul reigned during this period but we do not know how long. God rejected him and anointed David early in the days of Saul's reign. Also, the ark of the covenant remained longer than twenty years in Kirjathjearim, but the twenty-year benchmark was simply recorded to denote the end of the period of Samuel overcoming the Philistines.

The tribe of Benjamin was nearly annihilated in a civil war during the period of God being rejected as King: a man from Gibeah raped and killed a Levitical priest's concubine and this led to war. Benjamin was reduced in size from a people having 26,000 soldiers to a mere six hundred men, with no women and children surviving. It would be years before they would again be large enough to fight wars, and this detail, in conjunction with one other, helps to determine when their slaughter occurred: a man from the tribe of Benjamin fled from the army to inform Eli that the ark of the covenant had been captured (1 Samuel 4:12). An almost extinct tribe would not be fighting with the Philistines, therefore the civil war that decimated Benjamin could not have been before this battle. The Bible clearly says the other tribes wanted to see Benjamin restored, therefore, they would not let them join in battles until years had passed from their devastation. Benjamin's civil war against Israel had to have occurred after the ark was captured by the Philistines.

Again, the Philistine's capturing of the ark was likely a revenge battle for the three thousand leaders Samson had killed; Israel had been submissive to the Philistines prior to Samson. Based on the details, Samson must have died less than a year before Eli. Also, the last verse of Judges explains there was not a king in Israel at the time of Benjamin's plight; therefore, Benjamin and Israel fought sometime between the ark being captured and Saul becoming king. Saul alludes to this by explaining that he was from the least family in the smallest tribe of Israel: Saul was from the nearly annihilated tribe of Benjamin (1 Samuel 9:21).

Note: In the New Testament, the Apostle Paul gives approximate timelines for this period (Acts 13:16-22). He uses generalizations concerning the spans, saying, *"about four hundred and fifty years until Samuel the prophet."* The four hundred and fifty years best fits with the time from the Exodus until the end of the period of the judges (i.e., to the end of Samuel's reign as a judge in Israel, or to Samuel's death). There were exactly four hundred eighty years from the Exodus until Solomon began building the temple (1 Kings 6:1), leaving only thirty years to the benchmark Paul is referring. He was likely talking in guesstimates of Israel's departure from Egypt until Samuel's death. This matches closely being there were forty-three years from King David's ascension until Solomon began temple construction, and four hundred and fifty years is a reasonable approximation for four hundred and thirty seven years (480 - 43 = 437 years).

Paul next gave a forty-year space from Samuel to his reference, and again his end-marker is likely temple construction. This could not be an allusion to Saul reigning forty years, being that would require an additional forty years be subtracted and would make four hundred years a better approximation than four hundred and fifty years. Whatever Paul's reference, it was a response to the subject of the scriptures being read in the synagogue on the day he was answering, and he responded doing math on the spot without pen and paper (Acts 13:15-17). Furthermore, King Saul's reign could have only been a maximum of twenty years being David ascended twenty years after Samuel had subdued the Philistines.

The ark of the covenant was shown to have been captured by the Philistines only forty years before King David ascended. During those forty years, Benjamin warred with Israel and Saul became Israel's first king. This period would necessarily be when Israel reduced Benjamin to merely six hundred men who found only four hundred wives after the war (Judges 21:12). It would take time for them to regrow into a tribe having enough twenty-years-old males to fight wars (Numbers 1:3). For these reasons, Benjamin's war against Israel had to have occurred near the time the ark was captured by the Philistines, but as previously explained, it also had to have occurred afterwards. Soon we will see just how close together these events really were.

Saul became king when he was a young man (1 Samuel 9:2), had a son named Jonathan who was old enough to be a warrior (1 Samuel 13:1-3), and had a Benjamite father named Kish who was still alive: Kish and Saul would necessarily have been among the six hundred survivors of the civil war and Jonathan would have been born afterwards during Benjamin's rebuilding. Additionally, Saul had a forty-year-old son who succeeded him at death (2 Samuel 2:10).

Saul would have been at least twenty years old (fighting age) during Benjamin's war, and again, would have been among Benjamin's survivors. The interval from Benjamin's war until Saul became king would need to be long enough to allow Jonathan to grow from a baby to a fighting soldier, but short enough for Saul to still be young when ascending the throne. Based on the knowns, Saul reigned at most twenty years, probably less, and his forty-year-old son who succeeded him in 1070 BC, Ish-bosheth, meaning *"man of shame"*, had to be born in 1110 BC. Benjamin's decimation had to have occurred before Ish-bosheth's birth being all the women and children were killed in the civil war. Saul's *"man of shame"* must have been conceived just after the war in 1111 BC and born later that year, or the next.

> Note: King David's reign was forty years and six months, instead of an even forty years, thereby allowing Ish-bosheth to have succeeded Saul in 1070 BC after David's ascension, rather than 1071 BC.

Saul and Kish were residents of Gibeah where the Levitical priest's concubine was murdered and where Benjamin's war with Israel was ignited. The concubine was a resident of Bethlehem-Judah, and interestingly the hometown of Israel's second king, King David. God chose Saul from the small tribe of Benjamin to be Israel's first "man-king," and soon afterwards chose Jerusalem, a city in Benjamin's inheritance to be the place for his name to dwell. Perhaps Benjamin was receiving special favor to help recover from the losses of their disobedience. God's grace was abundant to Benjamin, sparing six hundred men who had defended rape and murder, and allowing them to rebuild and to produce the first king of Israel. What amazing grace and forgiveness!

Saul was given the distinct honor of being chosen as Israel's first king, however, he proved to be undeserving. His character is later revealed through his dealings with David, the humble young shepherd from Bethlehem-Judah. As we will see, the selection of Saul might also be a case of Israel reaping judgment for rejecting God as King. This period is one of the most challenging in the entire biblical record to decipher, and for this reason, the following verse has been the subject of many commentaries:

*"Saul reigned one year, and **when** he had reigned two years over Israel".* 1 Samuel 13:1 KJV

This translation seems redundant being two years of reign automatically includes one year but might make more sense if **"when"**, a word added by the translators, was removed. The Masoretic Hebrew text could be translated, *"Saul was the son of one year in his reign and had reigned two years over Israel"*, meaning that when Saul was in his first year as king of Israel, he had already reigned a total of two years over them. For this to be the case, Saul would have reigned over Israel during a year prior to becoming king, and the likely possibility is during the year of Benjamin's war with Israel. This is enthralling and maybe telling. Consider the following list of things we know about King Saul:

1. He was a resident of Gibeah, the location of the appalling rape and murder, and would have been at least 20 years old, or fighting age, during the time of Benjamin's destruction.

2. He and his father would both have necessarily been among the six hundred survivors.

3. He was taller than all the people of Israel and maybe they were afraid of him. (1 Samuel 9:2)

4. The sons of Belial did not like him. They said, *"How will this man save us?"* (1 Samuel 10:27)

5. Israel wanted a king suitable for leading in battle and they were pleased with the choice of Saul.

6. Saul hid when Samuel was going to present him to Israel. (1 Samuel 10:22)

7. Saul proved to have a murderous spirit in his dealings with David and in his murdering of eighty-five Levitical priests.

What did the sons of Belial know about Saul and why did they not want him to be king? This question is certainly worth pondering. The rest of Israel was incredibly happy to have Saul as king, but the sons of Belial were not. Could it be Saul was somehow involved with the murder and rape of the woman in Gibeah that caused Benjamin's plight and the sons of Belial were privy to the particulars? Was he involved in the refusal to turn over the guilty in Gibeah and thereby caused the death of 66,000 Israelites, or was he simply guilty by association? There must be some reason for the words, *"Saul was the son of one year in his reign and had reigned two years over Israel"*, and there also must be a reason for the attitude of the sons of Belial. Please consider the possibilities in view of the list above and form your own opinion.

Working backwards from the fall of Babylon in 539 BC, King David would have ascended to the throne of Judah in 1071 BC, or exactly forty years after 1111 BC. Using further constraints, the start of the period of the judges is limited based on the age of Joshua at his death: he was 110 years old. This leaves only a small window of forty years, plus or minus a few years, for the period between the ark being captured and the ascension of David. During twenty of those years Samuel judged Israel and subdued the Philistines (1 Samuel 7:2, 7:13-14). The Bible's details have bounded the period, requiring that the year 1111 BC was a huge year in the history of Israel. The ark of the covenant was likely with the Philistines while Israel fought against Benjamin.

The Year 1111 BC was a transition year between the Nazarites, Samson, and Samuel, and was the year that Eli died. It set the stage for Israel to get a "man-king," and it was likely the first year that Saul reigned, although not as king but as rebel, and probably worse. The Year 1111 BC was arguably the most eventful year in the Old Testament's history! One of the Psalms appears to have been written concerning that period (Psalms 78: 60-64). We can learn plenty from the chronology.

"In those days there was no king in Israel: every man did that which was right in his own eyes." Judges 21:25 KJV

CHAPTER THIRTEEN

KING DAVID

David spent the years leading up to his ascension as king of Israel on the defensive against the aggression of King Saul. Saul tried many times to kill him, but David was anointed by God. Each attempt to kill David only brought him honor and deliverance. We join the story of one such case:

> *And Saul pitched in the hill of Hachilah, which is before Jeshimon, by the way. But David abode in the wilderness, and he saw that Saul came after him into the wilderness. David therefore sent out spies, and understood that Saul was come in very deed.* 1 Samuel 26:3-4 KJV

David saw Saul chasing him in *"the wilderness"*, or Hebrew *midbar*, and sent men to confirm. This is another example of the Hebrew word *midbar* possibly being mistranslated. If David saw Saul in the wilderness (*midbar*), would he need to send men to confirm? Otherwise, if he saw him in a vision or dream (*midbar*) he would likely want to confirm. *Jeshimon* means *"desert"* or *"wilderness"* but is here translated as the proper name *"Jeshimon"*. Saul is pitched before *"the Jeshimon"* or alternatively, before *"the wilderness"*. *Jeshimon* and *midbar* are both used in these verses just as they sometimes appear together in other places in the Bible (e.g., Psalms 78:40, 106:14, 107:4, Isaiah 43:19-20). This would be redundant if *midbar* also means *"desert"* or *"wilderness."*

In the second book of Samuel, Joab was hotly pursuing Abner to kill him in revenge for his brother whom Abner had just killed moments earlier (2 Samuel 2:24-26). Abner gathered Benjamin together in the *"wilderness of Gibeon"*, or *"midbar of Gibeon"*, and asked Joab to quit his hot pursuit and he immediately agreed. Why? Joab later killed Abner in chapter three to avenge his brother but would not kill him when all of Benjamin was gathered with him (2 Samuel 2:27). The Masoretic text could be translated,

> *The sons of Benjamin gathered with Abner and were bundled as one, standing on the top of **Gibeah** as one.* 2 Samuel 2:25

Note: The King James Version translated Gibeah as *"hill"* but could have instead rendered it as the proper name, *"Gibeah"*, King Saul's home. The Hebrew text implies Abner would have been killed by morning if he had not spoken (2 Samuel 2:27), but what was it that he had spoken? Was he invoking a commandment, or *midbar*?

Benjamin was still a small, nearly extinct tribe and *midbar* might have been an agreement to let them rebuild. It had only been about forty-five years since the gruesome rape and murder of the Levite's concubine that led to their destruction. The location Abner gathered Benjamin was the wilderness of Gibeon, or *midbar* Gibeon, near Gibeah, the place Benjamin's problems had begun years earlier. Gibeon was the home of the Gibeonites (Joshua 9:3-15), so how could it be a wilderness? Did not God promise the children of Israel that they would possess cities and wells rather than wildernesses? Saul had wars with the Gibeonites who were probably still living in Gibeon at that time (2 Samuel 21:1-2). Does it make sense that Gibeon was a desert or wilderness? If this was a wilderness, from where did the Benjamites come to gather to Abner?

Benjamin was being decimated again and had already lost up to as many as three hundred and sixty men; it seems most reasonable Abner was invoking an agreement to protect Benjamin from extinction and Joab was afraid to dishonor it (2 Samuel 2:31). Why else would he give up such a hot pursuit of one who had just killed his brother? The invoked agreement might have had a name, *"Midbar Gibeon"*? Again, the battle slaughtering Benjamin years earlier had occurred in very nearby Gibeah.

Additionally, Abner spoke to the tribe of Benjamin before going to make an agreement with David to support him as king (2 Samuel 3:19). Why? Did he think he would be protected if the small tribe of Benjamin were on his side? Did he need Benjamin's approval before meeting with David to offer to establish him as king over all of Israel? He took twenty men with him to the meeting – perhaps all Benjamites? The evidence continues to accumulate in support of an alternative meaning for *midbar*.

As shown in the previous chapter, the ark of the covenant was captured and taken into the possession of the Philistines for seven months near the death of Samson, and the slaughter of Benjamin in Gibeah likely occurred just afterwards. While in the land of the Philistines, the ark caused much destruction and was soon returned. It first arrived in the field of Joshua and was then taken to the house of Abinadab in Gibeah (1 Samuel 7:1); the King James Version translated Gibeah as *"hill"* in that instance, but over forty years later when King David brought it to the city of David, they translated it as the proper name, *"Gibeah"*. Interesting.

The ark of the covenant remained in Gibeah, the location of Benjamin's plight, from shortly after the decimating battle until years later when King David brought it to the city of David. The ark had proven to be well capable of defending itself during its seven months in the land of the Philistines and had now returned to Gibeah. It would reside in Gibeah for more than 45 years to protect Benjamin during his rebuilding years.

King Saul and his son Jonathan both died in battle when Jonathan's son Mephibosheth was five years old (2 Samuel 4:4), and at that time, David became king over the house of Judah, ruling from Hebron; seven and a half years later David became king over all Israel. Upon hearing David had been made king over all Israel, the Philistines went to war with him but were defeated (2 Samuel 5:17-25). David then brought the ark from *the house of Abinadab in Gibeah*; this was about eight to ten years after he first became king over Judah. David wanted to build a house for the ark, but God would not allow him. God informed David that his son, Solomon, would build the house (2 Samuel 7:12-13).

David had been faithful to God and all his enemies were subdued under his rule. He gave an inheritance to Mephibosheth to show kindness to the house of Saul for Jonathan's sake (2 Samuel 9:1). This happened sometime during the range of ten to twenty-five years after he first became king of Judah: Mephibosheth, who was five years old when David gave him the inheritance, later fathered a young son named Micha (2 Samuel 9:12). Micha was born near the mid-range of David's forty-year reign, or approximately 1060 – 1045 BC.

With all his enemies subdued, things were going great for King David as he reigned from Jerusalem. All the land was in a state of rest until the king of Ammon died. Wanting to show kindness, David sent messengers to Hanun, the new king of Ammon, to offer his condolences for his father, but unfortunately his kindness was perceived as a spying mission. Ammon hired the Syrians to go to war with him against Israel, but David defeated them. After beating them, David made a peace agreement with the Syrians. The next year he sent Joab, the captain of his army, along with all of Israel's armies, to fight against Ammon, but King David remained in Jerusalem. While in Jerusalem, David had an affair with Bathsheba, the wife of one of his soldiers, and that betrayal plagued the remainder of his reign.

While Israel fought Ammon, David had the affair and Bathsheba became pregnant with his child. Hearing she was pregnant, David recalled Bathsheba's husband Uriah from the war with Ammon, trying to cover up his role in the pregnancy. King David ate and drank with Uriah and then sent him home to his unbeknownst pregnant wife in hopes of covering up the identity of the child's father. Uriah refused to go home to lay with his wife:

> *And Uriah said unto David, The ark, and Israel, and Judah, abide in tents; and my lord Joab, and the servants of my lord, are encamped in the open field; shall I then go into mine house, to eat and to drink, and to lie with my wife? as thou livest, and as thy soul liveth, I will not do this thing.* 2 Samuel 11:11 KJV

The next day King David tried again. He drank with Uriah, got him drunk, and told him to go home but again he refused. Running out of options, David sent Uriah back to the war carrying written instructions to Joab to have him put in a hot battle and to ensure that he be killed (2 Samuel 11:15-24). Later, after receiving news that Uriah was dead, David took Bathsheba to be his wife, but this was very displeasing to God (2 Samuel 11:27). Uriah had been faithful to Israel and to King David, but David had killed him, and consequently the remainder of his reign would be seriously affected.

God sent the prophet Nathan to reprimand David for his wrong and to explain that his illegitimate child would not live. Nathan used a parable to make the point clear, and his story is especially interesting being it uses three men rather than just Uriah and David: the third man might represent the spirit of lust that had overtaken him. King David truly repented, and God forgave him, but nonetheless there would be serious consequences. As a result of his unfaithfulness, Nathan prophesied the sword would not depart from the house of David, and evil would rise in his house in the sight of all Israel (2 Samuel 12:10-12).

After the death of the child, Solomon was born to Bathsheba and David, and God was well pleased with Solomon, displaying the awesome grace that God gives to those having true repentance. During the period of David's affair and murder, Israel continued to fight with the sons of Ammon, and Israel's

Captain Joab was winning the war abundantly. Joab sent for David to come join him in the battle against Rabbah or risk having all Israel name that city, "Joab." David's preoccupation with Bathsheba and Uriah had caused him to take his focus off the kingdom of Israel. Heeding Joab's advice he went to the war, conquered all the cities of Ammon, and then returned to Jerusalem. All of David's surrounding enemies were now subdued, but just as Nathan had foreseen, his next enemy would rise inside his own home.

David's firstborn son Amnon developed a strong lust for his half-sister Tamar, the beautiful sister of Absalom. By pretending to be sick, Amnon deceived King David into sending Tamar to nurse him, and when she was sent, he raped her. Upon hearing the news, King David was furious, although probably not as furious as Absalom: Absalom killed Amnon two years later in revenge and then fled for refuge in Geshur for three years (2 Samuel 13:38). The spirit of lust had again caused murder by David's house.

After three years in exile, Joab perceived David's heart was with Absalom, so he sent a woman to convince the king to bring Absalom back to Israel. Joab told the woman to pretend to be a mother mourning for a son who had been killed by another son and to ask King David for a judgment of protection for her remaining son. Joab's intent was to have David indirectly judge Absalom's situation. It worked. King David agreed to let Absalom return to Israel with the stipulation he would not see the king's face. Two years later Absalom sent Joab to arrange for him to stand before King David; now, five years after last seeing his father and seven years after his sister had been raped, Absalom met King David face-to-face. David forgave him in person (2 Samuel 14: 28-33), but it seems Absalom still resented King David for having sent Tamar to nurse Amnon seven years earlier.

After the meeting, Absalom gained followers by standing in the way leading to the king's gate and intercepting anyone coming to the king for judgment. He told people that unfortunately there was no one to judge for them but if he were in-charge there would be. Absalom stole the hearts of Israel from King David (2 Samuel 15:6). Soon afterwards but unknowns to David, a full-blown conspiracy to have him dethroned had developed; Absalom requested leave from the king's presence:

> *"And it came to pass after 40 years, that Absalom said unto the king, I pray thee, let me go and pay my vow, which I have vowed unto the LORD, in Hebron."* 2 Samuel 15:7 KJV

These forty years are confusing since King David only reigned a total of forty years, and seven of those years had just passed from the rape of Tamar, another eight to ten years were shown to have occurred prior to bringing the ark of the covenant to Jerusalem, and with even more years elapsing from the ark's retrieval until Mephibosheth was given an inheritance. Therefore, David had currently been king for at least twenty years.

Clearly this forty-year reference is from a point prior to David's ascension over Judah and probably from one of two events: 1) the ascension of Saul as Israel's first king, or 2) the anointing of David to become king. If the first possibility began these years, it would prove Saul's reign was less than twenty years, otherwise, if the more likely, the anointing of David by Samuel were the start, David would now be in the waning years of his reign. Being he was thirty years old when he ascended (2 Samuel 5:4-5) and being we have established a minimum of twenty years had now passed, and probably more, King David would have been a minimum age of fifty years at this point. Furthermore, he was probably at least twelve to fifteen years old when anointed by Samuel to be king, thereby making him now in his mid-fifties or older. The forty-year reference indeed fits well with his anointing by Samuel.

Rather than fight the conspiracy, King David chose to flee from Absalom. He ordered his ten concubines to remain and keep his house, had the ark of the covenant and the priests remain in Jerusalem, instructed his friend Hushai to return to the city to strategically assist from within, and allowed many followers to remain in their homes. He began issuing these commands near the brook Kidron in Jerusalem (2 Samuel 15:14-23) with the Hebrew word, *midbar,* appearing in these verses. Here *midbar* might be referring to the spoken commands of the anointed King David. Certainly, the brook Kidron and the Mount of Olives were not in a wilderness, they were in Jerusalem.

David fled initially with six hundred followers who were probably at least some of the original six hundred men with whom he fled from King Saul years earlier. He crossed the Jordan River the night of his escape and went to Mahanaim where provisions were waiting (2 Samuel 17:27-29), and curiously, the last words of these scriptures are *"in the wilderness (midbar)"*. If *"midbar"* was meant to be *"commanded word"* in this instance, it might be that David had pre-arranged the provisions. The people who supplied him were former enemies whom he had previously subdued in battles and with whom he had negotiated peace (i.e., 2 Samuel 17:27 identifies Rabbah of the children of Ammon). There would now be thousands of these former enemies, these non-Israelites, to join his six hundred men for a battle with the children of Israel (2 Samuel 18:1).

At his troop's request, David remained in Mahanaim while his servants went out to battle Israel. He divided his men into three groups and gave explicit instructions to deal mercifully with his son Absalom. The battle spread out across the entire country and a grueling slaughter ensued in which 20,000 men died: Israel was slain before the servants of David (2 Samuel 18:7) and Absalom died at the hands of Joab. Joab blew the shofar to end the battle and all Israel fled back to their homes to regroup. As word came to King David that his son was dead, he cried and mourned greatly. He truly blamed himself. He knew it was all a result of his unfaithfulness in the matter of Uriah.

After grieving, King David came and sat in the gates of Mahanaim, and all the people came out before him. The people reasoned they should reinstate him as king. David informed his nephew Amasa, who had just led Israel against him, that he would remain as captain of the host in the stead of Joab (2 Samuel 19:13). This shows not only forgiveness, but also that David somehow had insight that Joab had disobeyed him and had killed his son. With the appointment of Amasa, the entire tribe of Judah was united in a decision to restore David as king (2 Samuel 19:13-14) and they sent word for him to return to Jerusalem.

King David went to the Jordan River near Gilgal where a ferry was waiting to bring him home. All of Judah and half of Israel went out to escort him. After crossing the river and coming to Gilgal, all of Israel met the king and a quarrel arose between Israel and Judah. Perhaps Israel was concerned that David would be partial to Judah since only half of Israel had ushered him across. Whatever the reason, all but Judah left King David and followed a Benjamite named Sheba. An interesting point is *midbar* is correctly translated here as being the contentious words between Israel and Judah.

From Gilgal King David returned to Jerusalem and gave instructions to his new captain Amasa to gather the men of Judah and to return in three days to go after Sheba and quench Israel's rebellion. After three days, when Amasa had failed to arrive, David ordered Abishai, Joab's brother, to gather his men to pursue Sheba, and they did; they pursued to the great rock at Gibeon and there Joab killed Amasa and regained lead of the host. With Joab now in control, the host pursued to Abel in Bethmaachah and seized the city. A wise woman of the city negotiated with him and agreed to have Sheba beheaded and his head thrown over the wall. With Sheba now dead, Joab blew the shofar to end the siege and returned to Jerusalem and to King David.

Later there was a famine in Israel for three years and David inquired of Jehovah (YHWH) for an explanation. Jehovah answered that it was on account of Saul who had massacred the Gibeonites with whom Israel had made a covenant in the days of Joshua. David then asked the Gibeonites what they required to appease the situation and bless Jehovah's inheritance; they replied that seven members of Saul's family should be delivered and hung before Jehovah in Gibeah of Saul, the chosen of Jehovah. David agreed and sent seven of Saul's descendants to the Gibeonites, but he spared Mephibosheth in honor of his agreement with Jonathan. The Gibeonites hung these seven descendants of Saul in Gibeah, then David took their bones and those of Saul and Jonathan from Jabesh-Gilead and brought all to the sepulcher of Kish and buried them.

All these things were done at the command of King David and then Jehovah was entreated for the land (2 Samuel 21:14). This shows David was the king in authority and the one who asked the Gibeonites what they required: David gave the seven sacrifices to the Gibeonites, not Jehovah. Jehovah simply honored David's decisions as king.

Next, the Philistines again warred with Israel and King David went with the host to the war. In one of the early battles, David grew tired and was nearly killed, but was saved by Abishai. After this incident, the army told David he would no longer go out to battle since they did not want him to quench the light of Israel; obviously, David had grown old then. During these battles four giants were killed including the brother of Goliath. At this point, David was now delivered out of the hand of all his enemies and out of the hand of Saul (2 Samuel 22:1). It is likely that he wrote many of the Psalms during these waning years.

The remainder of David's reign involved him numbering all of Israel and Judah, and consequently, having to choose between three outcomes (2 Samuel 24). There are several apparent discrepancies between the accounts given in the second book of Samuel and the first book of Chronicles, so, before proceeding with the story, these anomalies are listed and addressed:

| Item 1 | 2 Samuel 24:1 | Jehovah moves David to number Israel and Judah | 1 Chronicles 21:1 | Satan provoked David to number Israel |
| Item 2 | 2 Samuel 24:9 | 800,000 valiant that drew sword in Israel, and 500,000 men in Judah | 1 Chronicles 21:5 | 1,100,000 that drew sword in Israel, 470,000 in Judah |

Item 3	2 Samuel 24:13	7 years of famine	1 Chronicles 21:12	3 years of famine
Item 4	2 Samuel 24:24	David buys the threshing floor of Araunah and oxen for 50 shekels of silver	1 Chronicles 21:25	David gave 600 shekels of gold to Ornan for the place

From the table above, there are obviously two distinct accounts that appear to be contradictory. The following table will now address each:

Item 1	There are numerous possibilities for this difference including that it could simply be a Jewish idiom in which the one allowing the provoking is credited with provoking, or possibly Jehovah and Satan both aroused David to number Israel. The Hebrew word "satan" means "adversary" and does not necessarily have to be translated as a proper name. Furthermore, in the account from the second book of Samuel, the anger of Jehovah might have provoked David. God's anger could truly be an adversary until one repents. Another point is the command to number Israel is given in the very next verse in each of these books (i.e., 2 Samuel 24:2 and 1 Chronicles 21:2). In verse one of both accounts the word *"number"* is the Hebrew word *"mana"* and could be translated, *"divide"*. Possibly verse one is saying David wanted to divide Israel, with verse two being the command to number them, and this would explain why Judah and Israel were counted separately, and why God, who wanted unity, would have been upset.
Item 2	The 800,000 valiant men that drew sword in Israel did not include the 288,000 appointed to the regular army serving the king (1 Chronicles 27:1-15) nor did it include the 12,000-horseman working the chariots (2 Chronicles 1:14), so adding gives 800,000 + 288,000 + 12,000 = 1,100,000 that drew sword in Israel. The 470,000 that drew sword in Jerusalem possibly did not include the 30,000 chosen from all Israel (2 Samuel 6:1), and this would give 470,000 + 30,000 = 500,000 men of Judah.
Item 3	There was a famine in the days of David for three years, year by year, and David inquired of the Lord for the reason (2 Samuel 21:1). The Bible does not say the famine lasted three years but rather had been going on three years when David inquired of the Lord. Also, it took nine months and twenty days, or nearly one year, for Joab to number Israel (2 Samuel 24:8). It is likely the famine continued until David was given the three options, making it now four years into the famine. The text does not say there will be seven future years of famine, but rather seven total years (2 Samuel 24:13). The famine might be what provoked David to number Israel; he might have wanted to know how many troops he had remaining.
Item 4	The fifty pieces of silver only bought the threshing floor and the oxen. David probably carried this much silver with him, and being he needed to act fast to stop the plague, he then bought the threshing floor and the oxen before later buying the entire site for an additional six hundred shekels of gold. He probably did not carry the 600 shekels with him. Also, Araunah and Ornan are likely two names for the same person.

These reasonable possibilities resolve the apparent discrepancies and even clarify this period (e.g., Israel had likely been in famine for four years at this time). With famine in the land, people were probably growing sick and dying. Realizing this helps portray the true picture of those times and to see the true heart of God.

An adversary (Satan) stood against Israel, and that could be the factor adding to Jehovah's anger (1 Chronicles 21:1). David gave the seven sons of Saul to the Gibeonites to be hung, and if this occurred during the first three years of the seven-year famine, and if it coincided with the numbering of Israel (2 Samuel 24:8), Jehovah's anger might be a result of the famine continuing even after David had appeased the curse of Saul. We simply cannot see into the spiritual realm and know its particulars, so this is one possibility, but there is a more likely reason. As previously shown, David did not consult with Jehovah on how to end the famine, but rather only inquired of its cause. Then as king, he alone sought the solution with the Gibeonites.

We know David was provoked to either divide or number Israel, and from the Hebrew writings, it was probably both. We are not told what he planned to gain by either. Was he planning a battle to eliminate the frail who were dying of famine? This seems highly unlikely based on David's character; therefore, the best answer is he probably feared another rebellion like that of Absalom, and he wanted to know what he would be facing in terms of numbers. Joab refused to count Benjamin and Levi: Levi was a tribe of priests, not soldiers, and Benjamin was probably still a small tribe that Joab did not want to include in battle numbers.

> *"But Levi and Benjamin counted he not among them: for the king's word was abominable to Joab."* 1 Chronicles 21:6 KJV

It seems that David simply doubted his anointed kingship, and this was counted to him as sin: he was afraid he would have to keep himself in power by his own might and did not consider the One who had appointed him. Whatever his sin truly was, David did not acknowledge it until he heard the numbers of Judah and the numbers of Israel, and then he repented and was given the three choices: 1) three additional years of famine, 2) three months of fleeing from his enemies, or 3) three days of pestilence.

David opted for the third option, he chose to fall into the hands of his merciful God rather than the hands of man (2 Samuel 24:14), so Jehovah sent a pestilence upon Israel and 70,000 died. Initially this seems cruel. Why would a merciful God plague and kill 70,000 of his people in a three-day plague? The answer looks different when considering the timing. The famine was bringing hardship to these 70,000 poor souls and God's mercy brought an end to their suffering. It is all a matter of how you choose to look at it.

The Lord Jesus taught that our faith moves mountains. Believing "God is cruel" can blind us, and then speaking foolishly can release negative faith and move bad mountains and set them right on top of us. Similarly, speaking positive in faith brings blessings. David was not in faith in the subject story, but he was the king and his words had power. He was what the people wanted, a man-king, so God had to work through him.

As the angel stretched his hand towards Jerusalem to destroy it, Jehovah repented ("repented" is the Hebrew *"nacham"* that can mean to pant, to groan, to draw the breath forcibly, to grieve) and said to the angel who destroyed the people, *"....it is enough: stay now thine hand"; and the angel of Jehovah was by the threshing place of Araunah the Jebusite."* 2 Samuel 24:16 KJV

Two descriptions are given for the angel: 1) the angel who smote the people, and 2) the angel of the Lord. These are not necessarily the same angel, but instead are possibly two separate ones. Regardless, the angel refrained and David bought the threshing place of Araunah. He also bought his oxen and offered burnt sacrifices and peace offerings, and the plagued was stayed from Israel. Several years later this became the site of Solomon's temple.

King David was a warrior and spent most of his life fighting. He usually had great faith and God worked many miracles, but still he was a man subject to human flaws. Upon discovering his sins, David was always quick to repent, and his life demonstrates the forgiveness of God. A fitting end for this chapter is from the first book of Kings:

> *"Because David did that which was right in the eyes of the Lord, and turned not aside from anything that he commanded him all the days of his life, save only in the matter of Uriah the Hittite."* 1 Kings 15:5 KJV

CHAPTER FOURTEEN

THE MILLENNIAL REIGN

"But, beloved, be not ignorant of this one thing, that one day is with the Lord as a thousand years, and a thousand years as one day." 2 Peter 3:8 KJV

Is God working a seven thousand years plan for mankind with time divided evenly into seven specific periods? Supporting evidence from the solved chronology will help answer.

1	2	3	4	5	6	7
1000 years	1000 years	1000 years	1000 years	1000 years	1000 years	1000 years

7000 years

God's plan for mankind is speculated to be on a precisely designed timeline of seven thousand years.

Jesus will soon return and reign on Earth for one thousand years during the seventh millennium, and this chapter studies the six thousand years that herald his arrival. From the chronology, the seventy-first Jubilee year was 2015 AD and coincided the last eclipse of the 2014-2015 blood-moon tetrad. Starting in that year, the beginning of each millennium is found by counting backward in increments of one thousand years.

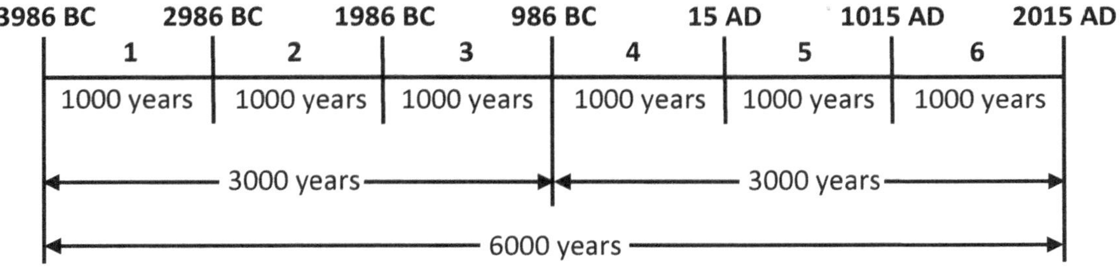

Six thousand years traverses from the conjectured year of original sin to the beginning of the recent Jubilee year, or 2015.

There is no "Year Zero", therefore, the one thousand years from 15 AD extends backwards to 986 BC, or the beginning of the fourth era and the midpoint of the overall 6000 years. Furthermore, the start of each millennium before the birth of Jesus (i.e., the BC Dates) have odd similarities when multiplying the numerals making up their years:

986 BC: 9 x **8** x **6** = 2 x **6** x **6** x **6**

1986 BC: 1 x **9** x **8** x **6** = 2 x **6** x **6** x **6**

2986 BC: 2 x **9** x **8** x **6** = **6** x **6** x **6** x **6** x 0.6666...

3986 BC: 3 x **9** x **8** x **6** = **6** x **6** x **6** x **6**

Each contains a pattern of 6x6x6: the year dividing the **two** 3000-year periods is the product of **two** times 6x6x6, as is the year 1986 BC, while the year 3986 BC is 6x6x6x6. From these patterns, the year 3986 BC, because it is near creation, will be investigated as being the year of Adam-and-Eve's original sin.

Applying the discovered and consistent date template, <u>month x day x century x year</u>, to the dates of the four eclipses from the recent blood-moons tetrad, and dividing these moon date products by the preflood, thirty-day moon cycles, gives:

April 15, 2014: 4 x 15 x 20 x 14 = 16,800; and 16,800 ÷ 30 = **560**

October 8, 2014: 10 x 8 x 20 x 14 = 22,400; and 22,400 ÷ 30 = **746.7**

April 04, 2015: 4 x 04 x 20 x 15 = 4,800; and 4,800 ÷ 30 = **160**

September 28, 2015:   9 x 28 x 20 x 15 = 75,600; and 75,600 ÷ 30 = **2520**

Note: The fourth blood moon year, or 2015, our reference year for the 6000-year graph, has additional confirmation in that it is a product of the special biblical number, 2520 (i.e., 9x28x20x15 = 30 x **2520**).

Adding the first three results gives the time of Moses' death just prior to the spring of 1466 BC: **560 + 746.7 +160 = 1466.7**. Next, adding the fourth result to these gives the beginning of the first millennia, **1466.7 + 2520 = 3986.7,** or 3986 BC, and is exactly 6000 years before the last blood moon date. "Wow" is not a strong enough word!

Our assumption that the sixth millennia ended in 2015 at the last blood moon and start of a Jubilee year produces amazing correlations on the solved chronology. For example, it has been shown in a previous chapter that Jesus was likely born November 1, 2 BC, making him 15 years old in 15 AD, or precisely midway through his earthly life that year. Jesus died on the Passover in 30 AD after being the Lamb of God for one year (see Luke 4:18-19, 3:23). Note: Instructions to Moses required Passover lambs to be one years old or less, so Jesus' ministry as the Lamb of God was one year (Exodus 12:5).

The start of the sixth millennia began in 1015 AD just prior to the death of King Arduino, the last native king of Italy during the Middle Ages: he died on December 14, 1015, with a solar eclipse occurring that very day. The ever-repeating date calculation for this date gives 12 x 14 x 10 x 15 = 25,200 (70x360). Arduino was dethroned one year earlier in Rome when the Pope declared Henry II the emperor of the Holy Roman Empire. Per our chronology, his deposition in 1014 AD was also precisely 2520 years after the Exodus from Egypt. The table below shows that each span began in a notable year.

Millennia	Began	Details
1	3986 BC	3986 falls exactly 10 years after creation. The number patterns suggest this could be the year Adam and Eve sinned. Again, 3x9x8x6 equals 6x6x6x6. The children of Israel began conquering the Promised Land in 1466 BC, or 2520 years after 3986 BC. The number 2520, or 7x360, propagates throughout time.
2	2986 BC	Noah was born in 2940 BC, or forty-six years after the second millennia began. Since he lived 950 years, Noah's entire lifetime fits entirely within the second period: he died in 1990 BC, or four years before the third millennia began.
3	1986 BC	Abraham offered Isaac in 1937 BC, or exactly 49 years (i.e., one Jubilee interval) after the third span began. Also, 1986 BC is the 2011th year of history, or 41 Jubilee cycles plus one year after creation (i.e., 41x49+1 years). The entire period from Israel being named until their separation into two houses occurred entirely within the bounds of the third millennia. The house of Israel began worshipping the golden calves in Samaria in 987 BC, the very last year of this period.
4	986 BC	The fourth millennia began in 986 BC at the mid-point of the 6000 years. Solomon died four years earlier in 990 BC, or exactly 1000 years after Noah. Again, 9x8x6 = **2 x** (6x6x6), and the year 986 BC divides history into two halves of 3000 years each.
5	15 AD	The fifth period began at the mid-point of Jesus' life on Earth: he was fifteen years old then.
6	1015 AD	King Arduino died one year after being deposed by the Pope in Rome. The date of his death multiplies to **2520** x 10 with the previous year, 1014 BC, the year he was deposed, being exactly **2520** years after the Exodus (1507 BC). Arduino died December 14, 1015, and **12 x 14 x 10 x 15 = 25,200**.
7	2015 AD	The seventh millennia began 2015 AD with the start of the Seventy-first Jubilee year and the final of four blood moons: the Jubilee year ended in 2016 AD during a major election year in the United States. Jesus will surely return early during this final millennium.

The solved chronology found Creation Year to be 3996 BC, or exactly 10 years before the beginning of the first millennia. Hidden in its numerals is a calculation yielding the second Sabbath-Year in the

Promised Land, or 1458 BC: 3x9x9x6 = 1458. This second Year-Seven also occurred precisely 10 Jubilee periods after Isaac was born.

> Note: Joshua began leading the children of Israel to their one-year-conquest of the Promised Land in 1466 BC, just like the one-year-ministry of Jesus in which he conquered sin during *"the acceptable year of the LORD"* (Luke 4:19). Furthermore, Joshua and Jesus are really the same name.

Our solved chronology found the eighteenth Jubilee to have begun in 583 BC, or 14 years after the first temple's destruction, and this is a biblical assertion that has eluded other chronologies for eons (Ezekiel 1:1-2, 40:1). This congruence alone puts the first Sabbath year in 1465 BC after a one-year conquest, matching that of Jesus' earthly ministry, and we have more evidence. The phone app <u>Jesus' Footsteps</u> provides an interactive walk-with-Jesus through his ministry, proving in detail that his ministry was just one year:

The acceptable year of the Lord was one year, or specifically 360 days, "a biblical year", not three or three-and-a-half years as commonly misunderstood (Isaiah 61:2 and Luke 4:19). He was crucified on the Passover in 30 AD. The Gregorian calendar, extrapolated to the first century, shows he died April 3, 30 AD, rose from the dead April 6, 30 AD, and first appeared to his disciples on the following morning of April 7, 30 AD. Amazingly, these dates are confirmed by numerical patterns:

> Crucifixion, Wednesday, April 3, 30 AD (Gregorian): **4 x 3 x 30 = 360**, or number of days of Jesus' one-year ministry as the Lamb of God.

> Resurrection, Saturday, April 6, 30 AD (Gregorian): **4 x 6 x 30 = 720**, having numerical correlation to the 72 hours that he was in the grave.

> First Appearance, Sunday, April 7, 30 AD (Gregorian): **4 x 7 x 30 = 840, or 12 x 70.** Twelve and seventy are the numbers of disciples in the two groups that Jesus sent out to preach during his one-year ministry.

Each millennium before the birth of Jesus is comprised of patterns of sixes. There are relations between man and the number six in the Bible, for example, man was created on the sixth day. In the book of Revelation, the number of the beast (i.e., six) is said to be the number of a man and his number is six hundred, sixty, and six. The number of the beast and the number of the beast's name are two separate numbers, and Revelation provides insight into the truth of the beast's name by giving us a method for calculating its number. It appears God's math ignores zeros and that six hundred, sixty, and six are variants of the number of mankind, rather than the long and superstitiously believed, number of the devil.

As previously explained, the book of Revelation instructs the wise to pebble the number of the beast, and later, with a second mention of the phrase, *"here is wisdom"*, shows the number of the beast to be six, since ***"five have fallen, one is****, and one is not yet to come."* The number six is also the number of man and is to be used in the calculation of the beast's name. The number of the sixth beast is six, plain and simple, and his number is to be pebbled to reach six hundred, sixty, and six, the variants of the number of mankind (i.e., again, God's math does not include zeros): you must cast six pebbles one hundred and eleven times to reach six-hundred-sixty-six, and this result provides the wisdom needed to understand the beast's name. Curiously, the number of the beast's name appears to be related to the age of Abraham when he offered Isaac.

Was Satan bound in 1015 AD to be detained for the sixth millennium rather than the seventh? Could the popular understanding of Revelation chapter twenty be wrong? Could Revelation chapter twenty be describing two periods, the sixth and the seventh millennium rather than just the seventh? A detailed study of those verses shows an alternating pattern of the definite and indefinite articles being used to describe the one thousand years. Jesus will return and reign on Earth during the seventh millennium as the King of Kings and the Prince of Peace! Mankind simply cannot establish peace without him, even as the initial years of these final one thousand years has proven. Will humanity burn the weapons of war for seven years before Jesus returns, or will Jesus instead return, and from Earth be the One commanding them to be burned (Ezekiel 39:9)?

If Satan were bound in 1015 AD, then the sixth millennia would truly be the "millennium of man." The Protestant Reformation began in 1517 AD near the very center of the sixth period. At that time man was returning to an understanding of the love of God and his grace rather than things of works such as "paying for indulgences." Unfortunately, the last century brought two world wars. Mankind simply cannot rule himself peacefully; he needs a king, the God King. Perhaps in God's perfection and holiness, he needed to give mankind a one-thousand-year opportunity, with Satan bound, to reveal the sheer hopelessness of our condition before Jesus reigns as king on Earth?

During the third millennia God promised Abram, who was childless, that he would multiply his descendants as the stars of heaven. Later in 1937 BC, he established a covenant with Abraham when he offered Isaac. Just a few years earlier Sodom and Gomorrah had been destroyed by judgment, and prior to that destruction, Abraham had asked God if he would spare those cities if he found 50 righteous people there. God replied that he would. Abraham further asked if he would spare if he found only 45, or 40, or 30, or 20 righteous people, and again the answers were all "yes". Finally, Abraham asked if he would spare for only 10 righteous, and again God affirmed that he would. However, Abraham never asked the ultimate question, "Would you spare them if only one righteous man were found there?" Abraham never asked, but during his offering of Isaac God answered as he passed over Isaac to a substitute ram caught in a thicket. God is merciful and Abraham learned that first-hand as Isaac was spared. Isaac was a type of the Savior, and if God found only One righteous man, all of mankind could be saved.

Exactly 430 years after Isaac was offered, Moses brought God's people Israel out of Egypt, but even so, they rejected God. In 987 BC the house of Israel betrayed him and began worshipping golden calves in Samaria, then 390 years later the first temple was destroyed in 597 BC. Exactly 666 years after that destruction, the second temple was likewise destroyed in 70 AD, or forty years after Jesus rose from the dead. These were two periods of iniquity, 390 years, and 40 years, and were both predicted by Ezekiel (Ezekiel 4:1-7): their sum is 430 years and matches the length of time from Isaac being offered until the Exodus began.

As has been presented, there was a ten-year period between creation and the first millennia. Similarly, there could be a ten-year period extended to the sixth millennia to initiate the weapons of war burning. If so, that would begin in 2025 AD? No one knows the day or the hour of Jesus' return, but time is designed and ordered, and it will end someday. Regardless of when, God is always Love.

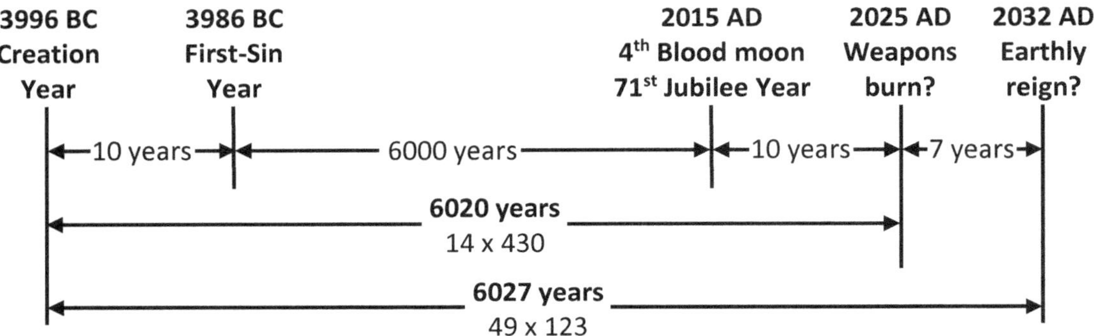

Six-thousand-year patterns continue towards two near-future dates whose events are yet unknown.

The 6000-year span is related to sinful man while the 6020 years, with its symmetrical ten years added, gives a pattern of biblical numbers. There are fourteen periods of four-hundred-thirty years, or 14×430, and the overall span of 6027 years has a relation to the forty-nine-year Jubilee cycle, or 49×123. Such wonderful, yet simple and perfect math; biblical math with the ingenious multiplier 123 and as orderly as one, two, and three. The numbers are prevailing and perhaps indicating that the Perfect God King is coming very soon!!!

CHAPTER FIFTEEN

NATURAL AGING OF A SUPERNATURAL CREATION

Scientific methods of discovery begin with conjectures that must be substantiated by evidence to develop strong arguments called theories. Most people today believe the age of Earth has been proven to be some 4.54 billion years old, but this is only a theory and is only as good as its foundation and supporting evidence. The primary idea of this belief is that Earth came into existence by natural processes, however, this first assumption contradicts the Bible that says it was created supernaturally six thousand years ago. Which is right?

As stated, at the onset, this book is not a scientific debate about dating methods, and furthermore we acknowledge there is scientific evidence supporting the billion-years-age theory. However, this book considers something that science does not: it assumes their first assumption could be wrong. The big bang theory has lots of merit, but many ignore that time itself could have been created during the initial expansion process. Science ignores the Bible entirely, and discards facts like sea life fossils being found on the top of mountains, yet those remains are still there attesting to the flood. Even many Bible-believers argue for an older Earth and try to explain the age discrepancies as matters of word evolution, saying *"days"* could mean *"eons,"* but this is in blunt contrast to biblical context:

> *And the ark rested in the seventh month, on the seventeenth day of the month, upon the mountains of Arafat. And the waters decreased continually until the tenth month: in the tenth month, on the first day of the month, were the tops of the mountains seen.* Genesis 8:4-5 KJV

Many formations found in nature are the result of natural processes, such as the Grand Canyon, but this does not mean that matter itself was formed naturally billions of years ago. Furthermore, the Bible's description of the flood can explain Grand Canyon, although if those processes are ignored, false theories can prevail. Many creationists argue the Grand Canyon formed within days by a rapid, horizontal flow of water during the abating flood, but science proves them wrong. The Grand Canyon is made up of sedimentary rock, requiring sediment to sit compacted in stagnant water for years to form. Sedimentary rock cannot form in rapid flowing water.

Bible-believers should reconsider the Genesis' account of the flood and understand its abatement was a slow process. The waters had decreased enough by the seventh month for the ark to come to rest on the top of the mountains of Arafat, but it would take several more months to completely dry up. As creationists admit their error based on misunderstanding scripture, scientists, knowing Earth contains many volumes of water below the oceans' floors, should also concede and consider the Bible in evaluating formation possibilities:

> *In the six hundredth year of Noah's life, in the second month, in the seventeenth day of the month, the same day were all the fountains of the great deep broken up, and the windows of heaven were opened.* Genesis 7:11 KJV

The Bible explains the flood waters came not only from the windows of heaven, but also from great depths below the floors of the oceans; geologists today believe there is more water below the ocean's floors than above them. Earth's gravity fuels the phrase, *"What goes up, must come down."* Whether most of the water came from *"the windows of heaven"*, above, or from *"the fountains of the great deep"*, beneath, it does not determine their final path, the water went down. The flood's abatement was not a rapid, horizontal flow, but rather a slow vertical one.

The topography of Grand Canyon is predominantly a flat-top profile situated at a high elevation of about seven thousand feet. The Colorado river in the floor of the canyon is at an elevation of 2500 FEET ABOVE SEA LEVEL. The following is a simple conjecture of how the canyon might have formed in only a few thousand years:

As the flood waters receded, sea-level elevation constantly decreased at a slow rate, and when the top of the oceans reached elevations just over 7000 feet, whirlpools began to form in the then-shallow waters above Grand Canyon's location due to Coriolis acceleration. These many whirlpools then grew into large and powerful circulating funnels cutting through the soft sediments as the waters made their way back towards the great depths of Earth. Debris collected in the low-pressure center inside the vortices and became entrained in the downward flow, then deposited in the fault lines (cracks) left by the great depths having been broken open. The abating water passed through the cracks leaving sediment that plugged the cracks, forming a great lake that drained ever-so-slowly, allowing sedimentary rock to form over hundreds of years in stagnant water.

This is a possibility, but unfortunately, one that has probably never been considered. The shape of the walls of the Grand Canyon appears as if they could have been formed by funnel-shaped whirlpools traveling along fault lines as the water descended for thousands of feet in its journey to the depths of Earth. The Grand Canyon region is known for having many fault lines. The science dating Grand Canyon could easily be wrong, and if so, it has done harm. Those "old-age" conclusions have been used-as-facts to support other theories.

While this book acknowledges that evidence exists to support the old-Earth theory, it also acknowledges there is much evidence showing the Bible is well structured and its dating record consistent, especially if properly translated and understood. The evidence supporting the Bible's claim of a young Earth is never contradictory: no biblical data is discarded and all the data fits. This is in stark contrast to science's constantly evolving evidence.

The numerically cohesive biblical evidence outlined in this book supports the Bible's assertion of a young Earth, and in this author's opinion, its evidence supporting its theory far outweighs science's evidence supporting science's theory. Supernatural processes outside of the realm called "time" simply cannot be evaluated by studies of natural processes.

CHAPTER SIXTEEN

"DON'T CHOP THE THROTTLE"

This book has provided an accurate-to-the-year chronology to be used as a reference for future Bible studies and has presented novel discoveries and ideas found from its use. These findings were results of spending many long hours, and along with that devotion came many questions: Why did you spend so much time studying the Bible? Why are there number patterns in the Bible and who put them there? How did you uncover them? What do the numbers mean? In this final chapter, I will answer some of these directly and others indirectly using personal stories from my life.

Nothing in the physical world requires more faith than flying on an invisible substance called "air" and I had the aviation bug since childhood. My dad was a private pilot who occasionally took me out to soar through the skies, and although it was scary early on, I grew to love it. A childhood friend and I even tried to make an airplane out of our bicycles, but that never really "took off", pun intended.

I earned a private pilot's license when I was around twenty but could not really afford to fly. One day while walking through a mall in Baton Rouge, Louisiana, I passed by an ultralight-airplane display, or motorized hang-glider as some called them, and I wanted to fly it. I talked with Dan, the plane's owner who had set up the display in hopes of selling them, but he was not interested in giving out free flights. I finally convinced Dan to let me work for him, for free, or rather for free flying. To make a long story short, I worked several months before he let me have my first flight, and even that was not supposed to be a flight, but instead to be a taxi around on the ground at the grass-strip airport.

"I'm going to let you taxi it around but don't takeoff. I repeat, don't take off!"

"Of course," I lied. "I'll just drive it down the runway!"

"Okay, and don't, I repeat, don't…but if you accidentally do…, takeoff…, Don't chop the throttle!"

Back then, and still today, I loved Bette Midler's song, the Rose, and lived a lyric from it: *And it is the soul afraid of dying, that never learns to live.*" Those words fueled me at twenty-years-age: I was unafraid; I was going to fly that airplane. I had worked long enough, flying was our agreement, not taxiing.

The grass strip in Port Allen, Louisiana was rather long, about 3000 feet, and at the end were tall power lines, the kind that are suspended from high steel stanchions. The ultralight plane was a canard-wing design powered by a thirty-five-horsepower snowmobile engine with a placard just above the pilot seat that said, "Minimum Weight 175 Pounds." The manufacturer made a smaller, less powerful twenty-horsepower version for lighter people like me, who weighed only 135 pounds at the time, or at least I weighed that before the flight. The little plane was a weight-shift aircraft with a motorcycle-style handlebar and throttle. While taxiing out, I reasoned,

"I ride motorcycles, I have my private pilot's license, I can do this."

I slowly taxied to the end of the grass runway and turned around. Now facing those tall power lines, I started taxiing back, but this time moving much faster. I decided to "pop-it-up on the back wheels and walk it like a motorcycle," just to get the hang of it: I opened the throttle and leaned back, and the next thing I knew I was over one-hundred feet in the air, climbing straight up, almost vertical: maybe the 175-pound placard did have merit, and perhaps in shock I somehow remembered it, so without delay, I "chopped the throttle."

The state fair has no thrill that compares with cutting a throttle to idle during a climb at greater-than-maximum-angle-of-attack, an attitude achievable only by a pilot weighing forty pounds less than the manufacturer intended: the climb-angle of that canard-wing ship immediately went from nose-up-to-nose-down and my heartbeat went from normal to first-place contender for a spot in the Guinness' Book of World Records, and at a speed faster than my brain could process. In the back of my mind, those last-pre-taxi-instructional-words-of-warning resurfaced just before impact, "Don't chop the throttle."

Descending vertically and almost at the ground, I opened the throttle wide-open and amazingly started to climb, no, not to heaven, but rather high into the realm just beneath. Now, going nearly vertical again, I reached at least three thousand feet before daring to reduce power, but this time did not abruptly close the throttle, but instead closed it ever-so-slowly, allowing the plane to gently level off. I learned to make turns, climbs, and descents, slowly and controlled, as I practiced for my first landing. The first try did not work out so well, I was landing crossways on the runway towards a ditch, so I flew around the pattern again. The second pass got better, and finally I successfully landed and taxied back to Dan, who was waiting calmly. I will never forget his first words, "Man you flew the hell out of that thing!"

Gerald Johnston flying one of Dan's ultralight airplanes in the early nineteen-eighties. This one is a slightly different model from the one in the story.

I had been dangerously close to the powerlines but somehow had avoided them. I soon learned to fly the ultralights safely though and kept flying them. Flying motorized kites was fun but I wanted to fly bigger aircraft for a living. I had joined the National Guard Infantry unit near my hometown and did well in training. I applied for the Army Helicopter Flight School and was accepted, but during the last physical exam, hearing loss disqualified me from military aviation. It seemed my dream had ended.

I changed gameplans and enrolled in engineering school at Mississippi State, and five years later earned a mechanical engineering degree. After working some years and finally having some money, I continued my flight training and received a flight instructor rating in airplanes. I bought a small airplane and taught lessons in the evenings after work and on the weekends. My dream revived as my aviation business grew, so I expanded into helicopters. After taking some lessons, I bought a small training helicopter on credit.

After getting my rotorcraft instructor's license, an aircraft inspector informed me that the helicopter was in much worse condition than I had been led to believe. In addition to that, word came that my engineering project had been cancelled. I found myself unemployed and financially overwhelmed. I was depressed but somehow was fighting the idea of bankruptcy, yet it started to look like the only option. I consulted an attorney who, after reviewing my finances, told me I was "below bankrupt", but through encouragement of a Christian friend, I chose instead to continue my fight. During those troublesome times, I was blessed to receive a seven-month assignment at an oil refinery near New Orleans, and that opportunity grew into a second project, enabling me to get a loan to repair the helicopter.

I hired a young instructor who was instrument rated in helicopters and things began to improve: I continued to work at the refinery and my new instructor was busy flying. He told me there was a huge demand for helicopter instrument pilots and encouraged me to get a second helicopter for instrument training. I agreed and negotiated a lease with an individual who had a helicopter, but it did not have the required instruments. In our agreement, I stipulated that his aircraft would be upgraded for instrument-training. The leased helicopter was then taken to a shop for the upgrade, but before it got completed, my young instructor moved on to a better job. Meanwhile, my project at the refinery was placed-on-hold, meaning I now had two helicopters and no income, except that I could give basic flight instruction.

My situation seemed hopeless, but one night an FAA Examiner called and asked if I had gotten the instrument ship up and flying. I explained that I had not, and that my instrument instructor had left. Perhaps he already knew because he said,

> "I'm having dinner with someone right now that might be able to help you. He is an instrument helicopter flight instructor and I'll put him on the phone, but first I want to tell you a few things about him."

> "Okay. I'm listening."

> He continued, "He is not only a flight instructor, but is also a medical doctor who is currently working as an airline pilot."

> "Wow!"

> "He is also a licensed aircraft mechanic, a guy who wears many hats. His name is Frank, and he is a Full-Bird-Colonel, Green Beret. I'm going to put him on the phone now!"

Suspense was building as this financially devastated and distraught pilot and engineer, who had served his country but had been rejected for Army helicopter training, waited on the phone. It seemed like forever, but really, it was only a minute or two before the colonel was on the phone,

> "Gerald this is Frank. We were just sitting here discussing your situation. Please understand that I'm not looking for a flight instructor job, but I might be able to help you. I might be able to train you for your instrument-helicopter-flight-instructor rating, but I must tell you right now, upfront, I cannot work with just anyone, so here is what we need to do: when you get your helicopter out of the shop, call me, and we will set up a meeting. I need to see the helicopter and you before I decide. If I can work with you, I will, if I cannot, please don't take it personally."

The timing was incredible. I was almost bankrupt, and to avoid it, he would have to agree to train me, and fast. A couple of weeks passed by, and I did not know what would happen. Finally, the helicopter instrument panel was installed and ready for use. I retrieved the helicopter and called the colonel who informed me to be at Lafayette Airport the next day with the helicopter. I woke up early and got on my knees before the flight to Lafayette, Louisiana. It was not a short prayer, but basically the message was,

"God please let this work out. Please have this man fly with me. I'm out of money and I'm out of time. I'm counting on you. Amen."

I flew to Lafayette and met Frank. I was a bit nervous as we sat and talked for a minute, but soon he agreed to help me, however there was a problem: the helicopter was a special trainer that required a special signoff for instructors, and he was not signed off. He called the FAA office to clarify, and they explained that he would need an FAA Helicopter examiner, authorized in that specific model, to sign him off before he could teach, and this would take time. The local FAA office did not know of anyone qualified to sign him off and my finances simply could not afford a delay.

While he was on the phone for what seemed like eternity, I recalled having met an FAA Helicopter Examiner three months earlier at a helicopter safety course I had attended in Los Angeles, California. The examiner from California was one of very few in the country who were qualified to make these signoffs and he would be my only hope. I needed to get in touch with him, and fast. I nudged Frank on the shoulder,

"Don't bother me, I'm on the phone."

"I know, but I know someone who can do this."

"Don't bother me!"

While he resumed the call, I turned and looked, and sitting in a chair reading a magazine, about twenty feet away, was Ray, the examiner from Los Angeles. I had "a twilight-zone moment!" Is this really him or am I going crazy? Is this the guy I had just nudged Frank about? I turned as white as a sheet. I looked at Frank who was still on the phone, and I just stood there, feeling faint and confused, and then nudged him again.

"What!" He said in frustration.

I cried out, "Hang the phone up!"

Frank quickly told the FAA to "standby", and while putting his hand over the receiver in disgust, he raised his voice,

"What?"

"Do you see that man right there? He can sign you off."

"What? Are you sure?"

I was not sure: I had only met him once and that was three months earlier and two thousand miles away, could it really be him? I approached and said,

"Excuse me sir."

He looked up, "You look familiar, do I know you? Wait, didn't we meet in Los Angeles in January? What are you doing here?"

"I live here, what are you doing here?"

He laughed, "I was just sitting here looking at this magazine and asking myself that very question. I haven't been on a flight like this in twenty years, but this morning, around eight, my boss walked into my office and told me I would be flying a flight to Louisiana today. I'm just killing time for about an hour before flying back."

By this time Frank had joined the conversation and we asked Ray if he could fly with Frank and sign him off. Ray looked at his watch and explained that he did not have enough time. Frank explained that sometimes you must make time, and they talked. During the conversation Ray told Frank that he was once a sergeant in the Green Berets, and that was all it took. Frank said, "Well Sergeant, I'm a special forces, Colonel; let's crank this little helicopter up!"

Two Green Berets to the rescue after one early morning prayer. I spent eleven to twelve thousand hours researching and writing this book because God is real, and he is merciful, and I love him. I want to know all I can know about the Bible, the book he gave us. Jesus Christ is not only my LORD and my God, but he is also my best friend. He wants to be everyone's best friend and he wanted me to write this book. We have all been through troubles, and I could write more, but the thing is, God is always good. He often gets blamed for the devil's deeds, and sadly, I too have blamed him. Through it all though, he has always loved me and has always answered my prayers, whether I understood the answers or not. He always has a great sense of humor, proving his love and forgiveness. The following story demonstrates this well.

For the first-time ever, Mississippi State University won a national championship in a team sport. We smoked Vanderbilt in the last two college baseball games this year, 22-2. Although we have had many good teams through the years in various sports, it is exceedingly difficult to win in the SEC West being Alabama, LSU, and other big names play there. Alabama seems to always win, unless of course, it is LSU. Anyway, I watched the Mississippi State Vanderbilt championship game with Jimmy, a friend who once played football at Ole Miss, and just as Mississippi State won this first-ever title, Jimmy left. Moments later he called me from the parking lot,

"Gerald, there is a man out here with a flat tire and you need to come help change it."

Three minutes into my first national championship celebration and I am outside changing a flat tire for a man who turns out to be an ex-football player from Bear Bryant's National Champion Crimson Tide of Alabama. I know God was laughing!

Some might think that was just a random chance occurrence, but it was not. The very next time I went there, another unfortunate fellow had a flat tire, again, the back right tire, and in the exact location in the parking lot. As he turned around, I saw on the front of his shirt, the letters, LSU, as in Mississippi State's rival, LSU Tigers, who hold many national championships. God's sense of humor is better than mine; I let the LSU man change his own tire.

Championships come and go, just like flat tires, but the love of God is everlasting. I hope to have answered some of the questions I set out to answer. The Bible is an ancient book and God knew that words could change in meaning over long periods of time, so he built structure into the text, a numerical skeleton to support translations and keep its message intact. No one can deny the patterns and the designs of time that have been presented in this book. The Bible was divinely inspired by God. I hope you have enjoyed the book and I thank you for having read it. Please be sure to check out the Appendices too. God bless you!

APPENDICES

Anno Domini History   Page 117

Number Correlations   Page 127

Moses' Tabernacle   Page 133

APPENDIX ONE

ANNO DOMINI HISTORY

<u>30 AD: Christianity began</u> – Jesus of Nazareth was crucified, and three days later, he rose from the dead. After his resurrection, Jesus continued teaching the apostles for forty days.

<u>70 AD: Destruction of Jerusalem</u> – Titus seized and destroyed Jerusalem and the second Jewish temple.

<u>96 AD: Jewish Tax</u> – After 96 AD Christians were exempted from the Jewish Tax, but Jews were still required to pay.

<u>285 AD: Roman Empire divided</u> – Emperor Diocletian divided the Roman Empire into two halves to improve manageability in governing the vast empire.

<u>312 AD: Constantine's conversion</u> – Constantine converted to Christianity and moved the capital to Constantinople (324-330). Non-Christians were required to pay for the city's construction.

<u>313 AD: Edict of Milan</u> – Constantine's edict brought an end to Christian persecution and enabled a rapid expansion of Christianity.

<u>325 AD: Council of Nicea</u> – Constantine convened the council affirming Jesus, the Son, was equal with God the Father and of the same substance. The council condemned the idea that Jesus was a created being inferior to the Father.

<u>380 AD: Trinity established</u> – Emperor Theodosius declared the Nicene Trinitarian Christianity to be the official imperial religion and the only one worthy to be called Catholic. The following year he summoned a new council at Constantinople to resolve schisms between the east and west to unite the orthodoxy of the Roman Empire's Christian religion to include establishing the Holy Spirit as the 3rd person of the trinity, condemning heresies, establishing diocese, and pronouncing Constantinople to be second in prominence to Rome.

<u>381–392 AD</u> – Theodosius strengthened the state religion of Christianity and by 392 AD he had become the sole emperor of the entire empire and the last one to reign over both halves. After Theodosius's death in 395 AD, the western half of the Roman Empire was irreparably divided from the east. Theodosius was the first emperor to submit to the power of the church.

476–480 AD: Western Roman Empire Falls –By 493 AD Italy had become the Kingdom of Italy under Germanic and Frankish rulers.

Middle Ages 5th to 15th century began with the Fall of Western Roman Empire

486 AD: Kingdom of France – Germanic Francs conquered area (presently France) and expanded to form the Carolingian Dynasty and finally to become the Kingdom of France by 987.

609 AD: Mohammad had his first otherworld visitation and began writing the Quran; twenty-three years later he finished writing, died, and the Islamic religion began. Even before he finished writing, Islam was a rapidly expanding religion and by 624 AD, it was pressing upon Jerusalem. Christians and Jews in Jerusalem saw this emerging religion as a threat and requested it be banned by government. By 630 AD the Muslims began invading the Byzantine Empire near Jerusalem and in 634 AD, just 25 years after Mohammad's first visitation, there was all-out war. Mohammad's first visitation would be only 116 years after the Kingdom of Italy was established in the place of the fallen Western Roman Empire. In 691 AD the Dome of the Rock shrine was completed on the temple mount in Jerusalem; the original dome collapsed in 1016 AD and was rebuilt in 1021 AD.

800 AD: Holy Roman Empire – Pope Leo III named the Frankish King Charlemagne the emperor of a new Holy Roman Empire and in 962 AD Pope John XII named the German King Otto-I the emperor after conquering the kingdom of Italy in 961 AD. Otto's latter years involved conflicts with the papacy and struggles to stabilize control of Italy. He tried to improve relations with the Byzantine Empire, but the Byzantines considered the creation of the Holy Roman Empire a slap in the face as they had fought for years for Christianity and were now being replaced.

983 AD: Otto-II became the first to call himself the Roman Emperor – Otto-II continued the work of Otto-I in subordinating the Catholic Church to Imperial control, strengthening Imperial rule in Germany, and extended the Empire's border into southern Italy. He defeated a major revolt from within the Ottonian dynasty who tried to claim the throne; his victory over the revolt excluded the Bavarian line (Henry II of Bavaria) from succeeding him, thereby providing succession for his own son. While trying to further expand the empire into southern Italy, Muslims who held territory in Southern Italy defeated Otto-II, and while preparing a counterattack, a major uprising by the Slavs broke out; Otto-II died during a campaign in southern Italy against the Byzantine Empire leaving his three-year old son Otto-III as Emperor thereby leaving the Empire in political chaos.

Prior to his death, Otto-II installed a non-Roman Pope John XIV (983-984 AD) who later intervened in the power struggle between the three-year old emperor and his cousin Henry II. Pope John XIV required the regency be given to Otto-III's mother while the emperor grew up. The Roman aristocracy used the turmoil as a chance to remove the non-Roman Pope and install one of their own, the Roman Antipope Boniface VII. Boniface who had been in exile in Byzantine, joined forces with Byzantine nobles in southern Italy, and with the aid of Crescentius-II (leader of the Roman aristocracy), he entered Rome and became Pope (or Antipope), and then imprisoned John XIV who died in prison four months later. After the death of Boniface, John XV became Pope (probably also with the help of Crescentius-II) and died a year later of fever.

Otto-III reigned from 983-1002 AD as King of Germany and 986-1002 AD as Holy Roman Emperor and King of Italy. He named his cousin Bruno as Pope Gregory-V. Gregory-V (996-999 AD) would be the First German Pope and the first non-Italian pope since 827 AD; He would be followed by the first-French Pope Sylvester II (999-1003 AD). Otto-III died of fever in 1002 AD, and having no children, his cousin Henry II tried to have the nobles and bishops give him the throne but was highly contested and unsuccessful. In the absence of an emperor, Italy began to break away from German control. In 1002 AD, Arduino, an opponent of the Ottonian dynasty, was elected king of Italy.

<u>1014 AD: Arduino dethroned</u> – Arduino, the last native King of Italy during the Middle Ages, was dethroned by Henry II in 1004 AD, but managed to regain his throne until 1014. In 1014 Henry II again prevailed against Arduino, requiring him to denounce his throne in Rome. The Pope crowned Henry II as emperor in 1014 AD, thereby ending the independence of the kingdom of Italy **(exactly 2520 years after the Jewish Exodus from Egypt using our chronology).** Arduino died the following year on December 14, 1015 AD, during a solar eclipse, and interestingly, using the pattern <u>month x day x century x year</u>, **12 x 14 x 10 x 15 = 25,200 or exactly 70 Biblical years (70 x 360)**. This coincides our theory of this year beginning the sixth millennia. There would not be another native king of Italy until the Italian reunification in 1861 AD.

<u>1032 AD: and forward</u> – All Emperors of the Holy Roman Empire would also be king of both the Kingdom of Italy and the Kingdom of Germany.

<u>1054 AD: East-West Schism</u> – A schism in "the church" resulting in the separation of the present Eastern Orthodox Church from the Roman Catholic Church.

<u>1059 AD: Papal Selection changed</u> – Prior to 1059 AD, popes were chosen by either their predecessors or by secular rulers, but after 1059 AD the Papal conclave system was established to elect new popes.

<u>1066 AD: Norman Invasion of England</u> – William the Conqueror (Duke of Normandy) along with Norman, Breton, and French soldiers, conquered the Kingdom of England.

<u>1095 AD: Crusades Began</u> – First of the wars by the Catholic Church aimed at reclaiming Jerusalem from Muslims and to reunite the Eastern Orthodox Church with Roman Catholicism.

<u>1215 AD: Magna Carta</u> – The Archbishop of Canterbury drafted the charter to make peace between rebel barons and the unpopular King John of England; it promised the protection of church rights, protection for the barons from illegal imprisonment, access to swift justice, and limitations on feudal payments to the Crown, to be implemented through a council of 25 barons. Neither side stood behind their commitments, the charter was annulled by Pope Innocent III, and then lead to the First Barons' War. The Carta was later reinstated and became part of English life but lost most of its vitality until the seventeenth century. It later influenced the thirteen colonists and formation of the American constitution in 1787 AD.

<u>1206-1368 AD: Mongol Empire</u> – The Mongol Empire emerged from the unification of nomadic tribes in the Mongol homeland under the leadership of Genghis Khan, whom a council proclaimed ruler of all the Mongols in 1206 AD. The Mongol Empire existed during the thirteenth and fourteenth centuries and was the largest contiguous land empire in history. Originating in the steppes of Central Asia, the Mongol Empire eventually stretched from Central Europe to the Sea of Japan, extending northwards into Siberia, eastwards and southwards into the Indian subcontinent, Indochina, and the Iranian plateau, and westwards as far as the Levant and Arabia.

1232 AD: Inquisition Began – an Ecclesiastical tribunal established by Pope Gregory for the suppression of heresy and well known for using torture. It later spread into other countries including Spain and Portugal where the primary focus was on force-converting Jews to Christianity. The office of Inquisition of Spain and Portugal spread in their areas of influence around the world including Mexico, Peru, and Africa, and continued until the Napoleonic Wars and the Spanish American Wars of Independence in the early nineteenth century. The organization still exists in the Roman Catholic Church today under the name "Congregation for the Doctrine of the Faith."

Hundred Years' War (1337–1453 AD) – Conflicts between rulers of the Kingdom of England and the Kingdom of France over right of succession to the throne of the Kingdom of France and resulting in England losing land in France.

1453 AD: Fall of Constantinople – End of the Byzantine Era as the Ottoman Turks (founded in 1299 AD) conquered Constantinople and became the Ottoman Empire.

1455-1487 War of the Roses – A fight for control of the throne of England.

1455 Gutenberg Bible – Johann Gutenberg holds the distinction of being the inventor of the movable-type printing press. In 1455, Gutenberg produced what is considered the first book ever printed: a Latin language Bible, printed in Mainz, Germany.

1492-1975 Spanish Empire

> 1469 AD: Catholic Monarch – Marriage between second cousins Queen Isabelle I of Castile and King Ferdinand II of Aragon was allowed by Pope Sixtus IV and thereby gave rise to the Spanish Inquisition.

> 1492 AD: Columbus – discovered America during a period of the Spanish Inquisition in which Jews and Muslims were persecuted in Spain.

> 1519-1522 AD: Magellan–Elcano circumnavigation – was the first around-the-world voyage in human history. The voyage began under the command of Ferdinand Magellan, a Portuguese, in search of a maritime path from Spain to East Asia through the Americas and across the Pacific Ocean and was concluded by Spanish navigator Juan Sebastian Elcano in 1522 AD. Elcano and the 18 survivors of the expedition were the first men to circumnavigate the globe in a single expedition.

1517 AD: Reformation begins – Martin Luther nailed his 95 theses to the door of the Church at Wittenberg Castle initiating the Protestant Reformation. The initial groundwork had been laid years earlier by Peter Waldo, John Wycliffe, and Jan Hus who was executed in 1415 AD.

1534 AD: Anglican Church Established – The Catholic Pope denied King Henry VIII to have his marriage to Catherine of Aragon annulled, so with the help of the English statesman Thomas Cromwell, he broke England away from the ruling authority of the Catholic Church, making the clergy then subject to the laws of England rather than the laws of the Roman Catholic Church. The 1534 AD Act of Supremacy required Englishmen to recognize King Henry as the head of the church, denying the Pope, and thereby creating the Church of England or the Anglican Church.

1542 AD: Inquisition – Papal office of Inquisition was reestablished to combat Protestantism. The Jesuits were established in 1540 AD to convert Muslims and to eliminate Protest-ants.

1545-1563 AD: Council of Trent – Held in response to the Protestant reformation, it was deemed one of the Catholic Church's most important councils and was described as the embodiment of the Counter-Reformation. Also, the Gregorian calendar was authorized during this council and was later instituted by Pope Gregory XIII in 1582 AD.

December 31, 1600 AD: East Indies Company – Following the defeat of the Spanish Armada in 1588, the British East India Company was chartered by Queen Elizabeth I for trading in the East Indies and began the rulings of the British Empire in India in 1757 AD. It was the oldest of several East India companies. With the Government of India Act 1858, the British government assumed the task of directly administering India in the new British Raj.

May 1607 AD: Jamestown, Virginia was established as the first permanent English settlement (Roanoke 1584 was first but did not survive) in America by the Virginia Company of London.

1611 AD: King James Bible– King James VI of Scotland became King James I of England and Ireland and the first monarch to be called King of Great Britain. He authorized a new English version of the Bible.

1618 AD: 30-Years War began – A series of wars initially between Protestants and Catholics principally fought in Central Europe and involving most of the countries of Europe. It was one of the longest and most destructive conflicts in European history, and one of the longest continuous wars in modern history.

1620 AD: November– The Mayflower carrying Pilgrims, or Anglican Separatists, landed in Plymouth Rock to form the Plymouth Colony that is now Plymouth, Massachusetts.

1648 AD: Peace of Westphalia – Ended the Protestant Reformation and the Thirty-Years War: The deadliest European religious war between Protestants and Catholics in the fragmented Holy Roman Empire.

1756-1763 AD: <u>Seven-Years War</u> – Involved every European power at the time except the Ottoman Empire. The war ended with the 1763 Treaty of Paris between France, Spain, and Britain and the Treaty of Hubertusburg between Prussia, Saxony, and Austria.

> <u>1762 AD: Treaty of Fontainebleau</u> – France secretly ceded to Spain all the Mississippi River Valley from the Appalachians to the Rockies; this agreement was kept secret during the 1763 Treaty of Paris.

> <u>1763 AD: Treaty of Paris</u> – Treaty between France, Spain, Portugal, and Great Britain after Great Britain's victory over Spain and France in the Seven-Years War, or as known in North America, the French-Indian War. Great Britain gained much of France's land in North America including the Louisiana territory from the Mississippi River eastward. Spain ceded Florida to Britain and Great Britain agreed to protect Roman Catholicism in the New World. The treaty began a period of British dominance outside Europe.

1775-1783 AD: <u>American Revolution</u> – Starting in the 1760s the colonies rejected paying British taxes without a voice in government, given rise to the phrase "taxation without representation." The American War of Independence began with "the shot heard round-the-world" resulting in the formation of the United States with the 1783 Treaty of Paris.

> <u>November 15, 1777 AD: Articles of Confederation</u> – The first constitution of the United States, though not fully ratified until March 1, 1781; the constitutional convention in 1787 made new federal laws.

1789-1799 AD: <u>French Revolution</u> – Following the Seven-Years War and the American Revolution, France struggled financially resulting in revolution. The Revolution overthrew the monarch government and established a republic that later became a dictatorship under Napoleon and a bloody period in Europe. The French captured the Italian peninsula in 1792 AD, a feat eluding previous French government for centuries.

1799-1815 <u>Napoleonic Wars</u> – Napoleon, a deist who had been raised Catholic, abolished the Spanish Inquisition in 1813. His emancipating of Jews made the Russian Orthodox Church think of him as "Antichrist and enemy of God." In 1815, just two years after the religious emancipation, Napoleon was defeated at the Battle of Waterloo resulting in Great Britain becoming the largest-ever world empire.

> <u>1800 Napoleon regains Louisiana</u> – Napoleon regains the territory west of the Mississippi River ceded to Spain in 1762.

> <u>1801 Concordat</u> – A reconciliation between Pope Pius VII and Napoleon solidified the Roman Catholic Church as the majority church of France. In April 1801 Napoleon said, "Skillful conquerors have not got entangled with priests. They can both contain them and use them." Although the Pope gained much from this agreement, the balance of power between church and state greatly benefitted Napoleon. French children were issued a catechism teaching them to love and respect Napoleon.

1803 Louisiana Purchase – France sold the Louisiana Purchase to the United States.

1806 End of the Holy Roman Empire – Dissolved by Francis II after his defeat by Napoleon at the Battle of Austerlitz.

1808-1833 Spanish-American Wars of Independence – The Spanish American wars of independence were numerous wars against Spanish rule in Spanish America that took place during the early nineteenth century after the French invasion of Spain during Napoleonic Wars in Europe.

June 18, 1812 AD: the War of 1812 – War between the United States, then being eighteen states including Louisiana who had just become a state, the United Kingdom, Britain's North American colony allies, and Indian allies. The War ended with the battle of New Orleans in 1815.

1815–1914 AD: "British Peace" – A period of relative peace in Europe and the world during which the British Empire became the global hegemon and adopted the role of global policeman. The United States issued the Monroe Doctrine in 1823.

1839-1860 AD: The Opium Wars – was a collective term for two wars in the mid-nineteenth century involving Anglo-Chinese disputes over British trade in China and over China's sovereignty. The disputes included the First Opium War (1839–1842) and the Second Opium War (1856–1860).

1861-1865 American Civil War

1881 AD: the Hebrew language was revived – Eliezer Ben Yehuda, born Eliezer Yitzhak Perlman, immigrated to Palestine, moved to Jerusalem, and began reviving the Hebrew language.

1898 Spanish American War – was a conflict fought between Spain and the United States in 1898. Hostilities began in the aftermath of the internal explosion of the USS Maine in Havana harbor in Cuba leading to United States intervention in the Cuban War of Independence. American acquisition of Spain's Pacific possessions led to its involvement in the Philippine Revolution and ultimately in the Philippine–American War. The 1898 Treaty of Paris resulted in which terms favorable to the United States were negotiated allowing it temporary control of Cuba and to be ceded ownership of Puerto Rico, Guam, and the Philippine islands. The cession of the Philippines involved payment of $20 million ($600 million or more in today's currency) to Spain by the U.S. to pay for infrastructure owned by Spain. The Philippines would not become an internationally recognized independent state until 1946.

1899 Zionist Federation of Great Britain and Ireland – The Zionist Federation (ZF) was established in 1899 to campaign for a permanent home for the Jewish people.

December 23, 1913 Federal Reserve - The Federal Reserve System (also known as the Federal Reserve or simply the Fed) became the central banking system of the United States. It was created on December 23, 1913, with the enactment of the Federal Reserve Act in response to a series of financial panics (particularly the panic of 1907) that showed the need for central control of the monetary system if crises were to be avoided. Over the years, events such as the Great Depression in the 1930s and the Great Recession of the 2000s led to expansion of the roles and responsibilities of the Federal Reserve System.

1914 WWI began – WWI began when Archduke Franz Ferdinand of Austria was assassinated on June 28, 1914, resulting in Austria-Hungary declaring war on Serbia; the first world war escalated when Germany declared war on Russia and then on France, and the UK declared war on Germany after they invaded Belgium. WWI was the third deadliest war in history and ended the period of Britain's world domination. The United States remained neutral until 1917, then Italy left the Triple Alliance and joined the Allies of the Triple Entente and both the United States and Italy declared war on Germany. Britain declared war on the Ottoman Empire November 5, 1914, and Zionism was first discussed at the British Cabinet November 9, 1914.

1916 Sykes–Picot Agreement – A secret agreement between the UK and France with Russian assent and based on the premise the Triple Entente would conquer the Ottoman Empire. The agreement determined how the Ottoman land would be divided.

1917 Balfour Declaration – British Foreign Secretary Arthur James Balfour communicated the Balfour Declaration to the leader of the UK's Jewish community Lord Rothschild for transmission to the Zionist Federation. The declaration was a single paragraph in the letter to Rothschild stating Britain favored the establishment of a Jewish national home in Palestine, but without prejudice concerning the civil and religious rights of existing non-Jews in Palestine or rights and political status of Jews in other countries. The Balfour Declaration would be incorporated in the Sevres peace treaty with the Ottoman Empire and in the Mandate for Palestine.

October 30, 1918 Partition of the Ottoman Empire – World War I ended November 11, 1918.

1919 Paris Peace Conference – The meeting of the Allied victors following the end of World War One to set the peace terms for the defeated Central Powers following the armistices of 1918. It took place in Paris and involved diplomats from more than 32 countries and nationalities. The conference called for establishing the League of Nations, provided the German and Ottoman overseas possessions would become mandates primarily to France and Britain, and made five peace treaties with the defeated Central Powers including the Treaty of Versailles which disarmed Germany.

January 10, 1920 League of Nations – The LN was established as a result of the Paris Peace Conference ending WWI.

1920-1948 Mandatory Palestine – The British (and initially French as well) had civil administration of this territory and was formalized by the League of Nations in 1923 as the "British Mandate for Palestine" with two ruling areas: 1) east of the Jordan River and 2) west of the Jordan River known as Palestine. During this period, the Jewish population greatly increased in Palestine from 76,000 to 608,000. May 15, 1941, the Palmach, or specialized Jewish soldiers, were established in the Hagana, or Jewish regular-trained military unit during this period, that became the basis of the present Israeli Defense Forces, or IDF.

July 24, 1922 Mandate for Palestine – The draft of the **Mandate** for **Palestine** was formally confirmed by the Council of the League of Nations on July 24, 1922, supplemented with the September 16, 1922 Trans-Jordan memorandum, and then came into effect on September 29, 1923 following the ratification of the Treaty of Lausanne.

November 1, 1922 AD: End of the Ottoman Empire – The Ottoman caliphate was abolished on March 3, 1924 and the Lausanne treaty went into effect on August 6, 1924. From the month x day x century x year template for these dates: March 3, 1924: 3 x 3 x 19 x 24 = 3888 + 6x6x6, and for August 6, 1924: 8 x 6 x 19 x 24= 3888 + 6000 +6000 +6000. That is a strange pattern, and by the way, 3888 is the largest number that can be written in standard-notation Roman numerals, maybe Rome was reviving back then?

Soviet Union – December 30, 1922 to December 26, 1991– The Soviet Union had its roots in the October Revolution of 1917, when the Bolsheviks, led by Vladimir Lenin, overthrew the Russian Provisional Government which had replaced Tsar Nicholas II. In 1922, the Soviet Union was formed with the unification of the Russian, Transcaucasian, Ukrainian, and Byelorussian republics. Following Lenin's death in 1924 and a brief power struggle, Joseph Stalin came to power in the mid-1920s. The 1922 Treaty of Rapallo between Russia and Germany (i.e., Weimar Republic, 1919-1933) secretly arranged for Germany to rearm their military contrary to terms of the Treaty of Versailles.

1928 The Muslim Brotherhood was formed.

1929 Great Depression– began with the sudden devastating collapse of U.S. stock market prices on October 29, 1929, known as Black Tuesday.

1939 Great Depression ended with the start of WWII – The Empire of Japan, aiming to dominate Asia and the Pacific, was already at war with the Republic of China in 1937, but the world war is generally said to have begun on September 1, 1939 with the invasion of Poland by Nazi Germany and subsequent declarations of war on Germany by France and the United Kingdom. WWII was the deadliest in all of history with estimates being as high as 85 million deaths.

1945 WWII ended – The war in Europe ended with an invasion of Germany by the Western Allies and the Soviet Union, culminating in the capture of Berlin by Soviet and Polish troops and the subsequent unconditional surrender of Germany on May 8, 1945. Following the Potsdam Declaration by the Allies on July 26, 1945, and the refusal of Japan to surrender under its terms, the United States dropped atomic bombs on the Japanese cities of Hiroshima on August 6, 1945, and on Nagasaki on August 9, 1945. With Operation Downfall having been planned and invasion of the Japanese archipelago imminent, plus the possibility of additional atomic bombings, and the Soviet Union's declaration of war on Japan and invasion of Manchuria Japan surrendered on August 15, 1945, ending the war in Asia, and cementing total victory for the Allies. The Soviet Manchurian operation was their last campaign of WWII and largest of the 1945 Soviet-Japanese War, with Soviet gains including Manchukuo, Mengjiang, and North Korea.

October 24, 1945 UN established – United Nations was established to replace ineffective League of Nations and to prevent another world war.

<u>1947 UN Partition Mandate</u> – Palestine would be divided into independent Arab and Jewish states. The Arabs rejected the plan and immediately after it was adopted a civil war broke out and the plan was not implemented.

<u>1948 Israel formed</u> – At the end of the British Mandate; Israel declared statehood and war with the Arabs immediately began.

<u>Korean War – June 25, 1950 to July, 27 1953</u> – Korea was ruled by Japan from 1910 until the closing days of World War II. In August 1945, the Soviet Union, because of an agreement with the United States, declared war on Japan three days after the US dropped the atomic bomb on Hiroshima, and liberated Korea north of the thirty-eighth parallel; the U.S. forces subsequently moved into the south. By 1948, as a product of the Cold War between the Soviet Union and the United States, Korea was split into two regions, with two separate governments claiming legitimacy of all Korea, and neither side accepting the border as permanent. The conflict escalated into war when North Korean forces—supported by the Soviet Union and China—moved into the south on June 25, 1950. The United Nations Security Council recognized North Korea's act as invasive and called for an immediate ceasefire. On June 27, 1950, the Security Council adopted a resolution dispatching the UN Forces in Korea. Twenty-one countries of the United Nations eventually contributed to the UN force, with the United States providing nearly ninety percent of the military personnel.

APPENDIX TWO

NUMBER CORRELATIONS

In this appendix some amazing number correlations from the completed chronology will be presented. These numbers and their relationships show a consistent pattern to time. This is simply a partial list that will hopefully continue to grow by the insights of those who study the Bible and who use the chronology. This section is not intended as a casual read, but rather an item-by-item detailed study. You may ask, "Why are you multiplying the numbers like this?" The answer is to show the Bible is structured and the biblical timelines are on a well-designed matrix far beyond random chance.

1. **3996 BC – Creation year has several peculiarities.**

    a. $666 \times 6 = 3996$
    b. $3 \times 9 \times 9 \times 6 = 1458$. The Year 1458 BC is the second Sabbath year (or second Year-Seven) in the Promised Land; the first Sabbath year, or 1465 BC, occurred right after the year-of-war that conquered the land. This second Sabbath year was the first Year-Seven after a completed seven-year cycle in the land.
    c. Abraham was born 3996 years before modern Israel became a nation.

2. **3986 BC – Could this be the year Adam and Eve sinned?**

    a. This date is exactly 10 years after creation.
    b. $3 \times 9 \times 8 \times 6 = 6 \times 6 \times 6 \times 6$
    c. 3986 BC is exactly 6000 years before the Year 2015 AD (a Jubilee) and the last blood moon in the recent blood moon tetrad. The blood moons have a consistent <u>month x day x century x year</u> correlation to the Year 3986 BC and to the Year 1466 BC, the beginning of the Promised Land conquest.

3. **1656-year interval from Adam to the Flood** matches the span from the birth of Moses to the destruction of the second temple in 70 AD. Notice the six numeral sixes that make up these spans of 1656 years ($6 \times 6 \times 6 \times 6 + 60 \times 6$ years).

4. **The Year 2340 BC** is the year of the Flood. Like the 1656 span, six numeral sixes make up the number 2340, or $(6 \times 6 \times 6 + 6+6+6) \times 10$.

5. 2239 BC to 2000 BC – God divided the languages at the tower of Babel in the days of Peleg.

    a. The chronology shows the lifespans were shortened by half beginning with Peleg. Peleg and his descendants only lived about half the length of their post-flood ancestors after the languages were divided.

    b. We are not told the exact year God divided the languages, but it is interesting that from the time Peleg is 66 years old (2173 BC) until the Exodus from Egypt in 1507 BC is exactly 666 years, indicating the span of bondage from Babel until freedom was related to the works of man. Peleg is the sixth post-flood generation with Noah being the first.

6. 2048 BC – Birth of Abraham (i.e., born 1948 years after Adam)

    a. Isaac is born 100 years later in 1948 BC.

    b. Their birth years added together equals creation year: 2048 + 1948 = 3996.

    c. The present-day nation of Israel was established in 1948 AD.

7. 1937 BC – Isaac was offered as a sacrifice

    a. Abraham was 111 years old, and Isaac was eleven.

    b. The 430-year period given in Exodus 12:40-41 begins with this event. We are told the 430 years were exact to-the-day and the day in Exodus was Passover. Apparently, this was also a Passover and truly the first one as God passed over Isaac.

    c. The Year 1937 BC is 42 Jubilee cycles plus one year after creation. This only occurs if Isaac is eleven years old when offered.

8. 1908 BC – Isaac marries Rebekah

    a. 1908 BC was 401 years before the Exodus from Egypt. This fulfilled God telling Abraham his seed would sojourn in a land not theirs for 400 years. Before his marriage to Rebekah, Isaac was not yet traveling from Abraham. The point being that thirty-one years passed from Isaac being offered until he and Rebekah began sojourning in *"a land not theirs"* such that there is no contradiction between Genesis 15:13 and Exodus 12:40-41.

    b. Isaac was 40 years old when he married Rebekah and their marriage was 401 years before the Exodus. This is strong scriptural support for his age being eleven years at the time Abraham offered him being that happened 430 years before the Exodus. Genesis 15:13, 25:20, and Exodus 12:40-41 do not conflict after all.

9. 1758 BC – Jacob went to Egypt at the age of 130 years

    a. Joseph is reunited with his family for the remaining 71 years of his life.

    b. After Jacob arrived, the children of Israel were in Egypt for 251 years; the Exodus was in the 252nd year of the span in Egypt that began with Jacob's arrival (252 is a multiplier in the special biblical number 2520). Joseph's siblings likely arrived the year before Jacob, therefore they arrived in Egypt 252 years before the Exodus.

c. Jacob arrived in Egypt exactly 300 years before the first Sabbath cycle was completed in 1458 BC: the second Sabbath year in the Promised Land began in 1458 BC.

10. **1687 BC – Joseph died**

a. Joseph died exactly 180 years (60+60+60) before the Exodus. An unspecified period later, but within 100 years from his death, forced labor began for the children of Israel since Joseph could no longer protect them.

b. Moses was born exactly 100 years after Joseph died, a nice even one century, and set by Isaac's age being eleven during the sacrificial offering.

c. 1687 BC is exactly 700 years before Jeroboam caused the house of Israel to sin by worshipping the golden calves in 987 BC. The Year 987 BC is nearly an even 3000 years after 3986 BC, the likely year of Adam-and-Eve's first sin. 3986 BC is exactly 6000 years before 2015 AD, the beginning of the 71st Jubilee. Again, 3986 BC has the following: 3x9x8x6 = 6x6x6x6. There are exactly 2520 years from 3986 BC, the proposed original sin year, until Joshua began conquering the Promised Land in 1466 BC. Note: 2520 days is seven biblical years, 7x360=2520: This biblical number is a repeating pattern throughout history.

11. **1507 BC – The Exodus occurred exactly 430 years after Abraham offered Isaac to establish the covenant.** The house of Israel went into the Diaspora in, or just before, the fifteenth Jubilee year, or 730 BC: the fifteenth Jubilee occurred exactly 777 years after the Exodus.

12. **1466 BC – Moses died near the beginning of this Hebrew year (February-March).** The Israelites began conquering the Promised Land in the spring of 1466 BC using the modern Gregorian calendar metric.

a. 1465 BC was the first Sabbath year in the Promised Land; the land kept a year of rest just as the children of Israel had conquered the land (Leviticus 25:2). This was precisely seventy Jubilee cycles before Israel recaptured Jerusalem in the 1967 AD Six Day War. Note: One is added to the span to go from BC to AD being there is not a Year Zero. A detailed explanation of Jubilee cycles is given near the end of chapter two.

b. 1458 BC was the Second Sabbath year in the Promised Land and the first after the first completed seven-year cycle in the conquered land. This Sabbath year has a special numerical relation to the creation year, or 3996 BC: 3x9x9x6 = 1458. Also, exactly 490 years, or ten Jubilee periods, earlier, Isaac was born in 1948 BC.

13. **1431 BC – The period of the Judges of Israel began.** This period is not a critical-line path in solving the chronology but can be back calculated from the critical-line result.

14. **1416 BC – The First-ever Jubilee year began in the spring of this year.** See the year 583 BC discussion later in the list for more confirmation. Again, a detailed explanation of Jubilee cycles is given near the end of chapter two.

15. 1111 BC – One of the most eventful years in the history of the nation of Israel. This year is comprised of only the numeral "one" like the one-hundred-eleven-year and eleven-year ages of Abraham and Isaac when the covenant was established.

   a.   The biblical character Samson died that year.
   b.   The priest Eli died that year.
   c.   The ark of the covenant was taken captive by the Philistines that year.
   d.   The tribe of Benjamin was nearly annihilated while the ark of the covenant was with the Philistines that year.
   e.   The Philistines return the ark of the covenant: two milk cows pulled the unmanned cart and mysteriously returned it to a field in Benjamin's inheritance. The tribe of Benjamin had just been reduced to only six-hundred men during a civil war with their brethren.
   f.   Exactly eleven years before 1111 BC was the seventh Jubilee year, or 1122 BC.

16. 1027 BC – Solomon began construction of the temple 430 years before Nebuchadnezzar destroyed it.

   a.   There were 390 years from the year the house of Israel began worshipping the golden calves until Solomon's temple was destroyed (Ezekiel 4:1-7 and 2 Chronicles 11:17), and there were 40 years from the start of temple construction until the worshipping of the golden calves. Adding these together gives 430 years, or 390 + 40 = 430 years.
   b.   The Bible provides a cross-check; the records from the books of Kings and Chronicles show 419 years from onset of temple construction until the Babylonian captivity began, and the temple was later destroyed in the eleventh year of the captivity. The cross-check agrees, 390 + 40 = 430 years matches 419 + 11 = 430 years.

17. 597 BC – The temple was burned by Nebuchadnezzar. This was 390 years after the house of Israel began worshipping the golden calves, thereby fulfilling an Ezekiel prophecy. Interestingly, exactly 666 years after the first temple's demise, the second temple was also destroyed (70 AD). Secular history places the destruction of the first temple in 586 BC, but this disagrees with the Bible: Babylon fell in 539 BC and the seventy year captivity ended shortly thereafter in 538 BC; therefore, the captivity began in 608 BC (538 + 70 = 608), and eleven years later, the temple was destroyed in 597 BC.

18. 583 BC – This year was the eighteenth Jubilee. It occurred fourteen years after Solomon's temple was destroyed.

   a.   The combined message of Ezekiel 1:1-2 and Ezekiel 40:1 require the fourteenth year after the city was smitten to be a Jubilee year, therefore, we can place all Jubilees from this confirmed year.
   b.   A back calculation puts the first Jubilee in 1416 BC, therefore the second Sabbath year would be 1458 BC with numerical correlation to the year of creation 3996 BC (3x9x9x6 = 1458), just as if the Bible's author had intentionally placed it there. Also, 1458 BC is exactly 490 years after Isaac was born.

   c.   The land rested during the first Sabbath year, or 1465 BC, while the Israelites rested from conquering the Promised Land. The initial conquest by Joshua lasted one year.

Closing comments: The chronology was developed based on the Hebrew Masoretic text. Other ancient manuscripts (i.e., the Samaritan Pentateuch and the Greek Septuagint) give different timelines for Genesis chapters five and eleven. A comparison of the differences reveals a pattern that suggests both other sources were based on the Masoretic text but were adjusted by one hundred years for each generation. Perhaps this was done to give credit to Noah for his work on the ark and for saving mankind from extinction, or to Noah's son Shem who was age one hundred when his first post-flood son was born.

After Peleg's sixty-sixth year, only fifty years were added to the Masoretic periods rather than one hundred years; the lifespans also decreasing by fifty percent after Peleg, and this match supports the hypothesis that these were adjustments based from the Masoretic record. The reasons for the adjustments are purely speculations.

From the chronology, numerous patterns of biblical numbers have been found throughout history. These are surely few compared to those yet to be discovered. The patterns proclaim that all human history has been ordered by God. Through these numbers we can see that God is ultimately in charge of all things and their seasons. As Solomon wrote,

> *"To every thing there is a season and a time to every purpose under the heaven:"*
> Ecclesiastes 3:1 KJV

APPENDIX THREE

MOSES' TABERNACLE

This appendix is included for those who love numbers and for those who simply want more proof. Moses was given detailed dimensions and assembly instructions for the tabernacle including the dimensions of the curtains, boards, and beams (Exodus chapter 26). It is important to follow the instructions carefully to see the configuration of the finished tabernacle.

The tabernacle's structure consists of the boards overlaid with gold, the inner sidewall curtains, the outer sidewall curtains, or tent, the front cover (not depicted), the veil separating the holy and the most holy parts within the boarded section, the roof or overhead tent covering, and nine pillars (not shown). The top view layout below shows the arrangement with the boarded section being the innermost dark lines, the middle and lighter lines are the inner curtains, and the outer lines are the outer curtains. The thin dark line is a veil that separated the Holy from the Most Holy.

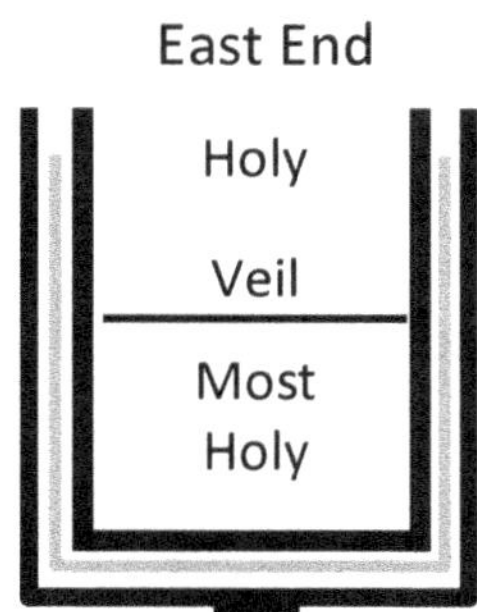

Top View of Moses' Tabernacle
Front facing East

The inner curtain (light lines) does not cover the entire boarded section of the tabernacle as will be shown during the assembly. The outer curtain consists of eleven individual curtains (or sheets) while the inner curtain has ten sheets (Exodus 26: 1-12). The dimensions of each are shown below.

Individual Tabernacle Curtain Dimensions: Left side is outer curtains and Right side is inner curtains.

The outer curtain was to be assembled with five sheets coupled together and six sheets coupled together:

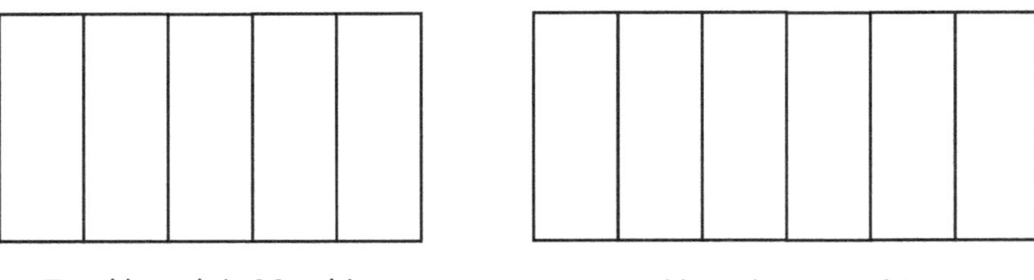

Outer Curtains assembled into groups of five and six sheets.

The sixth sheet was to be folded in half and doubled onto the face of the assembly, and fifty loops were to be added in the folded edge. Note: The King James Bible says, *"...and shalt double the sixth curtain in the forefront of the tabernacle"*, but it is more properly translated, *"...and will double the sixth curtain against the face of the tent"* (Exodus 26:9):

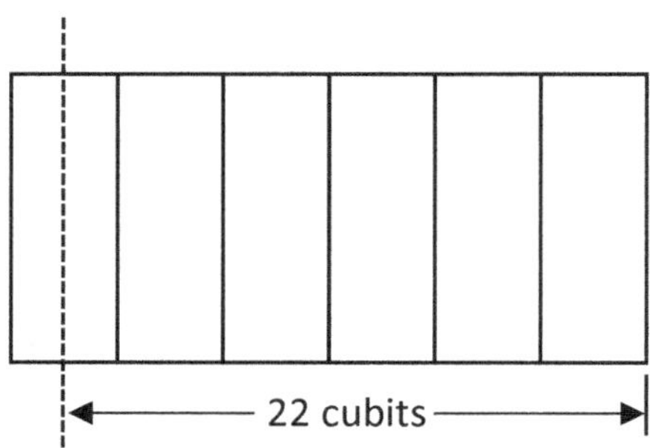

New length of six sheets from edge to fold is 22 cubits.

The two assemblies were to be joined together by attaching the edge of the five-sheet group to the loops of the six-sheet group (Exodus 26: 9-11):

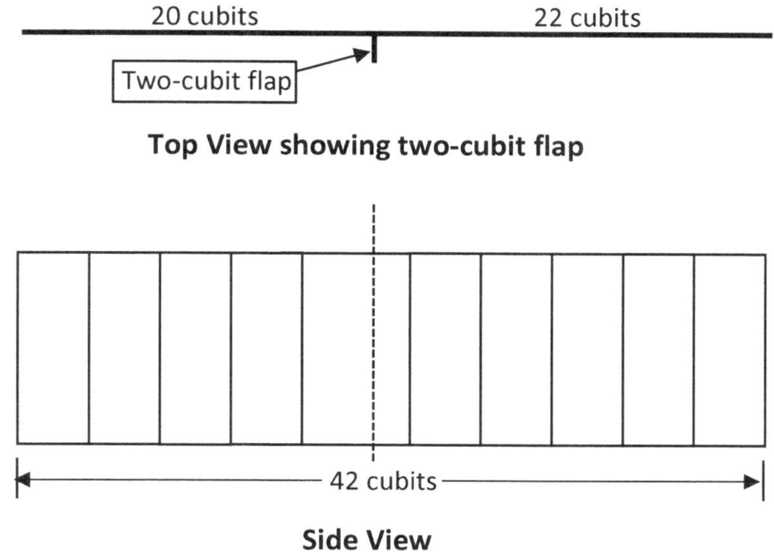

Top View showing two-cubit flap

Side View

Eleven Outer-Curtain-Assembly's length is 42 cubits plus a flap.

The top view (above) displays the two-cubit flap that remains after they were joined, and it was to lay over the backside of the tabernacle:

East End

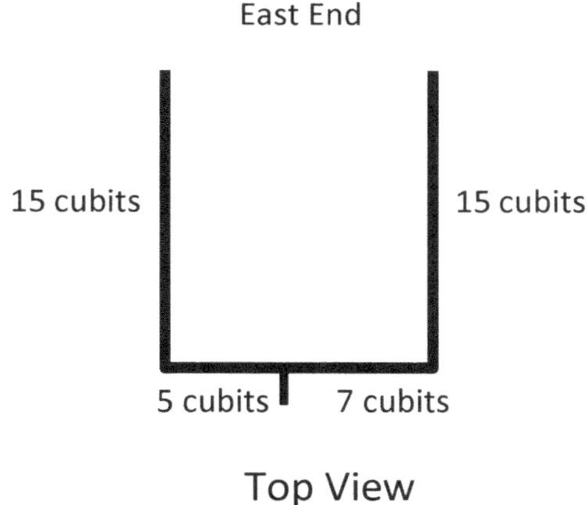

Top View

Total length of the outer curtain is 42 cubits, and the length of the flap is two cubits.

The boarded section contained forty individual planks of the same dimensions, one-and-one-half cubits wide and ten cubits high (Exodus 26: 15-16). Each board was to be assembled in pairs, one above the other (Exodus 26: 17-21). There were to be twenty boards on the south side and twenty boards on the north side (Exodus 26: 18-20) meaning ten pairs on each side. Note: The Hebrew text explains this better than the English.

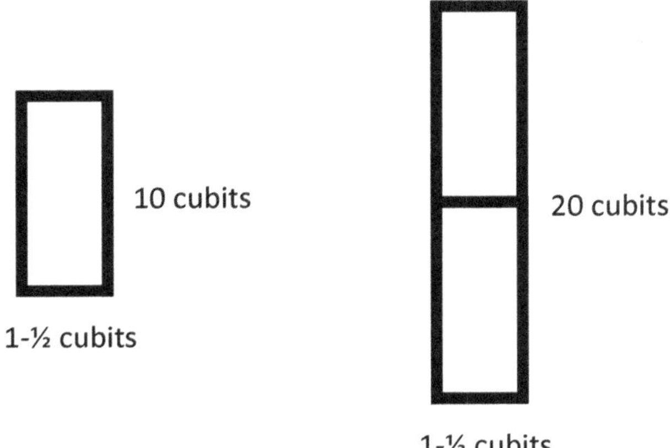

The North and South walls were made up of a total of 40 individual boards (i.e., left above) to be assembled into twenty vertical pairs (i.e., right above), or ten pairs for each wall.

The instructions for the west side were different (Exodus 26:22-25): Its boards were presented in pairs and required six for the back and two for the corners for a total of eight pairs of boards across the back, or west side. Simply put, there were ten pairs on the north side, ten pairs on the south side, and eight pairs on the west side.

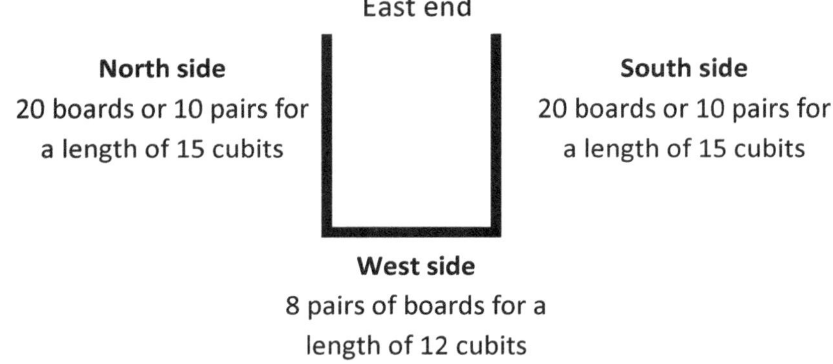

Top view of the board assembly showing ten pairs of boards on the north side, ten pairs on the south side, and eight pairs on the back, or west side.

The assembled lengths of the boards and the outer curtains are each 42 cubits, therefore the outer curtains precisely covered the temple walls.

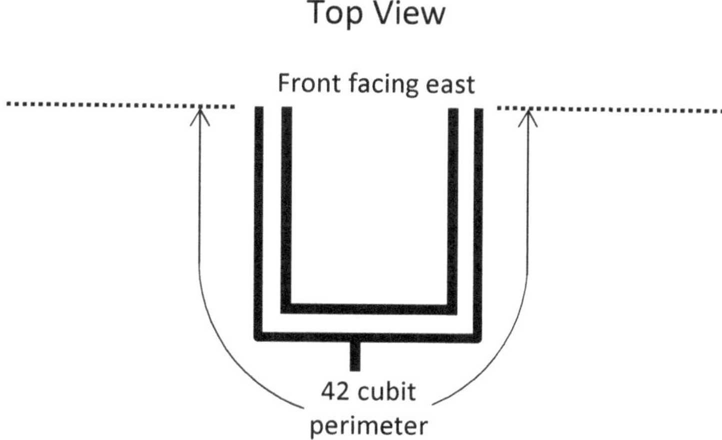

The length of the boards is exactly equal to the 42 cubits length of the outer curtain assembly and are therefore precisely covered by the outer curtains.

The inner curtains were assembled in two groups of five sheets each with each sheet being four cubits wide and 28 cubits long. The halves were joined, and their total length was two cubits less than the length of the outer curtains, and being the outer curtains were 30 cubits high, its height would also be two cubits shorter than that of the outer assembly. With both the inner and outer curtains suspended from a common height of 30 cubits, the inner curtain would hang two cubits from the ground as illustrated:

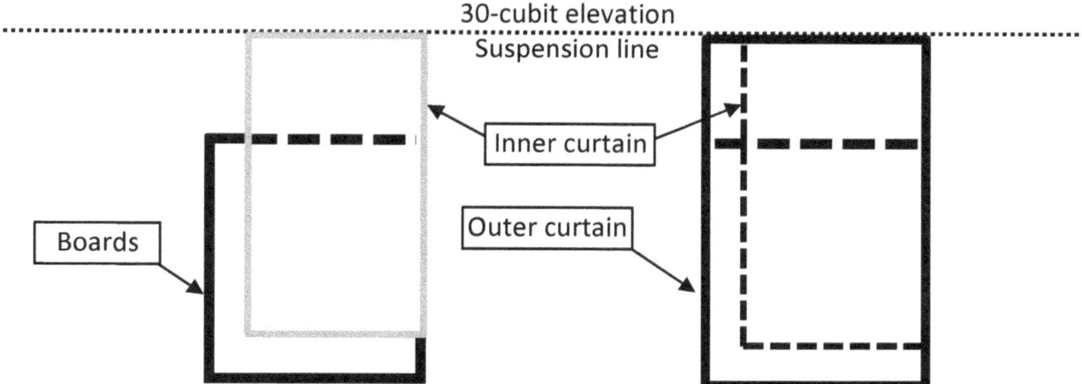

Two North Side Views Looking Southward: The view on the left omits the outer curtain to reveal the inner curtain is not completely covering the boards. In the depiction on the right, the outer curtain is displayed, showing it precisely covers the boards.

The next graphic is a top view looking down at the assembled tabernacle. The length of the inner curtain is two cubits shorter than the boarded section and the outer curtains, and the two-cubit flap folds precisely across the seam connecting the two halves of the inner curtain, one cubit either side of the seam (i.e., the dashed line is the inner-seam location). The four circles in front of the veil are pillars sitting on silver foundations to support the veil, and the five darker circles are pillars sitting on brass foundations supporting the front cover (Exodus 36:36-38). Note: The actual configuration of the pillars is not specified.

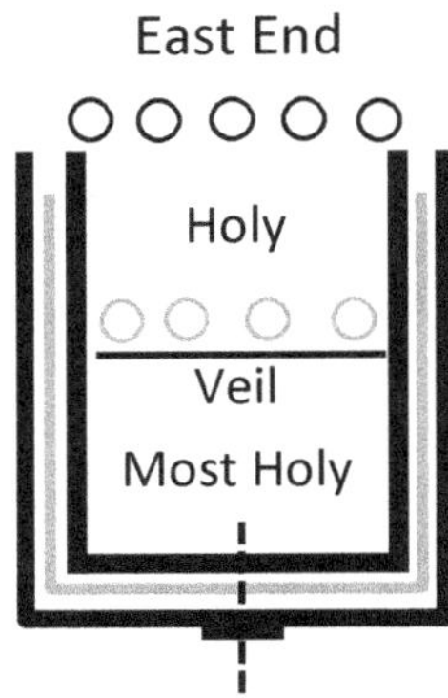

Top View of the Assembled Tabernacle facing to the east.

The dimensions of the final configuration have numerical correlations to other biblical numbers:

1. The open area on the front of the tabernacle is 360 square cubits. Prior to Noah's flood, there were 360 days in a year and Jesus' ministry as the Lamb of God was 360 days in agreement with God's stipulation to Moses that the Passover lambs were to be lambs of the first year. Jesus was crucified and died on the Passover in 30 AD, or Wednesday, April 3, 30 AD. As previously shown, multiplying **month x day x year** for that date gives 4 x 3 x 30 = 360. The phone app Jesus' Footsteps shows in detail the length of Jesus' ministry and is recommended for further study.

2. There are 100 silver foundations, or sockets, in the tabernacle: 40 in the south wall, 40 in the north wall, 16 in the rear wall, and one under each of the four pillars supporting the veil. There are five brass foundations, one under each of the pillars supporting the front curtain, for a total of 105 foundations in the tabernacle. The number of **foundations** matches the number of days in 3 ½ biblical months, or 105 days, which is also 2520 hours, a **foundational** biblical number (3.5 x 30 = 105 days, and 105 x 24 = 2520 hours).

    The book of Daniel has an Aramaic expression *"... time, times, and the dividing of time..."* (Daniel 7: 25), and the origin of the Aramaic word for *"time"* has a root (Strong's number H5708) meaning *"menstrual flux"* indicating the time period is likely intended to match a menstrual cycle, or about one month. If so, these three-and-a-half times are likely three-and-a-half months, or 105 days, or 2520 hours. This opens new possibilities for Daniel's Aramaic message.

3. The area of the outer-side curtain is 1260 square cubits, or 42 x 30 cubits, matching the 1260 days and the 42 biblical months mentioned in the book of Revelation. Note: 1260 is exactly half of 2520, our foundational number in item two above. The inner side curtain area is 11.111...% less than the outer side curtain. The theoretical ages

of Abraham and Isaac at the time of his sacrificial offering were 11 and 111. Furthermore, our Chapter-Three theory makes a strong case for the length of Jesus' life being exactly 11,111 days.

4. There are eleven curtains in the outer curtain, matching Isaac's age when offered, and one of these curtains, the sixth, is folded leaving a two-cubit flap. The flap covers the seam of the inner seam evenly, one cubit either side, or one-and-one as in the repeating "one(s)" patterns.

5. The total area difference between individual sheets of the inner and outer side curtains is 6.666…%. This number has been thoroughly discussed; it is the number of mankind.

6. The top view cross-sectional area is 180 square cubits (60+60+60). The volume of the boarded section is 3600 cubic cubits (60×60). The number of man is prevalent.

7. The area of each board pair is 30 square cubits, and the length of the outer side curtain is 30 cubits. The months were each 30 days long prior to Noah's flood.

8. The entire perimeter of the outer court is 300 cubits with a gate opening of 20 cubits on the center of the east border. The opening is 6.666….% of the entire perimeter. (Exodus 27: 9-18)

9. The lengths on either side of the outer-curtain seam on the back wall are five cubits and seven cubits. Jesus broke five loaves when feeding the 5000 and seven loaves when feeding the 4000.

10. The perimeter length of the inner curtain along the back wall is 12 cubits and its sides are each 14 cubits (i.e., the inner curtain is two cubits less in total length than the outer curtain). Dividing each of these lengths by the four-cubit widths of the individual sheets gives 12÷4 = 3 and 14÷4 = 3 ½. Jesus was in the grave for three days and appeared to his disciples after three-and-a-half days. Also, the two witnesses of Revelation lie dead in the street for three-and-a-half days. There are two occurrences of the three-and-a-half quotient, or one for each side, and thereby matching the number of witnesses in Revelation, and only one occurrence of the three quotient from the backside.

11. There are a total of 21 individual curtains, 15 structural bars, and 56 individual boards in the tabernacle. Multiplying these numbers gives (21+15) x 56 = **2016**. 2 Chronicles 2:2 also has a numerical product that correlates to 2016 if multiplying the workers mentioned: 70,000 x 80,000 x 3,600 = **2016**0000000000. The seventy-first Jubilee ended in **2016**, the year the United States abstained from vetoing the United Nations resolution to divide the land of Israel.

GLOSSARY

Confidence   The probability for known evidence being valid.

Cuneiform   Ancient inscriptions preserved on the Nabonidus and Cyrus cylinders dating the fall of Babylon to October 539 BC.

Exodus   An event in which approximately two million Israelite slaves were freed from captivity to begin a journey to the Promised Land. All twelve tribes of Israel made the Exodus journey.

Galeed   Location where Jacob and Laban made an agreement concerning their land boundaries. Galeed was the northern boundary of ancient Israel.

Hypothesis   Conjecture, hunch, guess, possibility.

Jubilee cycle   A forty-nine-year period continuously propagating through time. A detailed explanation is provided at the end of chapter two.

Jubilee year   "Fiftieth year" that concludes the forty-nine-year Jubilee cycle. A detailed explanation is provided at the end of chapter two.

Promised Land   Also known as the land of Canaan, this was the Israelite's new homeland conquered after leaving Egypt during the Exodus and after wandering in the wilderness forty years.

Proof   The evidence supporting conjectures, hypotheses, and theory.

Probability   Percent-confidence in known evidence to elevate hypotheses to theory.

Sabbath year   Same as Year-Seven and is a year of rest for the farmland occurring every seven years as mandated by God. It is referred to as a Year-Seven in the Jubilee explanation given at the end of chapter two.

Tabernacle   The worship tent made by Israel during the Exodus. It was later replaced by Solomon's temple.

Tanakh   Also known as the Old Testament, this is the Hebrew text of the Bible.

Theory   An idea proposed in the absence of data and supported by evidence. Scientific law requires there to be no unknowns; therefore, theory is the highest hierarchy of proof for a conjecture.

Transfiguration   A New Testament event in which Jesus, Moses, and Elijah appeared on a mountain after Jesus was transfigured into a shining being whose brightness was like that of the sun.

Year-One   First year of work in the recurring Sabbath-Year counts. The count restarts at the end of seven years just as weekdays do at the end of seven days.

Year-Six   Sixth and final year of work in the recurring Sabbath-Year counts. The count restarts at the end of seven years just as weekdays do at the end of seven days. The produce of every Year-Six was blessed to yield enough food for three years (Leviticus 25:20-21).

Year-Seven   Year of rest for the farmland in the recurring Sabbath-Year counts. The count restarts at the end of seven years just as weekdays do at the end of seven days. Year-Seven is synonymous with "Sabbath year."